"It is an interesting biological fact that all of us have in our veins the exact same percentage of salt in our blood that exists in the ocean, and, therefore, we have salt in our blood, in our sweat, in our tears. We are tied to the ocean. And when we go back to the sea—whether it is to sail or to watch it—we are going back from whence we came."

—John F. Kennedy
America's Cup crew's dinner, September 14, 1962

Waterborne

A Slow Trip Around A Small Planet

by

Marguerite Welch

SEAWORTHY PUBLICATIONS, INC. • MELBOURNE, FLORIDA

Waterborne
A Slow Trip Around A Small Planet
Copyright ©2019 by Marguerite Welch

Published in the USA and distributed worldwide by:
Seaworthy Publications, Inc.
6300 N. Wickham Rd
Unit 130-416
Melbourne, FL 32940
Phone 310-610-3634
email orders@seaworthy.com
www.seaworthy.com

Library of Congress Cataloging-in-Publication Data

Names: Welch, Marguerite, 1940- author.
Title: Waterborne : a slow trip around a small planet / by Marguerite Welch.
Description: Melbourne, Florida : Seaworthy Publications, Inc., [2019] | Summary: ""Waterborne" is the story of an artist, an engineer and a Labrador-three entirely different personalities-who abandon a stable middle-age lifestyle for a pitching deck and the possibility of pirates. Challenged by culture clashes, gear failure and sudden storms, their story is as much a sea saga as travel memoir, celebrating the interior as well as exterior journey and the joys of an inquisitive engagement with the world-a timely subject in today's climate of increasing tribalism"-- Provided by publisher.
Identifiers: LCCN 2019022907 (print) | LCCN 2019022908 (ebook) | ISBN 9781948494250 (trade paperback) | ISBN 9781948494267 (epub)
Subjects: LCSH: Welch, Marguerite, 1940---Travel. | Sailors--United States--Biography. | Women sailors--United States--Biography. | Travelers--United States--Biography. | Women travelers--United States--Biography. | Voyages and travels.
Classification: LCC GV810.92. .W45 2019 (print) | LCC GV810.92. (ebook) | DDC 910.92 [B]--dc23
LC record available at https://lccn.loc.gov/2019022907
LC ebook record available at https://lccn.loc.gov/2019022908

Dedication

*This book is dedicated to
my three best friends and
intrepid sailors:*

Michael, Sam and Jack

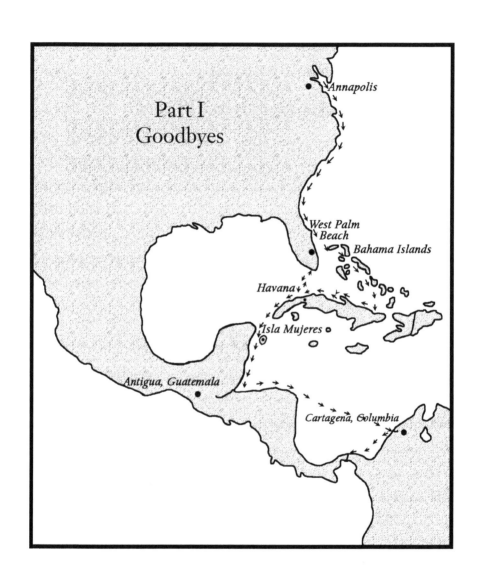

Part I
Goodbyes

Annapolis

West Palm
Beach

Bahama Islands

Havana

Isla Mujeres

Antigua, Guatemala

Cartagena, Columbia

I was in it for the ride, for the thrill, for the fear, and for the absolute certainty of the uncertain. I still am.

> *"There is no happiness for him who does*
> *not travel. . . . The fortune of him who is*
> *sitting, sits, it rises when he rises, it sleeps*
> *when he sleeps, it moves when he moves.*
> *Therefore, wander."*

From the *Rigveda,* a collection of sacred Vedic Sanskrit hymns

The Dream

THERE ARE STILL SOME MOONLIT, STAR struck nights on the boat when I look up at the sky, study the compass, listen to garbled voices on the VHF and wonder were we really gone for 14 years? Are we still gone? Was it just a dream, that world that only exists in my mind now—my memories, my heart. It's as if I made it all up but I didn't. It's a fact that after thirty-three years of marriage, two careers for Michael, two sons and many reincarnations of myself, we abandoned everything and everyone we loved to explore the world in a small boat. "Why?" you might ask. "Why not?" I might reply.

We had always had sailboats, from a 20-foot day sailer on Mission Bay in San Diego in 1965 to our present 38-foot Shannon Cutter, bought as an escape vehicle when, after a thirty-year career in the Navy, Michael retired and needed a new adventure, a new command. We named her *Ithaca* after Odysseus' home island in the Ionian Sea, never believing that someday we would actually go there.

At the close of his retirement ceremony at the US Naval Academy, Michael walked down the steps of Bancroft Hall wearing his uniform for the last time. The next day he was piped aboard his new command, much reduced in size but not necessarily in responsibility. Thus began a yearlong "practice cruise." The initial seven-day passage from Norfolk to Bermuda was our first serious offshore experience. Finding Bermuda in the middle of the Atlantic by taking sun sights with a sextant seemed to me more miracle than science. It was not the first time or the last that I was infinitely grateful to have married a naval officer.

That year taught us a lot about ourselves and our boat. A horrendous three-day storm on the way to Puerto Rico taught us endurance and proved to be a useful measure of what we and the boat could survive. It also revealed who got seasick and who didn't and what not to say about it. Most importantly, we began to learn how to live together in a small space without killing each other. In truth, a lesson we are still learning. Happily, we also learned that we both loved the lifestyle, the sailing, the adventure, the unexpected challenges of every day. But, we weren't ready to run away from home forever. Not yet. Michael would often say he felt like he was "skipping school." I had no problem with "skipping school," but I acknowledged that we still had responsibilities at home—namely, kids in college and a mortgage to pay.

We went home. Michael bought a business suit and took a job in defense contracting where he was challenged, successful, and promoted rapidly. We bought a used car and moved back into our house. I started an event planning and design business, did community volunteer work and art projects. *Ithaca* waited at the end of our pier until the time was right for an even grander adventure.

Eight years went by. Life was good, but terra firma had slowly and seductively entrapped us with its tentacles, and the big "Six O" birthday was roaring toward us like a freight train. We cruised around the bay on *Ithaca* and fantasized about longer journeys but it was hard to cut all the ties and go. Then we met Hans at the Annapolis boat show, who said: "There are lots of places in the world you can go in a plane, but for the ones you can't, you need a sailboat and a wind vane steerer." That he was the vendor for Monitor wind vanes did not invalidate his observation. He hooked us.

We had the sailboat. We bought the wind vane steerer, ever after affectionately known as "Hans." For the next fourteen years, Hans saved us valuable battery power by replacing the electronic autopilot when there was wind enough to sail. When there was too much wind, he often held a course better than we could, silently steering us across the sea to distant landfalls and islands that had no airport.

The day we bought the wind vane steerer we really didn't have a plan. As a matter of fact, we never really had a PLAN. We just thought, let's head out in a generally westerly direction for a couple of years and see what happens. We imagined we would be gone for three years maximum, vaguely thinking about a circumnavigation but not committed and certainly NOT telling anyone we planned to sail around the world.

* * * * *

The hardest step was to leave home: rent the house, move out, depart—indefinitely. For Michael, it meant leaving a prestigious and rewarding job, for me leaving grandchildren born and unborn, a rose garden, arts career, personal space and preconceived ideas of identity and lifestyle, which are harder to leave than your dog, who I refused to leave. For many years to come, leaving home was hard. We tried to fly home once a year for a few weeks, usually around Christmas, but in some ways, that made it harder. We had to keep leaving over and over again.

Many marriages don't make it, whether because of infidelity, children on drugs, lost jobs, unpaid mortgages, miscommunication, or just plain lack of love. I would add to that list of challenges fourteen years of living on a small boat with the same man. In our case, no two people could have been more different. Picture the Owl and the Pussy Cat, plus a dog, in an 11 by 38-foot boat that sometimes felt as small as a large closet. Often the unhappy alternative of a life raft was the only means of escape.

The Owl was an engineer, a fighter pilot, a Navy Captain, a man used to giving orders and being in charge. A man used to living with thousands of other people in the confines of an aircraft carrier, where camaraderie is the currency of survival. A gregarious Naval Academy graduate, class of 1961, who loved his Navy buddies like brothers. The Pussy Cat was an artist, a loner, not inclined to "join" a team or a ladies group, lead anyone, or be president of anything. It never occurred to her to go to a high school or college reunion. She was a people watcher, not a participant. Her best friend was usually a book. The dog was a black Labrador named Jack who wagged his tail at everyone, except cats.

The Owl took his tools, tide tables, books on engine repair, refrigeration, navigation, and electrical systems. He filled the lockers with spare parts for every system on the boat. Bilges bulged with plastic bags of nuts and bolts, pumps, injectors, water filters, fuel filters, a heat exchanger, and a spare alternator. The Pussy Cat brought books on varnishing and sail repair but mostly novels, poetry, and numerous guidebooks for the Bahamas, Cuba, and Mexico—about as far away as she could imagine going. She cradled her camera gear in bubble wrap, stowed three empty journals under the bunk, and stuffed watercolor paper, pens, brushes, paint, glue, and a cutting board into a 2-foot by 2-foot locker. The dog brought his dinner dish.

The Owl was a passage maker, always anxious to move on to the next place. The Pussy Cat was a traveler, a lingerer who wanted to learn languages, eat local food, visit remote villages. And the dog? The dog just wanted to go swimming and play ball.

On October 28, 1998, they sailed away for a year [years?] and a day to the land where the Bong-Tree grows . . ."

Hugging the Shore

ALL THE LAST-MINUTE ITEMS WERE STOWED; Jack, our four-legged mate, was aboard; mooring lines were taken in . . . and Ithaca slowly pulled away from our pier in Annapolis. My best friend, Sharie, waved and shouted, "Watch out for miracles." That morning we had learned about one miracle already on its way in the form of a new grandchild due the following summer—a going away gift. I cried, and for a brief minute reconsidered the journey, but it was too late. We raised the genoa and sailed south down the bay toward the Intracoastal Waterway, or ICW.

Seen from the air, the East Coast of the United States south of the Chesapeake Bay curves like a backbone. The sea flows between vertebrae of land and spreads inland like a spider web of veins and arteries that have been the lifeblood of local commerce for hundreds of years. One thousand and ninety miles of rivers, estuaries, bays, marshes, and man-made canals make up the inland waterway from Norfolk to Miami. Traveling the ICW in a small, slow boat with a deep draft is as frustrating as it is exhilarating. Big ships and small boat traffic, unmarked sandbars and submerged debris, erratic tides and foul currents are just a few of the hazards. From the bustling cities of Charleston, Savannah, and Jacksonville to tiny waterman towns and flat, boring, buggy swamps, each place presents a challenge for the yachtsman and possesses its own unique history, romance, and beauty.

At 1:30 p.m., November 2, 1998, we passed by Mile Marker #1 at the mouth of the Elizabeth River in the historic Navy town of Norfolk, Virginia. Even Jack stood at attention on deck as we motored by the aircraft carriers while Michael looked wistful and nostalgic but stood tall as only a Navy man can. Having navigated past the small sleepy towns of the lower Chesapeake Bay, we were now challenged by seacraft of every type: container ships, ferries, tugboats, large powerboats, and small sailing dinghies, all constrained by a narrow channel and poor visibility. Tension slackened when we finally passed into the long canal that leads to North Carolina's Currituck Sound. Then, on to Coinjack, the shallow, rough waters of the Albemarle Sound, and Oriental, where we took a break for a few days to wait for mail from our mail-forwarding service and to do mini repairs. Even though we left with all systems "go," there is always SOMETHING to fix or shop for on a boat.

* * * * *

My ancient plastic corner garbage sink strainer was cracked and curled. Peelings and coffee grounds leaked through and clogged the drain. In Oriental it became a major quest. Unfortunately, it was Sunday. The streets of the forgotten waterfront town were empty except for a cluster of Latinos in colorful clothes congregated by the grocery store: girls in hot pink, boys with hair slicked and boots polished—little blotches of brightness in an otherwise gray scene.

We tied Jack to a lamppost and went into the antique/junk store where sagging shelves held piles of assorted detritus from years gone by. Surely I could find an "antique" sink strainer here, a remnant from a grandmother's kitchen. Three women were gathered around a potbellied stove chatting leisurely. The gray-haired proprietress was seated in a leather La-Z-Boy. An afghan spread over her shoulders reminded me of the crayon-colored squares we knitted in grade school to make quilts for the soldiers during the Korean War. She looked up and smiled. "Mornin.'" Her friend sat in a straight-backed cane chair, legs crossed at the ankles, fingering a pearl necklace as she asked where we were from. A younger woman, perhaps her daughter, stood next to her polishing a little silver cup. The lady in the pearls said, jokingly, she had just thrown away a similar sink strainer.

"Why you lookin' for an old thing like that anyway?" the proprietress enquired while her hands deftly peeled potatoes on the newspaper spread across her lap. "It's so convenient. I loved it," I replied. The woman rocked back in her chair and smiled then continued her conversation with her friend. The soft accents and genteel demeanor of the women seemed a bit incongruous in the midst of bent metal coffeepots, lamp skeletons, and broken baby cribs—afternoon tea in a graveyard. I wanted to sit down with them and chat a bit about the "doin's" of the day.

On the walk back to the boat, I noticed all the houses and shops had rocking chairs on their porches but no one sitting in them. I thought about the erosion of time, of being in a place that had once been vital and full of life but now nothing was left but an old boot, a pile of pots and pans, a torn crocheted bedspread, a broken bike . . . Like my mother's half-empty house, full of sad memories and marks on the rug where furniture once stood. But at least here, in the dark center of that store, dignity and love still lived, or appeared to, unlike my last memories of mother's house full of anger, regret, and misunderstanding. The conflict with my sister after our mother's death was and still is to this day an utter mystery to me.

* * * * *

November 16, 1998, White Hall Creek, South Carolina

We are anchored in a flat, treeless marsh. A hazy sun hangs low on the horizon. The sky bleeds into silvery pink ripples. A chorus of birds calls to each other like clumps of children at a slumber party. One group gets settled then another group from a different area of the swamp starts chattering. Soon other groups join in and a chaotic din spreads across the marsh like an invisible cloak of crickets hiding in the flat watery reeds. Suddenly silence again, except for the lazy slap, slap, slap of wavelets against the hull. Tomorrow we will pass Palm Island. Finally palm trees, our measure of "going south" and "one sheet nights."

* * * * *

Charleston, Beaufort, Savannah—gracious Southern towns of sad history, soft accents, and antebellum grandeur verging on the cliché, antique stores on every block cluttered with sterling silver heirlooms, period furniture, and old master paintings. The grand Georgian architecture, the curving stairways, columns, screened porches with ferns and wicker rockers, elegant dining rooms and chandeliers, formal front parlors, postage stamp town gardens—everything reminded me of mother. Her sense of style, knowledge of antiques, and love of silver, even though in later years and more diminished times she had to polish it herself. Of course I read *In the Garden of Good and Evil*, and now saw its characters on every corner.

From Charleston, at Mile Marker #422, to the Florida State line, Mile #714, the ICW's system of narrow canals and dredged cuts gives way to a system of wide river mouths, sounds, and coastal inlets. The landscape of low, marshy grassland is remote, uninhabited except for plentiful shore birds, waterfowl, and great blue herons standing sentinel along the mudflats. Occasionally a group of porpoises would swim along the hull and surf the bow wave. Big sand dune hummocks and huge oak trees covered with Spanish moss left no doubt we were in the Deep South.

From time to time we were in a place long enough to have our mail-forwarding service send whatever mail had accumulated. With every package I anticipated a letter from my sister, but as the months and then years went by without word from her, I began to realize that the death of our mother was not just the death of one person but two. I never understood why she had stepped away so abruptly and refused to be comforted by me that day on the fishing boat in Monterey Bay. For her, grief sparked long-forgotten animosities and jealousies, like invisible cancer cells, which bloomed into an incurable malignancy and left no room for love, understanding, and forgiveness. She had been my best friend but now she didn't know me, and I guess I didn't know her.

She was angry from the moment of mother's death. I had suddenly become a stranger in her eyes who threatened to usurp her rights to our entire family history. I was going away on a sailboat. Why did I have any interest in mother's house, furniture, family photographs, or possessions? Of course I did. She was my mother too, and everything was suffused with the memory of her. It was very hard to let go. It wasn't just stuff. It was a life. The memory of which I wanted desperately to share. But my sister didn't. The settlement was messy and painful. I always thought that, with time, we could get over it, but she couldn't. In spite of all the years that have passed, however, there will always be a small, unmendable hole in my heart where memories of our laughter live and hope persists.

Mail or no mail, we moved on, and we were in Florida by December. Michael tried his best to distract me, but I couldn't shake my sadness.

December 21, 1998, Fort Pierce, Florida

Mother died a year ago today. The hurt is like Jack's cut foot that I've been watching heal—so deep and painful, at first he could barely walk, and yet, slowly it has healed from within, even though repeatedly aggravated by fits of licking when it started to bleed again, but, as someone wrote, "the body wants to heal itself." It will heal; not ever disappear, but it will get tough enough to walk on. I have to stop licking this pain, put sadness aside. Leave my tears in storage with my handkerchiefs. Still no mail from my sister. I wonder if she is reading my letters.

Rowed Jack ashore in the early morning light. A pod of bottlenose dolphins thrashed the water, puffing and swooshing among a school of small fish, a flurry of silver in the shallows. Then stillness.

> *"The heart retains its scars longer than*
> *most parts of the body."*

From *The Carpet Wars* by Christopher Kremmer

*   *   *   *   *

Leaving the boat in West Palm Beach, Florida, we drove to Naples for a family Christmas. Son Danny, as yet unmarried; son Pete, his wife Tracy, and daughter Alexis; as well as assorted members of Tracy's family gathered for a last family reunion before Michael and I headed out into "the wild blue yonder." Everyone was full of anticipation about the new baby and our impending big adventure. On our last day in Florida we all went to Tiger's Tail beach for a swim. Watching Alexis paddle about in the water made me realize once again what I was leaving. I swam up and down the beach until my shoulders ached. Delicious warm turquoise water caressed my skin. The pattern and rhythm of breathing, stroking, legs propelling my body over the white, sugar-fine sand was like a healing meditation.

While I was swimming, I sensed a presence and rolled over to see a pelican gliding just above my head, reminding me of the pelican flyover in Monterey a year earlier. The next day we drove back to West Palm Beach and set sail for the Bahamas on January 17, 1999.

Islands in the Sea

T HE BAHAMAS ISLANDS, OR CAYS (pronounced keys), are flat, scrubby, sandy islands that dribble down from the southeastern coast of Florida across the Tropic of Cancer, fringing large, shallow sandbanks like long thin scribbles, forming curlicues of island groups and small settlements wherever there is land enough to live. Each has its own individual character: from the hustle-bustle of Grand Bahama Island to minuscule Man-O-War Cay in the Abaco region, which was settled by Loyalists in 1780 and still remains a tiny, tidy church-going, all white, "teetotaling," fishing and boat-building community proud of its heritage and tradition.

Long renowned for groundings, pirates, and smugglers, the real treasure of the Bahamas lies in the shallow, warm, gin-clear water where gardens of mounded golden brain coral, purple spiky sea rod, undulating sea fans, orange tube coral, and thick, velvety, appropriately named elkhorn coral provide shelter and food for all manner of sea creatures—among them, swarms of finger-length baby parrotfish, big fat smiling triggerfish, red squirrelfish, blowfish, and yellow tail. Shy eels poke their heads out between reef crevices, and giant grouper hover in the shadows. Sadly, the fish are thinning and the coral is often visibly bleached by pollution, but in certain places the underwater landscape is still a magical watercolor world.

We left Riviera Beach Marina in West Palm Beach at 6:30 p.m. at the tail end of a torrential rainstorm. Based on Florida weather, we anticipated a mellow 10 knots out of the east and 2-foot seas, but it was not to be. Instead, 20–30 knots on the nose kicked up a nasty chop, and the mellow passage across the Gulf Stream was a brutal bash. By the time we finally pulled into West End, Grand Bahama

Island the next morning and completed the check-in procedure, we were exhausted. Twenty-four hours later I was lying on the warm deck in my bathing suit watching *Ithaca*'s shadow tracking us in the sand 20 feet beneath the keel as we ghosted over the shallow transparent water of the Bahama bank, genoa billowing in a light breeze, Jack asleep at the helm while "Henri" (our French electronic autopilot) steered a steady course to Great Sale Cay, the Gulf Stream terror of two nights before a dim, bad dream. I felt like a big happy fat seal peacefully sunning herself on a distant shore.

By 5:00 p.m. we were anchored in Great Sale Cay, quietly drifting in 6 feet of water so clear it seemed you could reach over the rail and pick up a starfish. All was blissful silence until Jack started lobbying for a beachside bathroom, urgently crossing his legs and looking mournful as only a Labrador can. Nothing to do but inflate the dinghy and motor to a deserted island where we surfed onto a pebbly shore. Jack jumped out of the boat before it touched land and ran to the nearest casuarina tree. Then, as the sun went down, turning the water to pale purple, all three of us celebrated with our first swim in Bahamian waters. That night we sat out on deck after dinner and watched the stars reflected in the still water seamlessly blend into the sky—a planet unto ourselves, spinning in the unending universe. We had reached Paradise.

With morning came a rude awakening from our idyllic dream: salt water in the engine cooling system. A leak in the heat exchanger, maybe? Nothing to do but press on to Green Turtle Cay and get it fixed. Little did we realize how typical this pattern would become.

* * * * *

On a mission to get our engine cooling system repaired, we were not ready for the "laid-back" nature of island culture on Green Turtle Cay. When we came alongside the fuel dock on Tuesday, a lanky old-timer leaning against the fuel tank smoking a cigarette called out, "Ahoy mate, what can we do for you? Name's Ian." In the midst of explaining our heat exchanger problem, Kevin, the dock master, sauntered down the pier and spied the Navy insignia on Michael's ball cap. " Hey man, were you in the Navy?" he enquired leaning down to shake Michael's hand. That was it. All conversation about our engine problem ceased as the three of them relived the Vietnam War for the next forty-five minutes.

Finally, a pause in the conversation gave me a chance to call up, "Is there an engine mechanic around?" Michael took the cue and followed up with an explanation of what we needed. Kevin scratched his bristly chin and volunteered George, the "island mechanic," but "it's damn hard to find him."

Our quest for George involved a lengthy island walkabout and new challenges for Jack, who for the first time in his life saw roosters, chickens, and goats at which he warily growled. Cats, on the other hand, were always fair game for chasing had I not had him firmly tethered to the end of a leash. The real challenge were the "Potcakes," island dogs that as the result of haphazard mix-master breeding have evolved into a consistent look and temperament. They are all mid-sized, brown, short-eared, and short-tempered, with an instant hostility to strangers. It was pitiful to watch Jack, a gregarious Labrador who thought all dogs were possible playmates, bound up to them, tail wagging with friendly expectations, and be instantly rebuffed and attacked.

By Wednesday we had finally corralled George in a local beach bar and persuaded him to take a look at the heat exchanger, which he diagnosed as needing a special part. Two days later, still no part. "Maybe Monday," George said. The part had been sent to another island, but he "never got around to picking it up." So we rode around the island on our bikes for a couple more days, slowly getting in the groove with island time. We ate conch burgers at Miss Laura's, biked to the bank, stopped at the hardware store, the grocery store, then biked to the other side of the island to check out the beaches and the Green Turtle Club. We ate cracked conch and drank numerous Kaliks at the Wrecking Tree, visited the Model Workshop, the Wine Shop—which had every kind of rum you could imagine—the Cemetery, the Jail, and the Albert Lowe Museum. We were back in the "cruising" mode, more or less.

Several more days passed while we exhausted all the tourist sights and still no heat exchanger. Then a disappointing trip to the post office to pick up our long anticipated mail package, which contained nothing but bills, took us down a few more notches on the enthusiasm meter. Michael threw the envelopes on the table.

"I don't know how we can afford this adventure."

"Anything from my sister?"

"No."

"Anything from home?"

"No."

"Come on. Let's go for a drink."

Our new friends Kevin and the Gully Roosters were playing at the Roost. I took my camera. A tall blonde with slightly knocked knees, wearing a short black dress, staggered up to the bar. Everyone seemed to know her and called out, "Hey Jackie, Happy Birthday!" as she lurched around the room in a "celebration" mood, dancing provocatively with "Smithy," a large, bald black man. They were well matched on the dance floor, but Jackie, gold jewelry jangling, exuded a New York attitude in contrast to the mellow "whatever" style of her partner. Her friend, a brunette with short cropped hair, had also over-celebrated and clung to the neck of a shirtless black man near the door. Most of the other black people hung out in the back room or on the porch. A middle-aged cruiser couple drank beer in the corner while their Australian sheepdog watched the scene from under the small round table. Slowly, more people started to dance, and soon Jackie and Smithy were dancing in the center of the floor while all the other yachtie types were doing a rather drunken Congo line around them. I snapped a few photos and found Michael at the bar talking to a local fisherman.

Five days later the heat exchanger was installed, the engine was flushed out, and all systems were up. After a final bike ride around town, we stopped at the Wrecking Tree for a "Wrecker"—cousin to the "Goombay Smash," another equally brutal island rum drink. A young black fellow on a bike stopped by our patio table to chat. Now the assistant minister at the Methodist church, he had lived in Green Turtle Cay all his life. When we told him we were leaving the next day, he warned us to listen to the weather. A 150-foot steel boat had turned over at Whale Cay the year before when the "rage" was on. We had heard plenty about the rage—huge waves that break across the pass to Marsh Harbour, on the eastern side of Great Abaco Island. Luckily for us, that morning Ellie, a regular on the cruisers' net, had reported "the Whale is calm and likely to remain so for a couple of days." So calm, in fact, that the next day we motored in flat seas all the way across the Sea of Abaco to Marsh Harbour. We were learning that the pattern of high wind one day, no wind the next was typical of the area.

*   *   *   *   *

The town of Marsh Harbour was built around a large, shallow, but well-protected, harbor that is a haven for cruising boats during the winter season. A center for commerce and tourism. We spent several weeks there hanging out with cruising friends, meeting new ones, and making the rounds of restaurants, bars, marine stores, and food stalls while we waited for a good weather window to head south.

On our last Sunday we took a rickety yellow school bus to the Creole Catholic church for Mass. We and two other yachties were the only white people there. The rest were Haitians, many clearly very poor. The music was a combination of tambourines, bongos, and an electronic keyboard played haphazardly by a young boy who, from what I had understood on the bus, had forgotten his music book. Songbooks were few and in tatters, and everything was in Creole French, which was a bit difficult to follow.

The priest was not present so the bus driver, a community elder, gave a very long and impassioned "sermon"—so long that everyone started saying "Amen" way before he finished. Without the priest, the congregation was like a group of children in need of a supervising parent, restless and disorganized, but the music pulsed with a unified passion. A young girl in an orange shirt and skirt decorated with sailboats led the singing.

Everyone was dressed in their best clothes no matter how old and worn: dark little girls, bundles of bright taffeta and ruffles. One woman who wore a "Minnie Pearl hat" and a bright red polka-dot dress put a dollar in the collection plate, which was a hardship, and had to make change. A three-year-old boy saw his grandfather playing the tambourine on the altar and toddled up to hug his legs. A young woman next to me, wearing in a turquoise and white lace dress with a little black pillbox hat perched at an angle on her head, swayed, clapped, and sang boisterously—making me feel not only underdressed but not sufficiently rhythmic. Next to her a small, ebony-skinned man dressed in white linen pants, a black shirt, gold-rimmed glasses, and delicate gold necklaces looked unusually prosperous, the old lady in wrinkled hot pink next to him a dramatic contrast.

At the part of the Mass where, at home, everyone tenuously turns to their neighbor to shake hands and say "peace be with you," here everyone suddenly stood, clapped and stamped their feet, singing, parading through the aisles, and hugging each other be they friend, family, or stranger. Clearly it was their favorite part of the service and practically impossible for the bus driver to convince the congregation to settle back in their seats.

After Mass, everyone lingered, filing out of the church slowly as if not wanting to leave the place where they had felt such joy and community. Many of the parishioners greeted us warmly and we, too, felt disinclined to leave our new friends and the genuine spirit of love. Sunday Mass back in Annapolis, Maryland, by comparison seemed a bit tepid and dull.

As practicing Catholics, Michael and I always looked for a place to go to Mass on Sunday no matter where we found ourselves in the world. This quest often led to unexpected adventures and linguistic challenges. But whether the Mass was in an obscure chapel on a side street in Aden, Oman, or the magnificence of St. Peter's Cathedral in Rome, was said in Arabic or Latin, attended by five people or five thousand, we always felt united with our fellow worshipers through our common faith and fundamental belief in God's love and redemption. So often, in good times and bad, that experience helped us get through the journey and brought us closer together when we may have been drifting apart—an experience which continues to this day. It is the glue that holds our marriage together.

Back then, in February 1999, however, we still had a long way to go. Little did we realize how far and how long. Then we were mainly concerned with moving down island from the Abacos, hopscotching along the giraffe neck of Eleuthera and south through the string of pearls of the Exuma chain to Long Island and Cuba.

The Pearl of the Antilles

C UBA STRETCHES HER LONG ARM FROM HAITI in the Caribbean across the Gulf of Mexico, fingertips pointing toward the Yucatán Peninsula like God creating Adam in Michelangelo's painting on the ceiling of the Sistine Chapel. Since 1492, when Christopher Columbus mistakenly assumed Cuba was part of Asia and deemed it "the most beautiful land human eyes have ever seen," its history has been plagued with political and cultural clashes that have produced a unique and vibrant country. The particular blend of African and Spanish culture is reflected in a lively and multifaceted people whose language, architecture, music, and art are passionate and sophisticated. Called the "Pearl of the Antilles," Cuba's landscape is equally varied and rich with beauty—from shimmering cordilleras to the rolling green sea of sugarcane fields waving in the tropical breeze.

Day and night music pours out of every window, a continuous sound track to daily life. Ethnomusicologist Fernando Ortiz called Cuban music a "love affair between the African drum and the Spanish guitar," which has spawned such lively rhythms as rumba, mambo, cha-cha, salsa, and son (the Cuban equivalent of American country music). Music is the lifeblood of the Cuban people, who seem to come out of the womb dancing. There must be as many Cuban musicians as there are doctors, which in 1998 numbered one for every 270 citizens. Since the Revolution medical care has been free and some of the best in the world. Illiteracy, like extreme poverty, is a thing of the past. The problem with leveling the playing field, however, is that the level is low. People live in very crowded and oftentimes unsanitary conditions, with little hope of getting a better job or improving their existence. Passionate, vibrant music is their main joy, refuge, and escape.

The dual Cuban economy is another and more curious irony. In 1999 there were both "dollar stores," where US dollars were the operative currency, and "pesos stores," which took the local currency, but there was nothing to buy. Dollar stores had food, appliances, and household goods—not as abundant as the most meager store in the United States, but at least there was something. The bottom line is that you had to have dollars to buy anything. The only way you got dollars is if you worked in the tourist trade or had a relative in the United States who could send dollars. So, in essence, even though Cuba is a communist country where everyone is equal, some are a lot more equal than others, thus making jobs in the tourist industry highly competitive.

As we were soon to discover, nothing in Cuba is ever exactly as it may appear. Your waiter is really a cigar salesman, your new best friend wants you to marry his sister, your taxi driver takes you to his grandmother's for lunch instead of to the museum. As we traveled around the world, we discovered that this was not unique to Cubans, but they win the award for doing it with the most charm and believability—set to music.

* * * * *

On May 13, 1999, a line of thunderstorms chased us into our first Cuban port, Bahia Naranjo, a large, remote bay surrounded by mangroves, backed by jagged mountains. It was stunning after the scrub of the Bahamas. Stepping over a squadron of disoriented flying fish who had crashed on deck during the passage, I dropped the anchor just as a large fish jumped three feet in the air, flashing gold in the setting sun, a derelict catamaran with a Canadian flag the only other witness.

After a boatload of ragtag "officials" finally finished checking us into the country, with their little scraps of miscellaneous paper and stubby pencils, Sheldon, the "skipper" of the catamaran, rowed over and introduced himself. A tall, thin, scruffy blond-haired "long-timer," he had spent a lot of time in Cuba and was anxious to inform us about the political situation, which had tightened recently vis-à-vis tourists and Cuban "fraternization." Now, he reported, "Girls are jailed for talking to tourists. Gone are the days when you could have Cuban friends on your boat. Cuban citizens aren't even allowed to enter the big tourist hotels." He also informed us that it was no longer possible to rent a private car and driver, which used to be really cheap. Under the new rules, everyone had to use the official taxis, which were much more expensive. "Most of the tourists are here on package tours and never go anywhere outside their glitzy resorts. But don't worry, you can go anywhere as a tourist and not get hassled."

Sheldon's friend Gil joined us later and filled us in on his Cuban girlfriend, who lived up on a hill overlooking the bay. Referring to her as his "wife," he said, "She cries whenever I leave, so I never tell her when I am going. She comes to the marina looking for me and cries until I return. She really loves me. Every day she climbs up in a tree next to her house and looks for the boat." When he described how she cooks on an open fire in her house with a dirt floor, Sheldon asked, "Why don't you buy her a stove?" Gil replied, "Gathering firewood and watering the floor gives her something to do."

Looking at me, Sheldon said, "It's hard to get used to the different morality here, girls constantly offering themselves to you. To them 'I love you' means 'glad to meet you.'"

This was all a bit disheartening: their attitude toward women, the repressive political environment, the slight shabbiness of it all. Nonetheless, it was interesting to learn that the Cuban government was happy to have us here even though our government was not, and that as long as we spend dollars, we were all friends. The next day we hauled our folding bikes out of the cockpit lockers and went exploring, leaving a patient but disgruntled Jack on board to guard the store.

Cuba is a beautiful but treacherous place for bikes we were soon to discover. All the people who were not driving around in their '50s Chevy were mostly riding bikes, which came in every form, often draped with other riders either perched in front on the handlebars or seated behind on little ledges. Sometimes the bike was rigged with a chair on the side for an extra person. One young girl balanced sideways behind the handlebars with one arm around her *novio* (boyfriend)—we supposed—her long thin legs delicately crossed at the ankles as she ate a huge papaya. mothers carried their babies in their arms or propped them on the handlebars. No wonder all the men are so thin, all this peddling of their womenfolk everywhere.

Sometimes carts were rigged to the bikes to carry people or sugarcane or wood or a slaughtered pig. It is picturesque until you realize how hard life is for everyone. Just getting from place to place often involved hours of waiting on the side of the road for a bus that never came, or hitching a ride in the back of a crowded truck. Yet everyone was dressed nicely, the women especially. If not wearing tight pants and spandex tops, they were dressed neatly in skirts, blouses, and tidy shoes, which got splattered with mud when a bus went by, which happened often as the roads were so cratered with potholes it looked as though a major mortar battle had just recently occurred. In the rain they were deadly.

One weekend we rented a car and headed inland. It was a challenging adventure full of potholed, steep, difficult roads and all the hazards of driving in Cuba's chaotic traffic: bikes, carts, broken-down buses jammed with people, carriages, motorbikes, pigs, oxen, mules, and chickens crossing the road. Cuban cowboys rode on small delicate horses—horse and rider usually thin—either in groups or alone, machetes at their sides, rolled-up cowboy hats partially hiding their handsome gaunt faces and bushy black mustaches.

Not only were the roads sketchy and the traffic challenging, but navigation for a foreigner was complicated by the lack of road signs and inconsistent maps. Somehow we found our way to Bayamo through sugarcane fields, clumps of royal palms, and banana plantations that stretched out to peaked hills. Then the land gradually flattened to sprawling pasture sparsely dotted with herds of cows. Approaching Santiago de Cuba, we crossed the foothills of the Sierra Maestra Mountains and dropped down to the city, which slopes along a curving bay on Cuba's southern coast.

After several detours we found ourselves in the Vista Alegre part of the city, originally a wealthy suburb with shaded trees and lovely old houses. Now all these houses are occupied by several families, and spacious backyards are crowded with little bungalows. We spent the night in one of these bungalows with its simple but clean room, bath, and terrible bed. Our hostess, however, was charming and completely unfazed by our furry traveling companion, Jack.

After getting settled, we clinked glasses of rum and congratulated ourselves on having successfully negotiated this first leg of our adventure. Then we went to the local cultural center, Casa Carib, where Jose Angel, the director, cooked a meal specially for us. We sat at a little card table under a shuttered window in what had once been the dining room of a grand house. High ceilings, floral murals painted on the walls, and tile floors opened out to a main hall supported by columns on each side and lit by dusty chandeliers. The dining room itself was dark. Jose brought out individual baked whole fish on a bed of cucumbers, artfully arranged on Styrofoam plates, with a plastic fork and knife jauntily stuck upright in each fish. It looked surprisingly elegant in spite of the crude materials and was very tasty, if a bit bony.

Jose was a charming man of medium height, slightly bald, with café con leche smooth skin and a round expressive face that went from melancholy to playful with a little "mas o menos" in between. His dress pants, carefully pressed long-sleeve pinstriped shirt, and innate aristocratic graciousness made us feel that we were special guests in his house. Then he brought out his guitar and I fell in love. I asked him about the difference between son and trova and he played some of each. I still couldn't tell the difference. A fellow with a red shirt and red straight-brimmed hat joined him on little bongos. It was difficult to sit still, eat politely with my plastic fork, and not fly off my chair with the intoxicating rhythm.

Later on there was to be a folk music performance. When we moved into the great hall, waiting for it to start, one of the performers approached us with her young son. A thin woman in a red knit dress, her hair in a tight bun perched like a bird's nest on the top of her head, looked at us with large expressive eyes. She smiled an overly familiar, toothy smile and aggressively pinched the boy's cheek. "He is such a good boy." Her eyes watered while I struggled through some appropriate reply in Spanish. She moved closer, stood on tiptoe, and whispered in my ear. "Could you buy me a beer and some juice for my son?" Michael went to the bar and brought back a small can of juice and a cold Cacique.

From behind the bar, Jose narrowed his eyes and stared at her. The mother and child wandered off, but minutes later she returned, as if she had forgotten something. She grabbed my arm, pulled me toward her face, and whispered, "I need money for the boy," jutting her chin toward her son standing by himself against the wall. Jose glared. She caught his eye, let go of my arm, and moved back. Just then the lights went down. She drifted off. The performance started and, thankfully, everyone saved face.

Old, fragile chairs that looked like they couldn't stand the weight of a thin Cuban much less a fat tourist soon filled up with some of both as the Folklorico Group began to sing and dance a program of spirited Afro-Cuban music. The dances were fast, energetic, and sexy, the dancers outfitted in simple but charming costumes. The first number included several "old men," characters with canes and powdered faces sneaking up on the laundry girls (a traditional dance we were to see performed with variations everywhere in Cuba.) The second had to do with seductive bread sellers, with their swishing hips and come-hither gestures. The third was a wild rumba, not to be confused with our tame-by-comparison ballroom dance version.

I was not off the hook, however. During a break, the lady in the red knit dress approached me again. Before she could say anything, I slipped two dollars into her hand. She shook her head, disappointed at what, I suppose, she considered a meager sum, and walked away. Jose, watching from behind the bar, frowned. Later I tried to explain: "What could I do? I felt sorry for the boy." Jose nodded. "No problem," he said, masking his assaulted pride.

Our Man in Havana

A STRONG WESTBOUND CURRENT FROM THE Atlantic squeezes through the narrow channel between the Bahamas and Cuba. It flows east to west along the north coast of Cuba eventually merging with the northbound Gulf Stream. This coastline between Bahia Naranjo in the northeast to Havana on the northwest is dotted with outlying reefs, atolls, islands, and shallow bays. Both the availability of comfortable anchorages and the favorable current make a westward passage to Havana the optimum route. As we made our way along this protected coast, we were often the only boat anchored in the still green waters of these isolated mangroves.

Our Cuba cruising guide advised to check in with the Guardia Frontera every night, but no one ever answered our radio call. Mostly we just saw random fishermen. Occasionally a lone man, wearing some remnant of a camouflage uniform, would appear in a small boat and ask to see our papers and then write down the information in a tattered notebook. We often saw a lighthouse or ramshackle guardhouse surrounded haphazardly by barbed wire but rarely a guard. Once, in Paradon Grande, an unattractive cay with a spectacular harlequin lighthouse, Jack and I were surprised on the beach by a boatload of what we thought were fishermen. When they pulled their boat ashore, a tall, thin, shadowy man in random camouflage sprinted toward us. Jack growled. I clipped him back on his leash. As the man got closer, I saw a holstered gun on his hip and heard loud spitfire Spanish. From his gestures it was clear he wanted us to get in our dinghy and go back to the boat NOW. We left without asking why. Explosives on the beach? Drug smuggling? I never knew, but it was a huge relief when the dinghy started on the first pull.

On the barren Cayo Santa Maria there stands a large sign announcing "Welcome to Cayo Caiman—Socialism or Death." One morning a crowded fishing boat came putt-putting into the anchorage and dropped the hook. The fishermen then spent the morning bathing and doing laundry while I tried not to watch. A few hours later they pulled up their anchor and motored directly toward us waving and yelling, *Buenos dias*! (Good day). A tall, dark-skinned man in skimpy red underwear stood on the cabin top waving and blowing kisses. Socialism or Death?

Only in Veradero, one of the largest tourist resorts in the Caribbean, did a string of officials take interest in us for a few hours, snooping around the boat, asking for cigarettes and "a little something for the children." When I offered a can of Play-Doh we had on board for some boat fix-it project, the customs officer sneered and stomped back onto the pier in a huff.

He must have unleashed some bad karma on *Ithaca*, though, because for the rest of the day Michael and I dissolved into petty arguments. The heat, humidity, and mosquitos had aggravated our anxiety about our malfunctioning batteries, the beating heart of boat life. Under the tension, our relationship eroded, and the smallest issue stirred up a hailstorm of confrontation. As we approached the fuel dock, I yelled, "I'm not ready. I don't have the fenders over." *Ithaca* plowed forward. "You're coming in too fast. We're going to hit the pier."

I scrambled to get the boat hook and tripped over a line. "I told you to stow that line," Michael yelled. Crack. The bow pulpit hit the piling. "I told you, you were coming in too fast." Michael backed off and made another approach as I positioned the fenders, and we slowly eased alongside the pier. Still fuming I went below and banged some sandwiches together, which we ate in silence waiting for the fuel truck to come. This stubborn storm dogged us for days until, finally, we could get off the boat and onto our bikes and get some space.

The ride into town along a street carpeted with vibrant red blossoms from the overarching royal poinciana trees was a visual balm. But we also needed food and a phone booth. We found some staples in a dollar store and a phone in one of the resort offices. When we called home we learned that our first grandson had been born and named Calvin after my father, who had died several years before we left. The red petals in the street blurred through my watery eyes, and I almost fell off my bike with happiness as we cruised around looking for a bar in which to celebrate, the happy news of our grandson having blown away our anger like a cold front on a stormy afternoon.

The next day we headed west again toward Havana and arrived at Marina Hemingway on June 8th, on the tail end of a huge thunderstorm with 30-knot winds and big rolling seas. Wet, but happy.

*   *   *   *   *

For four centuries Cuba was the gateway to Spain's vast American empire, and its major cities still reflect that history in beautiful albeit crumbling Spanish colonial architecture which in some cases dates back to the sixteenth century. Founded in 1519, Havana, the largest city in the Caribbean, is one of the oldest cities in the Americas and one of the most romantic, with narrow cobblestone streets, gracious squares, and dusty, pastel-colored buildings that even in their ruinous condition are still stately. Along the Malecón—a sweeping harborside walkway between the city and the sea—thousands of personal dramas play out every night under the stars and the city lights from high rises and colonial buildings whose colonnades and balconies seem to crumble before your eyes in the blowing spray from waves crashing against the seawall. In places the city looks like the aftermath of a war, whole buildings reduced to rubble. Yet it is clean, no garbage in the street, no sewer smell.

Our first day there we had beer at Los Dos Hermanos across from the Port Captain building overlooking the harbor. Afterward we walked to Plaza Vieja lined with aristocratic eighteenth-century residences, their wide covered galleries, arches, and balconies partially hidden under plastic indicating a heroic attempt at restoration—a herculean task because countless buildings and neighborhoods like this are beyond repair or impossibly impractical to restore. I wondered what this city had been like when my fifth grade friend's stepfather and his family lived here. Which had been his house and where were the family sugarcane fields? Years later, living in the United States with a new family, he had become so depressed at the loss of it all that he ultimately took his own life. Socialism or Death indeed.

In spite of the ravaged conditions of the city, we loved wandering about. Many of the buildings had been turned into museums, and a few little shops around the Plaza de San Francisco hinted at the upscale Gucci-type boutiques that would surely sprout there eventually. Refreshingly void of the usual grot shops and tourist trinkets, Havana had not yet become a Disneylandesque theme park parody of itself like so many places around the world. One good thing about the embargo was that cruise ships did not call there. For this the visitor was grateful and willing to forgive the terrible food at government-run restaurants, the hustlers, the poor transportation, and the bad roads.

But again, nothing was ever quite as it appeared. One day as we were sitting on a stone bench in front of the National Capital, modeled on our US Capitol, a delightful young couple approached us. How charming we thought as they chatted us up in accented but understandable English. Then suddenly the conversation swung to buying watches or taking a tour of the city. When we refused, the friendship evaporated as quickly as it had materialized, and they shuffled off in a huff. Minutes later the woman returned. "Hey, Yankee, some dollars for dinner?" We looked at each other, frowned with dismay. "Sorry, we don't have any money," Michael said, turning his pockets inside out. After she left, he turned to me and said, "It's interesting that there are so many hustlers here but no one obviously living on the street like we have in our cities."

"I know," I agreed, "but I still always feel guilty. They certainly need it more than we do, but then you feel mad because you've been tricked."

It was a moral conundrum we faced often and never resolved.

Later we headed to the famous Hotel Ingleterra and the bar/restaurant El Floridita, Hemingway's watering hole, now, unfortunately, swarmed by tourists. Next door, however, we found an equally charming bar where we sat by an open window drinking mojitos and watching an afternoon rainstorm pass by, the romance of the moment marred by the straggling boys staring at us with outreached hands. On the way home we stopped at a dollar store and bought two steaks. Back on the boat we watched the news about Kosovo on CNN and felt like we were a million miles away from where we had just spent the day. An ad about having beautiful toenails struck me as particularly excessive when so many people have a hard time just buying shoes.

∗ ∗ ∗ ∗ ∗

Life in Marina Hemingway was filled with the usual mix of minor boat-mending projects and local excursions often aided by our "right-hand man" Lazaro, who was an unending source of information, advice, and friendship. His story reflected the tragedy that had become Cuba after the Cold War ended. Educated in Russia as a mechanical engineer during the years when Russia was a key economic and political supporter of Cuba, he spoke fluent Russian and English and was a man of great stature and dignity. Now the only job he could find was as a "boat boy" doing odd jobs around the marina—boat cleaning and minor maintenance—for $5.00 a day. For this he pedaled his bike two hours to work every morning and two hours home every afternoon no matter the heat, rain, and humidity.

Once we found him, we always had work for him to do on *Ithaca*, and he and Jack became inseparable. Lazaro would spend the day washing the boat, doing small projects, and polishing all the stainless while Jack lounged on the pier and "talked" to him. Or, Lazaro talked and Jack listened with his head cocked attentively and the tip of his tail tapping the pier for emphasis. There were numerous treats, of course: belly scratches and back rubs. They were best friends, especially when Jack got into trouble.

We had been on a road trip to Pinar Del Rio and the mountain resort of Aguas Claras. It had been rainy and steamy. The open-air thatched roof restaurant was draped with bougainvillea, but the watery red sauce smothering bony fish (the stable of government restaurants) had been predictably tasteless and the legion of begging whining cats depressing. The house drink, a concoction of sugar, soda, and two kinds of rum, softened our mood a bit. But the dreadful omelet the next morning made us grumpy again in spite of the very reasonable $24.00 a night accommodations. After a long, difficult drive back to the marina, there was another test while we were hoisting duffle bags and groceries aboard a bucking deck.

Jack must have been feeling the stress, too, because our usually mellow, unflappable Labrador suddenly barked with alarm. Then a child cried. We turned to see a seven-year-old and his bike lying in a tangle on the pier and Jack calmly staring at him. Two seconds later irate parents began yelling at us. "Did you see that? Your dog bit James." Incredulous, I said, "What? Jack wouldn't bite a kid. He loves children." "Well, he knocked him over," Mom asserted as she untangled the little darling from his tipped-over wheels. I suggested, "Maybe your son startled Jack riding by so close to the boat. It just isn't his nature to be aggressive." "Well, he knocked James over. He might have bitten him. Look at this blood on his arm."

Mom was getting a bit rabid. Dad said, "Well, we need to call a doctor." A crowd gathered. Marina officials appeared. A doctor was called and a vet summoned. Jack nonchalantly snoozed on the deck while we politely apologized and tried to reassure everyone that Jack was not a kid killer.

Michael remained calm and low key as he always does in a crisis, but inside I could tell he was seething. (The wisdom of having a dog on board was a periodic discussion that I always dreaded.) I made excuses for Jack. Michael made excuses for the irate parents.

"He didn't really bite the boy. The boy fell on Jack and startled him so he growled and snapped," I insisted.

"This is just another example of how crazy it is to have a big dog on a sailboat."

"I'm exhausted. This is all very hard. Thank heavens for Lazaro. He is so cheerful and so sweet with Jack. Consoling him and telling him he is a good dog. He IS a good dog."

We were polite to each other, but distant, and went to bed early.

The vet came the next morning, examined Jack, and took some blood. Our trip to Trinidad was postponed because we had to wait four days to see if Jack had any disease.

June 19, 1999, Marina Hemingway, Havana

Nothing from the vet, so we are assuming Jack passed his blood test. This morning it looks like the parents and the boy have left the marina. Whew. Things are better today. Last night we went to the Hotel National for a "truce" drink. It is really quite a grand place where Batista hung out up on a hill in Vedado overlooking the malecón. Later we went to the One Eyed Cat for dinner. By 11:30 everyone was coming out to walk along the malecón, lovers, bike riders, people hugging, kissing, drinking, staring, waiting, watching. We leaned over the seawall and silently, hand in hand, watched the waves crash against the rocks below. I know Michael is right about Jack, but it breaks my heart to think about giving him up. I just can't.

* * * * *

By July it was clear our batteries were dying and beyond resuscitation. Unable to locate new ones on the island, we decided to make an overnight run to Key West to purchase new ones. When we returned to Cuba it would only be for a brief stop to get a better angle across the Gulf Stream. So this was good-bye to a place and a people we had grown to love. We were especially unhappy to say farewell to Lazaro, who had become a good friend and companion to all three of us. Waving good-bye at the end of the pier with his great grin and upbeat spirit, he represented all that was both celebratory and sad about his country.

Epping Interlude

W E SET OFF FROM MARINA HEMINGWAY
on June 28, 1999, raised the sails in a lively wind,
and flew all night by the light of a full moon. At the
time, the Cuban embargo dictated that Americans could go to
Cuba but could not spend any money. Hmm. Careful to hide
any evidence that we had, we poured our last remaining Cuban
rum into wine bottles and hid receipts or anything that looked
remotely like it came from Cuba. Fortunately, the Yacht Club at
Marina Hemingway gave American sailors a letter upon leaving
the country that stated that you and your vessel had been guests
of the marina and they had paid for everything. Double hmm.
We were still a little nervous.

The Agriculture and Immigration officials in Key West came
out to the boat immediately and took all my fruit and vegetables but
didn't come aboard. Then we walked to the Customs office, where
the official asked a lot of questions, gave us a long lecture about how
we should not be traveling to Cuba, and then asked us if we had
"the letter." "Now, you're not going back there, are you?" he gruffly
questioned. Michael said firmly, "No sir" as I thought, "Absolutely
yes." Then we were dismissed. Whew. We could have brought back a
case of cigars and no one would have been the wiser.

So there we were, back in the land of plenty, and it sure was.
The first thing I noticed was all the stores bulging with stuff: forty-
nine different kinds of breakfast cereal and as many different kinds
of tennis shoes. Loud, twanging cowboy or country music poured
out of every waterfront bar, and semi-dressed tourists crawled over
the street like Cuban ants. I was grateful for lettuce, asparagus, and

broccoli, though, and we both were grateful for West Marine and new batteries.

*   *   *   *   *

A few days later we left Jack with a vet in Key West, rented a car, and drove north to Islamorada to collect our mail from our mail forwarding service. Despite my having sent her many postcards, there was nothing from my sister. She was the last remaining person in my immediate family. She had not spoken to me, written, or answered my letters since the final settlement of mother's estate. Suddenly, at fifty-eight, I felt like an orphan. I loved her, missed her, and felt doubly bereaved.

I was not a cheerful traveling companion as we continued up the East Coast to visit family in Annapolis. While in Annapolis, our younger son announced his engagement, and our new grandson was baptized on the Fourth of July. I hoped his being welcomed into the church with fireworks was a good omen. It certainly would have delighted my always slightly irreverent father, his namesake.

Then we drove to Utica, New York, to visit Michael's mother, who was in a nursing home.

July 16, 1999, Hamilton, New York

I am sitting in Michael's sister Susie's downstairs apartment looking out the window at a sea of rolling green hills. It is 6:30 in the morning, quiet except for the ticking of a grandfather clock and the low murmur of a television. Michael's mother died last night. Her death put everything into a different perspective, more urgent and yet less significant. Live life, because it is short. Accept life for what it is. Michael is always so silent about his feelings. It is hard to comfort him. He is always the person who comforts others by his stillness and forbearance.

*   *   *   *   *

Margaret had been waiting for us at the elevator in the nursing home when we last saw her six days before. She was wearing a pink dress, her hair recently curled, and she was lively and alert during our visit. She laughed when I told her that everyone in Cuba called Michael "Papa" because he looked like Ernest Hemingway, with his graying beard and spirited eyes. She followed along with our chatter about family events and recent travels, less interested in what we said than in enjoying the fact of our presence. When Michael started talking about how much we missed our house and I missed my garden, she looked straight into my eyes, smiled wanly, and nodded. I wondered if she was thinking about the vegetable garden she and "T," Michael's father, had planted up on the hill behind their house, where they would cart twenty-five gallon jugs of water every day to keep the garden thriving. Or perhaps she was thinking of the wisteria that grew on a pergola outside her kitchen window, or the apple trees that bloomed every spring. Even though she never mentioned them, her wistful smile said it all. At that one moment I felt we shared an understanding of what our lives are about and I knew it was good-bye. Now I felt as though I had lost my own mother again.

* * * * *

July 30, 1999, Boca Chica Marina, Florida

Thank heavens for our new awning shading the top of the cabin where I sit. A light breeze ruffles my hair and staves off the horrible heat. For the past couple of weeks I have been plagued by increasing surges of anxiety and feeling like I can't breathe. We have been in so many different places in the last month or two, and experienced so much family drama, I am at a loss to put it all in perspective. In a few days we will head out again on the next leg of our adventure. I hope that when we get going again I will be so enthralled with new sights and things to learn about that this breathing anxiety will disappear. I know it has a lot to do with the weather. When it is so hot and humid, you feel like you are drowning. The fact that mother died of smoke inhalation, not able to breathe, and then seeing Margaret in her coffin has thrown me into that dark pit again that takes all my strength of will to combat.

Talking to Michael helps even though I feel so stupid. Poor guy, among his other duties as ship's captain, navigator, chief fix-it man and humorist he has to be the ship's psychologist too.

I wish I could patch things up with my sister. We don't have time for unkindness. Life is so short. I pray every day for her to find the kind of happiness and peace I have on good days, which are most of the time.

* * * * *

By August 12th, we were cruising along the northwest coast of Cuba to Maria Gorda, the closest departure point for Isla Mujeres, an island off Cancun on the Yucatán Peninsula of Mexico.

Isla Mujeres and Marshall

THE GULF STREAM, WHICH PASSES BETWEEN the western tip of Cuba and the Yucatán Peninsula, can be a temperamental body of water. We were lucky and clawed across it in a southerly 2-knot current just ahead of a tropical wave that would have turned the "stream" into a "maelstrom." Making that short passage, we not only crossed a turbulent body of water but also passed through another prism of Spain's multifaceted four-hundred-year domination of the New World where, although the language is the same, the history and culture are quite different. Cubans are predominantly Spanish/African. In the Yucatán region of Mexico, the mixture is Spanish/Mayan Indian, and Mayan features are distinctly apparent in their descendants, who are short, square-shaped people with solemn, round faces. It is a physiognomy you see throughout Central America along the Classic Route of the Maya, which we were to follow for the next six months.

Where Cuba pulses to the beat of African rhythms and the Spanish guitar, Cancun and the coastal towns to the south beat to the tune of the tourist dollar in large noisy resorts strung out along the Gulf of Mexico. Where Cuba's shops are spare, Mexico's shops bulge with all the consumer items of a flourishing Western economy. Where Cuba is lush and verdant, the Yucatán is dry and dusty. In Cuba, Michael was called "Papa" for his resemblance to Hemingway. In Mexico, he was called "Meester Wheeskers."

Landfall on Isla Mujeres (the "Island of Women") off the coast of Cancun commenced with the obligatory call on the Port Captain, a charming, polite Spaniard. A marathon check-in procedure ensued: first to the "Migration" (or Immigration office); then the bank, where we paid our entrance fee directly to avoid graft; then the "Sanitation" (or Health Inspector's office); then the Customs office, which was closed for lunch. An hour later, after ceviche and a beer at a nearby beachside restaurant, we presented our passports at the Customs office and were instructed to go to the stationery store to Xerox four copies each of our *Zarpe* (cruising permit), boat documentation, and insurance papers. Finally, five hours later, we returned to the Port Captain with our stack of signed documents legalizing our entry into the country. Every time I wait in line at a Customs kiosk in the airport I remember how difficult it really CAN be to enter a foreign country.

Once we were legal and comfortably situated in the anchorage, we attacked the town. The abundance in the shops was staggering after the scarcity in Cuba. The shelves were bulging with every kind of item you can imagine. The stationery store had shelves of notebooks, wrapping paper, and pens, things often not available in the best dollar stores in Cuba, where even the Customs officers wrote on random little scraps. Donuts, little cakes, interesting looking pastries, and some rather obscenely shaped bread loaves were piled in tempting mounds at the Panderia, where we bought bread and a few of the pastries, thinking they were a dessert sweet, which we tried after dinner. Turned out they were very spicy meat pies—a bit of a shock when you are expecting baklava. All part of the adventure but it reminded us how hard it had been for us to get bread in Cuba, where bread is free if you are a native and is served in the restaurants if you are a tourist. But we, being neither, had to beg for it.

Isla Mujeres was by turns a quiet village and a party town, with at least three restaurants and bars to every block. When the daily ferry would arrive from Cancun loaded with day-trippers, the atmosphere was a little like a perpetual carnival. In spite of this, it had a certain disheveled charm, even though building debris cluttered the streets and stray dogs ate from overflowing garbage cans—something we never saw in Cuba.

For cruisers, Isla Mujeres was an eddy off the mainstream route south along the coast of Central America to the Panama Canal. It was an easy life if you weren't planning on going anywhere, and most weren't. It was a perfect place for weary, beached-up single-handers, where inexpensive alcohol, a movable feast of available women, and easy access to marine services provided a cheap and congenial cruising community. Almost too cheap and too congenial. Like a watery vortex it swept in all the flotsam and jettison of the cruising world like so many dead leaves and broken branches. Once there it was hard to leave. Some sailors passed on to other ports of call, but many became velcroed to the pier.

Michael liked it because the tequila was $8.00 a half gallon and the mix $4.75 a quart. I liked it because the grocery store sold cheap avocados, mangos, tomatoes, and bananas, and there were numerous *lavanderias*: we once had thirty-two pounds of laundry washed, folded nicely, and put in big plastic bags for $9.00. A bargain, in our book, that we rarely saw anywhere else in the world. Jack liked it because there was a beach nearby with palm trees and a great swimming hole where we went to play several times a day. We stopped for a week and ended up staying five months, partly because of Jack.

We had been there only a couple of days when I discovered a bookstore/cultural center run by two young American women, Molly and Genevieve. It became my place of refuge while Michael cruised the *ferreterias* (hardware stores). One sultry afternoon I was sitting at a small table outside, reading—bare feet cooled by the chipped tile floor, Jack asleep under my chair, his leash looped around a table leg. My eyelids drooped from the warm air and cold beer. A fly landed on Jack's nose. He shook his head and opened his eyes to see an inquisitive cat sauntering by. He lunged, knocking over the table, beer, and book and jolting me into consciousness. The cat disappeared over a low wall and Jack lay sprawled on the tile floor amid the debris, licking his leg. Michael had to carry him back to the dinghy pier.

X-rays showed some kind of ligament tear. Medication wasn't helping. You could tell Jack was in pain. The vet said he needed to stay off his leg, get off the boat, and stay quiet. Fortunately, the marina had a small room, which we rented, and Jack and I became flat mates while Michael "kept the home fires burning" on the boat. I was sad for Jack because he was suffering and felt banished. Secretly, however, I loved having a place of my own and an excuse to study Spanish with my new bookstore friend Isabell. In truth, Michael and I needed a break from each other.

Thus, we settled into Marina Paradiso, made friends, and called it home for a while. The open-sided, thatch-roofed *palapa* at the junction of two piers was the social hub where yachties congregated for happy hour, boat talk, American football on someone's old television, beer drinking, and the occasional movie. At the palapa you could get your hair cut for $2.00, get advice about how to fix your alternator, or share a sandwich or a case of beer. It didn't take long to bond with the handful of regulars.

Max, a weathered wastrel on an equally trashed sloop named after his long-lost girlfriend, Maria, was one of my favorites. Looking a little like the Rolling Stones' Keith Richards, his hard living had not yet entirely obscured his once handsome face. Rob was a big bald tough guy who always had an angle, a beer in his hand, and an escape story. Another regular was Bob, who lived on a fading trawler and seemed to have lost himself when he lost his wife. And then there was Marshall, a fellow cruiser who lived on a boat next to us in the marina.

One day I asked Marshall over for a beer to thank him for keeping our fridge stuff while we had been away on a road trip, never realizing that I was opening a book of stories that would stay with me for years. Marshall was probably in his 80s, a bit frail, but still quite the ladies man with a charming slow Texas drawl. In spite of his freckled pale skin, rusty-gray hair, and bristly chin, you could tell he still had "it," even if his thin legs with almost no calf muscles, spreading middle, narrow shoulders, and squinting, light-sensitive left eye betrayed his years. He confessed he had trouble remembering dates and names, which mildly bothered him, but so did I. None of these little imperfections kept him from making regular visits to Cuba to visit his special girlfriend or to flirt with whatever skirt or short shorts flipped her flip-flops along the pier by his boat.

In the course of our conversation I learned that he had a thirteen-year-old son who had been born in Cabo San Lucas. "I was between wives looking for things to do. I met Rosalee on a ski trip. We were married a week and a half later." When they divorced, she wanted the boat but several years later decided to sell it. Marshall wanted to buy it back and went to see Rosalee about it. They were on the boat together. "All got very romantic and son Alph was conceived," he recounted. They reunited. Rosalee had a place in Cabo where they were when Alph was born. Marshall said to the doctor, "He'd better be white," and the baby was, according to Marshall, "as white as a light bulb next to all the other little Mexican babies." Rosalee later succumbed to cancer and Alph went to live with Hannah, Rosalee's daughter by a previous marriage, who "loved the boy from the day she saw him as a newborn when she was nineteen."

Wistfully he recounted how Alph came to visit him on the boat from time to time. "Once Alph had a pet barracuda named Ralph who lived under the pier. One day he was very excited to catch a big fish off the end of the pier, but Ralph snapped the fish in half just as Alph brought it to the surface. Only the head was left." Marshall stared at the water. A seagull bombed its prey with a splash. He looked away. "Rosalee died at home. I always regretted I didn't do that with my mother. Then we sent the boy to live with Hannah." Marshall's reminiscing was sort of like listening to an audiobook in installments. Every time we got together we heard another couple of chapters, not necessarily in chronological order.

When I asked Marshall why his boat was named *Luft Gangster*, another amazing story unfolded. He had been an air crewman in World War II. When his plane was shot down in Poland, he was taken as a prisoner and marched for three months back to Germany. The first German words he ever heard were *Luft Gangster*, meaning "air gangster," spoken by the German cavalry officer who found him hiding in the woods after he bailed out. According to Marshall, all Germans thought all Americans were gangsters.

Actually, it would make a great script for a movie. His life kept happening over and over again in flashbacks, with little changes here and there every time a new cruiser arrived in the marina. I almost filled a whole notebook full of Marshall stories: how he helped build a glider when he was a boy; his great-grandfather buying land in Texas for $1.00 an acre; and how his only daughter, "a lovely little thing," was killed in an automobile crash with two other girls and a professor on the way back from the library when she was twenty. Another child, a son, died of a heart attack when he was thirty-five.

He never talked too much about his first wife, Mary, except to say that she was beautiful, half Cherokee, which he didn't know until years later. She was a very accomplished pianist. Marshall loved her father, "Mr. Smith," a Rhodes scholar who became a lawyer in Fort Worth. "He always came for coffee every Sunday morning before his golf game at the country club with his cronies and put his hat on top of the baby grand piano which was near our front door."

It's such a splendid detail. I can still see the whole thing in my mind's eye. If I'm not careful, this whole book will turn into Marshall's book.

The Route of the Maya

B Y SEPTEMBER, JACK HAD RECOVERED ENOUGH
to take a road trip. Armed with all the maps and guidebooks
I could find, we headed west across the Yucatán Peninsula,
through small dusty villages and faded colonial towns, visiting
famous monasteries and churches and staying in a variety of
accommodations that would accept a gentleman Labrador. The
big surprise was the local food, which went way beyond the
enchiladas and beans we called Mexican food at home. At a small
open-air restaurant in Vallalodid, for instance, we feasted on a
Mayan meat dish in pabil sauce, served on banana leaves, and a
huge salad. Dinner for two, including the cerveza, was $10.00.
Jack slurped up the leftovers.

My mission, however, was the Maya. I had been reading about
their ancient culture, architecture, and art that stretched back to 2000
B.C. and had survived until the Spanish Conquest. We were in the
heart of this history, and I wanted to see it all, a quest that we followed
throughout Central America from Belize to Honduras. While I
waxed poetic about the imagery and symbolism, Michael, being more
of a nuts-and-bolts guy, usually went along with a cheerful sense of
adventure and interest in more practical aspects of the history and
architecture, like, "How the heck did they build that?"

One thing that fascinated us both was "the ball game." The Mayan
sites were true cities, with political and economic organization and
structures as well as elaborate religious and social rituals. One such
religious/social ritual happened in the ball courts. Every city had at
least one, and the ball game played in it was not so much a sport or
spectacle as it was a ritual symbolizing the struggle between the forces
of life and death. It was kind of a cross between soccer and basketball.

As Michael Coe explains in his definitive book on the Maya: "Two teams of players hit a large heavy rubber ball to each other using only their hip or elbow or one side of their body. At the end of the Classic period two rings began to appear at the center on either side of the court. If a player got the ball through the ring he won the game." After the game, the losers, or their representatives, were decapitated.

Blood and worship were two sides of the same coin. Priests and kings often performed rituals of self-sacrifice by passing a rope of thorns through their tongues and spilling their blood. Double human sacrifices were performed by tearing out the heart of the victims to ensure that the "Sun would be born the next morning" and then decapitating them to produce a flow of blood to "slake the Earth's thirst" and guarantee its fertility. These rituals were an integral part of the Mayan iconography. In no other culture were violence and beauty so intricately interwoven: the ultimate metaphor of human life, birth and death. Curiously, in spite of the violent nature of the traditions and imagery—jaguars eating hearts, decapitations, and all kinds of brutal sacrificial rites—these mysterious and violent images had an abstract quality that kept me as the modern viewer a bit detached, unlike my reaction to the writhing dancers and sensual lips depicted in much Buddhist and Hindu art, which I had seen years before in Southeast Asia.

Chichén Itzá, the most famous site in the Yucatán Peninsula, was our first of many pyramid hikes, with its more than one hundred steep steps climbing straight up, literally breathtaking in the heat and humidity. Originally a small Puuc village in the eleventh to the thirteenth centuries, it became the most important city in Maya territory and the "Mecca" of Mayan pilgrimages. Both Mexican and Puuc styles were reflected in its pyramidal temples, elaborate friezes, steep staircases, and stark "Chacmool" sculptures of a stylized reclining man holding an offering vessel or tray. Serpent columns, sculpted stone mosaics, monster masks, and skull trophy heads were all themes that reappeared and were improvised on in the more obscure Puuc sites of Uxmal, Kabah, Sayil, and Labna, which we sought out in the following days.

What particularly fascinated me was the Mayan belief that the Earth was flat and four cornered. A different tree held up each corner, and the Ceiba tree held up the sacred center—a universal and timeless image: the tree of life, the family tree, the tree of the true cross. We are all connected. There were thirteen layers of heaven, each with a different god, and nine layers of the underworld, each with its own lord of the night—all very Dantesque. The flat Earth itself was thought to be the back of a monstrous crocodile resting in a pool full of water lilies. (I loved this image.) A double-headed serpent ruled the sky. This complex, dramatic iconography was reflected in every aspect of the Mayan culture and continues today in textile designs, religious rituals, and, to some degree, the layout of local towns.

We stopped in the old colonial town of Merida. In the center of town was a square with a church on one side, arcaded municipal buildings on the others, and a clock tower. Not unlike the layout of a Mayan ceremonial site. The huge tree in the center of the square reflected the Mayan idea of the Tree as the center of the World. There was also a fountain and, most interestingly, a basketball court. Each little town we passed through fit this formula to a greater or lesser degree.

It was all so fascinating, but the more excited I got, the more concerned Michael got about the boat, maintenance issues, and our overall schedule. I wanted to go on to Campeche; he wanted to go "home" to *Ithaca*. We stopped in a small village and tried to talk about it over *sopa de lima* and fajitas. He was recalcitrant. I pouted. Then there was Jack, who did not want to poop in the parking lot but there was no other place on the busy street. Everything was cement and people. So we got in the car and drove around to find an appropriate place to take him for a walk. We got lost. Finally, we stopped at a sports complex where there were lots of trees and grass. Jack happily relieved himself and we played ball while Michael tried to figure out where we were. Not so easy with sketchy paper maps instead of GPS and electronic charts. We both loved Jack, but sometimes it was like having a two-year-old in tow and often caused tension between us, as two-year-olds are wont to do. The rest of the afternoon there was little conversation in the car. Jack slept in the backseat. I looked out the window. Michael drove.

Food is sometimes the best antidote to anger, however, and our dinner at Los Almendros, a restaurant specializing in Yucatán food, did the trick for a time. A healthy helping of poc chur, pollo peril, cochinita pibil, and a spicy sausage called longaniza—served with an achiote sauce of chopped onions, sour oranges, tomatoes, hot peppers, and pickled onions—washed down with a couple of bottles of DosXX, restored our spirit of compromise, and we agreed to head back to the boat and save Campeche for another time.

September 11, 1999, Isla Mujeres, Mexico

Back in the marina, having picked up our mail in Cancun and sent off our broken autopilot. I have about given up on hearing anything from my sister. I just try not to think about it but still I feel a bit down. I really would like to be anchored off a nice beach where we could just jump over the side and go snorkeling instead of rail to rail with all these other boats. Although, it is pleasant to have unlimited electricity and water. M is in a bad mood because of the broken autopilot and mounting boat bills. We just keep getting hit with mountains of unexpected expenses. Stock market is up but we keep spending everything we are making in the stock account. Everyone grumpy on our anniversary. Not good.

Thirty-four years of marriage today and we are still learning how to do it. I am too sensitive about the "he always thinks he's right" syndrome. He does always think he's right. Maybe it's just a male thing. I think he doesn't give me any credit for knowing anything about anything—or, rather, anything important like "how to do" or "how to fix." I take it as a personal insult when I think my opinion is ignored or unwanted when perhaps it is more male stubbornness than anything personal. I just have to let it go. But it does seem like every time I suggest something, he automatically says "No" before he even considers my idea. He says I always say "What?" which drives him crazy, but I just can't hear him.

I always want to go further, walk further, see more, go around the next bend in the road. I hate to lose that enthusiasm and sometimes I think I give up too soon and we miss things that even he would like to have seen. But it's all a compromise. The world won't end if we don't get to Campeche. There are so many other places down the line to hold out for like Tikal and the Bonampak murals.

Rainy Season Blues

W E ENDED UP STAYING IN ISLA MUJERES until February while Jack healed and the rainy season passed. It was hot, humid, and wet. Mold seemed to grow on everything overnight. Boat projects, particularly varnish projects, were aggravatingly difficult. Michael would disappear into town to do email for hours while I sat around, read books, studied Spanish, and took care of Jack. My arthritic body ached from the dampness and my mental state echoed the weather—stormy, unpredictable, with brief periods of sunshine.

We were hanging around on Marshall's boat one night when Max and Rod stumbled aboard. "Been celebrating, Max?" Marshall asked. "Yeah. It's my birthday. Fiftieth as a matter of fact." He slumped down next to me. "Give us a birthday kiss, honey." I definitely was not in the mood for this. They were way ahead with the partying, but I smiled and gave him a little smooch because he seemed so down. For some reason, he started describing a movie with Robert Duvall called *Tender Mercies*. Rob cracked another beer. Max shook his head. "God, I hope I don't end up like that." I wondered, what exactly WILL his future be? It was all too depressing.

Later, back on the boat, Michael said, "I know you had different plans for your life. Thanks for coming with me and doing my thing instead." I answered, "I don't think about it too much like that. I just keep trying to find ways to be who I am and do something more with my life within the context of where I am." In actual fact, of course, Michael did a lot of things for me that he wasn't really interested in doing. I thought about it all night and whined in my journal the next morning.

October 31, 1999, Isla Mujeres, Mexico

It is frustrating to always feel like I am starting over. Just as far away from all my goals now as I was five years ago, ten years ago . . . I am putting a lot of effort into learning Spanish now. I hope it pays off and I can become somewhat fluent and we in fact spend significant time in Spanish-speaking countries. Not like all the effort I put into learning Mandarin Chinese. I miss doing art stuff. I just can't seem to find a way to work it in with our lifestyle. I miss photographing. I'm so used to working in black and white, when I get all these boring, faded photos back I wonder why bother. Why spend the money to get them developed. I really have to fight to hold on to my enthusiasm.

Sometimes I would really just like to be home, sitting in my swing with my grandchildren, working in my garden, playing in my darkroom, not here in this floating trailer park with a bunch of drunks.

*   *   *   *   *

The three-day music festival in town was a welcome break from our glum rainy season routine. We gorged on tacos from the food stand and watched children playing in the bandstand in the center of the square—sliding down the steps and making up games and chasing each other around to the music—while pretty girls paraded through the plaza obviously trying to catch the eye of the young bucks bunched together drinking beer and joking. A few couples danced. One particularly energetic pair was there every night, she flinging her hips and hair to the music until you'd think she would collapse from exhaustion. I brought my camera but couldn't seem to get up the energy to take photographs. I was so mesmerized by the music and the scene unfolding before me that I could not find a way to photograph the soul of this event. It was so cinematic, so in motion, so dependent on the pulse of the music. It was like trying to capture running water in your bare hands. So I wrote about it instead.

November 13, 1999, Isla Mujeres, Mexico

A father swings his child in the air, a middle-aged couple dance with the authority and rhythmic assurance that years together has created, tourists in awkward imitation, a solitary, stoic Mayan behind his cart stirring meat for tacos in time to the music, a little girl with a yellow balloon tied to her wrist skips through the crowd batting her balloon in all directions. A dancer in a long ruffled skirt twirled and swirled, her skirt billowing out all around her in ribbons of color, heels clicking. Another long-legged beauty in hot pink with a ruffled train, gold headdress, and very high gold strappy heels moved as if she didn't have a bone in her body.

Walking back to the boat, the neon lights of the carnival rides set up along the mini "malecón" illuminate the crashing ocean waves on the lee side of the island, the blare of the music garbled and amplified so that we can still feel the pulse of the bass halfway home to the marina. A steady wind stirs the palms overhead, which bow and weave to the music like drunken dancers. Rod and Max sit glassy-eyed drunk under a tree. Max beats the pavement with his feet. Meanwhile, Ed talks about his youth in New Jersey going to hear Tommy Dorsey.

* * * * *

Then it was Thanksgiving and I was trying to re-create mother's turkey stuffing with whole wheat Bimbo bread, chorizo sausage, and whatever I could find in the market. Michael watched the football game while I chopped and fried and stirred and tasted—and tasted again—adding more and more sage and rosemary to counteract the sweet taste of the Bimbo bread. About 3:30 we walked up to Molly and Genevieve's house on a cliff overlooking the sea. Everyone piled their plates high, made a toast to the cooks and everyone's various gods and homelands, ate, groaned, and went back for more. The party went on until 1:00 a.m. as people came and went. All of us sat out on the porch and watched the splendid moon rise up over the clouds.

It was a surprisingly special Thanksgiving with new friends gathered around who had become our extended family in this temporary home. In essence that was what our life was about then. We were drifters, picking up whatever little shiny stones we could find to build new connections, to shore up new pools of happiness that, though temporary, accumulated into a new landscape, constantly shifting underfoot, but boulders at the core kept us from falling through.

December 17, 1999, Isla Mujeres, Mexico

It is 7:00 a.m.—a beautiful cool morning, clouds tinged with the pink of a rising sun and sky growing ever bluer. The water is still and clear as a mountain lake. It is a treat to be alone and quiet with no particular plan for the next four hours.

In less than a week we will be flying home for Christmas and in a week more it will be the end of the 20th century. It seems appropriate that we have spent the last couple of weeks tracking down and learning about the Mayan culture that thrived at the beginning of this millennium. A people who spoke and wrote a mysterious language, left their history carved in little pictures on stone, fought wars over territory and power, governed their lives by ritual, myth, and faith. They stared at the same stars and marked time by the movements of the heavens, reaped, sowed, gave birth, died, beautified themselves with beads and feathers, loved their children, honored their dead. They still speak to us eloquently, if mysteriously, across the years through their crumbling architecture and handmade objects. Through these things we recognize our common human bonds. We see ourselves.

A tiny terra-cotta dog in a glass museum case is a touchstone. His rounded tummy, upturned nose, and pointed ears are so blissfully and lovingly articulated, I feel a contact with the person who made him. I feel the surface with my eyes, imagine smoothing the clay, and touch the hands of the past.

What will I leave behind to speak a thousand years from now to some astounded, mystified eyes, to say I am like you? We continue. Touch me. You are me. I am in you. Is this arrogance or is it God working through us all so that we recognize and want to communicate our spiritual nature as well as reproduce our physical selves. To make contact, to say this is how I saw it. This is how I felt.

We are one. We continue. We do not die. You take the torch from me like the children marching up the hills toward our Lady of Guadalupe in one endless stream, up and down the mountainsides. They pass the torch, the same flame into eternity where the dragon with two heads lives or the shining sphere of a Christian God, a Buddha, or Nirvana or naught. Take your pick, but it's a long way to go—many thousands of years, many mountainsides to pass the flame unless you believe as the Tancandon Indians that the world will end in March of 2018 when Shield Dragon's head will fly back onto his body with a bang and the world will end, exploding temples and teapots, tyrants and timid people into shining little particles of nothing.

But I don't believe it. The irony, the joke, the wonderment, and the miracle is that we do not die. It does not end. We humans think in terms of absolutes, beginnings and endings, up and down, good and bad, but God expressing Himself through human life is endless and beyond what we can understand, what we can put a beginning to or an end.

I stand here now on the threshold of an arbitrary time. In my hand a jade bead with round eyes and full lips speaks to me. I must put it in my mouth, bury myself, and wait to be found.

Millennium Memories

J ACK USHERED IN THE MILLENNIUM IN ISLA
Mujeres with Molly and Genevieve, our dog-loving buddies
from the bookstore, while we flew home for a spontaneous
holiday visit and a New Year's Eve celebration at our community
clubhouse, reconnecting with old friends as if we had never left.
At 11:45 p.m. we snuck out of the party and paid a stealth visit to
our house. Unbeknownst to our renters, we skirted around the
garage, tiptoed through the rose garden to the water's edge, and
sat on our favorite bench overlooking the river. Just as the last
seconds of the last millennium ticked off, we popped a bottle of
champagne and smooched in the moonlight like two teenagers
while fireworks exploded overhead. There was no place in the
world we would have rather been.

In spite of what was to come, that Christmas with family and
grandchildren was the most precious. Now, sixteen years later,
reading my journal entry written just after we returned to the boat in
January 2000, I find I still miss the same things.

January 10, 2000, Isla Mujeres, Mexico

*I miss: 101 Dalmatians in front of the fireplace; cold fingers around tea
cups after building a snowman; Alexis finger painting while I wrote
thank-you cards; baby Calvin putting his toes in his mouth, perfect brown
hair like a helmet on his square head, sparkling brown eyes and little tank
of a body going stiff and refusing to sit when you put him in the high chair;
Alexis' sea glass green eyes and expressive face like a fast-moving summer
sky; the halo of fine, flying blonde hair, the perky pink bow cockeyed on the
back of her head, hair escaping at the nape of her neck, and the dramatic
gestures; the way her pink lips purse together when she expertly mimics
her mother saying "that's rude" with a determined little hand on hip and*

body cocked sideways; the little sleepy body padding down the hall dragging "Elly" by a tattered pink ribbon in one hand and Pete's hand in the other to get "snuggie" in bed with Dad and a story. All that ended with heart wrenching hugs good-bye when we left to go back to the boat.

A week later we unexpectedly returned.

January 28, 2000, Annapolis, Maryland

Just yesterday we were back on Ithaca, now we are in Pete's house again. It's about 7:30 a.m. I am curled up in bed listening to the household noises as everyone slowly awakens. Pete turns a light on in the hall. Coffee pot gurgles, garage door opens and closes, toilet flushes, whisper, step-step-step softly down the hall again, car keys jingle, front door quietly opens and closes. Car motor starts. Alexis talks to her doll. Calvin starts little gurgling noises which increase in volume as he is ignored. Alexis whining. Calvin screaming now for breakfast and attention. Mom tells Alexis firmly "get dressed," Alexis says, "I don't want to" with a stamp of her foot. Now giggling, laughing and singing. Thunderstorm is over. Calvin is quiet, soothed by his bottle. Toilet flushes, voices drift off into the kitchen.

We are back in Annapolis because Michael's older sister Nancy is dying. I had almost forgotten for a minute until Alexis, sitting on a little stool next to me at the dinner table, looked at me with big serious eyes and said, "Is Da's sister better?" "How could I tell her No?" How could I say she would never get better? How could I explain that there was even such a thing as death? Such a thing as this deep sadness that grips the heart with an icy hand in the middle of a summer day. That she should ever have to know death's cruel revenge ravages my spirit more and yet I know, but for it, her face would shine the less.

That for all the loss of mothers and sisters and brothers and fathers, for all the pain of loneliness and mistaken paths, misspoken words, there is the still and always reward of renewed life, new chances, clean slates, the perfect unblemished hope in Calvin's smile.

* * * * *

Nancy died before we got to the hospital. It was a cruel loss for the whole family even though not unexpected, since she had been sick for quite a while and was clearly not doing well when, months earlier, we had all been together mourning the loss of Margaret, Michael's mother. On the drive back from Utica to Annapolis, memories seemed to pop out from every bend in the road. I couldn't seem to shut up and kept babbling on about the past while Michael listened silently and watched the asphalt spin out in front of us.

By the third of February we were back in Isla Mujeres preparing to move south. We were anxious to move on but sad to leave so many good friends whom we would probably never see again. When all the last-minute boat fix-its, shopping, and partying were finished, we all hugged each other, shed a few tears, shared a few jokes, popped a beer or two, and pulled away from the pier, waving and promising to write, relieved in a way to be on to something new. So many leave takings in the past couple of months had been exhausting.

More Maya

CRUISING SOUTH TO BELIZE, HIGH-RISE resorts and dreary fishing villages—many of which might have originally been Mayan towns later buried by Spanish settlements—now dominate the Yucatán Peninsula coastline. That the Mayan site of Tulum, 80 miles south of Cancun, survived is a minor miracle. Constructed in the late Mayapán period as the great Mayan civilization was coming to an end, it was probably still inhabited when the Spaniards arrived in 1518. Surrounded by a defensive wall on three sides, it's less than imposing "watchtower," perhaps derisively called the *castillo* by the Spaniards, still stares out at the greenish-blue Caribbean Sea from a high headland. Originally built to protect a small port and ward off attack from the sea, now its stucco masks and coiled snakes grimace at invading tourists, who have appropriated its signature winged "Diving God" flying down from heaven to receive the offerings of men as a scuba symbol.

Continuing south past Chetumal, we checked out of Mexico in San Pedro and worked our way inside the barrier reef that shelters the Belize coast with a jewel-like necklace of small offshore islands, atolls, and bright underwater gardens—a haven for divers and heaven for sailors in search of brisk sailing over flat seas undaunted by narrow harbor entrances, unmarked reefs, shallow water, and rough passes between offshore cays.

After a week in Cay Caulker, we were ready for a land adventure. A friendly veterinarian in Belize City agreed to keep Jack while we donned our backpacks and set off on a five-day trip inland via bus, taxi, truck, and boot leather. Known primarily as a dive destination, Belize, once the center of the lowland Mayan empire, is also an archaeological wonderland. More than six hundred sites have been identified, many still buried and unexplored. At this point I was deep into Mayan lore and wanted to see them all, or at least most of them.

Near the town of Nabitunich we met a woman named Margaret who ran a local clinic and the small resort lodge where we were staying. Over a couple of beers, we also met three men who were staying at the lodge. They were members of the Dayton Rotary Club, which had donated a van to Margaret's clinic and were there to build a little chapel adjacent to it. Two of the men, one of whom was an ex-FBI agent named Tony, had worked with Mother Teresa in Calcutta. He had had the job of collecting the dying from the railroad tracks every day to bring them into a shelter to be cleaned up and die with some kind of dignity. "The rule was we could only use primitive brooms made out of sticks to clean the filth and stench because Mother Teresa believed that we should not have anything more than what the people themselves had. It was a humility issue." We were stunned by the story and felt wholly inadequate in the presence of these men.

The next day they took us to the little chapel they had built and were hoping to have finished by the twenty-fifth of February, when it would be consecrated. Tony had made a Celtic cross for the front door out of an aluminum form stuffed with found objects and bits of trash—a thrift shop statue of St Joseph, two plastic Christmas angels, a dove of peace, and fragments of broken glass. Nothing more than what the people themselves had. It glowed with love. Using local discarded mahogany, town craftsmen had built pews and a lectern and carved a panel depicting the Last Supper for the front of the altar. Margaret had painted a statue of the Virgin, and stained glass windows had been copied out of fiberglass. Everyone had contributed something. They were all so proud of this humble little chapel, and we felt especially privileged to share their accomplishments with them. Later we learned that Margaret had been presented with a special award by Queen Elizabeth for her years of humanitarian effort in the area.

We waved good-bye and hiked down the path toward the bus stop in silence. In my journal I wrote: "I am often struck by these brief, intense encounters with strangers living wholly different lives.

We swirl around in our own orbit like revolving teacups in a carnival. We spin around and around bumping other cups and careening off toward the next one, in the circular, ever spiraling Mayan concept of time . . . but some teacups leave a lasting dent."

*   *   *   *   *

Continuing on the spiral, we crossed the Guatemalan border on foot and climbed into the back of a pickup truck, bouncing along a rutted dirt road for several hours until we reached the ferry to Flores. By this time we could hardly walk and fell into the nearest hotel that looked acceptable: not the most scenic, but cheap and exactly what we needed at the time—mainly a functioning bathroom.

Tikal, a short minibus ride from Flores, was the center of the lowland Mayan kingdom. Occupied from 900 B.C. to 950 A.D., it synthesized the cultural achievement of the late Pre-Classic and Classic periods. At one point an estimated ten thousand inhabitants lived within a radius of a thirty-minute walk from the center. Typical of the lowland Mayan settlements, Tikal's major structures were organized around a central plaza in a "triadic" pattern—a principle pyramid flanked by two lesser ones—representing a triad of gods. These pyramids were nosebleed-high jungle skyscrapers, however, with extremely steep stairs ascending from the central plaza to small, mysterious chambers at the top crowned by roof crests decorated with elaborate stucco relief. Other groups of structures lay scattered throughout the nearby forest, once connected by broad causeways that were now diminished to overgrown jungle paths. Bright, noisy toucans, bunched on branches overhead, looked down on us plodding along where majestic royal processions once passed. Strange raccoon-like critters with upturned flexible snouts scratched around in the undergrowth, and black howler monkeys, sacred to the Maya, called to each other eerily from the treetops sounding like disgruntled ancient Mayan spirits.

Mysterious and magical as the site was, it took some perseverance to absorb. It was hot. There was little information. Michael was anxious to move on, while I lingered over my guidebook and map unable to figure out where we were and what exactly we were looking at. I told him to just go on without me, but he waited, both of us annoyed at the other for different reasons. The rest of the day was dogged by an undercurrent of tension which gnawed at us unrelentingly, eating away the enthusiasm and adventure of exploring together.

July 15, 2000, Flores, Guatemala

I don't know why it is that no matter how romantic or interesting or exotic and unusual a place may be, one really has to be "up for it," attentive, undistracted by personal problems and open to absorbing a unique and different experience. I get angry at M when he isn't interested in what I'm interested in. But sometimes I am the one who is distracted, or uncomfortable, or bored, or angry, or tired. And sometimes I just can't sustain my own passionate interest because my feet hurt, I am ashamed to confess, even when I know I have this extraordinary opportunity. I am someplace I have never been and will never see again. I am angry at myself. There were magical moments at Tikal but I missed a lot.

* * * * *

Life story after untold life story passes before you on a bus, and the trip back to Cay Caulker was no exception: poor people living in mud houses with dirt floors, wearing tattered clothes, trying to raise and feed their children, find work, sell something to someone so they themselves can buy food in the continual battle to just survive without having to scrounge through garbage like the old woman I saw from the bus window, bent over in the smoke probing the garbage with a stick next to a dog doing the same with his nose.

All this against such stunning, dramatic countryside, such apparent natural wealth. When we got to the end of the line, we were the last off the bus except the two boys who were dead asleep in the back. Michael woke up one and he woke up the other, both hard to bring back into conscious world. No wonder, when their conscious world, even at this young age, is such a heavy burden that can only ever be truly laid to rest in sleep or, finally, in death.

After our trip to Tikal, we settled into *Ithaca* once more and continued south along the coast of Belize, cruising the offshore islands of the barrier reef, slowly working our way to Guatemala. By April 14th we had crossed "the bar" across the mouth of the Rio Dulce, checked into Guatemala at the port town of Livingston, and were heading upriver through a spectacular gorge of hanging vines and vegetation. White herons and yellow butterflies swooped across our bow. Fishermen cast nets from their *cayucos* and families paddled upriver under the shady overhangs along the shore. Clutches of thatched huts clung to the cliff side, and brown children dove off mossy logs half submerged in the dark water. Then, suddenly, the narrow gorge opened out like the inside of a candy Easter egg and we motored across a large bay called El Golfete, ringed by misty mountains in the distance. When the river narrowed again, small marinas and more pretentious houses lined the shore. After a sharp bend to starboard, we found Mario's Marina, which was to be our home for the next six months.

The Land of Eternal Spring

TUCKED WAY UP THE RÍO DULCE, WELL OUT of the hurricane belt, we felt protected from the weather if not entirely safe from the random marauders who were plaguing the river farther north. Daphne, the marina director, clenched a cigarette between her teeth and secured our lines to the pier while restraining a boxer mix who threatened to come aboard. Jack jumped off to her loving embrace and immediately made friends with the marina menagerie, wisely acquiescing that Daphne's cat was totally off-limits. Michael and I headed for the bar.

Like Marina Paradiso in Isla Mujeres, Mario's was a sailor's refuge populated by old circumnavigators, Caribbean veterans, sailors passing through like ourselves, and longtime liveaboards who had made Mario's their permanent home. The small pool, marina bar, and open-air restaurant were the gathering spots where everyone hung out, told stories, and exchanged information. I immediately noticed some unusually nice portraits of Guatemalan women hanging over the bar and was told the artist was Hank, an old grizzled sailor sitting off by himself with a young man who stared into his beer with the same intensity as the old guy. "That's young Hank, or 'Hank wanna be,' we call him. His real name is Robert. They've been hanging out here for years," Willy the bartender informed us. "Old Hank even has his name engraved on his bar stool. And this here's Gret and Hans. They're circumnavigators too."

"You folks just come in? Glad you made it okay. There's been some rough stuff goin' on around here. Last week we helped bring a Dutch couple into Roatan who'd been attacked by pirates off Honduras and their son shot. Pretty sad," Greta confided.

Michael and I looked at each other and raised our eyebrows. "I didn't think we'd have to worry about pirates till we got to the Red Sea," he said.

"Yeah, well, it used to be pretty safe up here but now upriver . . . I wouldn't take a boat up there," Willy volunteered.

Fortunately, the young couple on our right changed the subject and started telling us about the beauty of Holy Week in Antigua, the old Spanish city in the highlands where it was "Eternal Spring." It sounded a bit like Shangri La. Who could resist? Just to get away from the heat and humidity would be a treat in itself. Once settled in and reassured that it was perfectly safe to leave the boat in the marina, we were off in a dilapidated rental car with our buddy Jack riding shotgun.

The first part of the drive took us through green fields, palm trees, and tropical terrain that gradually became drier and more mountainous. Palm trees gave way to cactus, and brown hills were covered with dead bushes studded with what looked like cotton balls. Slowly it got cooler as we approached the urban sprawl of Guatemala City and took the exit for Antigua. The road continued to wind up into cool mist, pine trees, and the world where springtime was everlasting. Five hours later we bounced over the cobblestone streets, past blocks of walls, windows, and colorful doors, to find our way to Jack's "hotel" at veterinarian Cynthia Buskie's premises, where he would stay for the week while we hung out at the Casa Azul, a few blocks away, for the Holy Week celebrations called Semana Santa. From the balcony of our room we looked down on a rose-bowered courtyard, small swimming pool, and fountain. Over the garden wall and beyond the sea of red tile roofs rose a cathedral and a volcano looming through the mist.

* * * * *

It was Good Friday. The town was thronged with people. Finding a place for dinner was a challenge. After dinner we walked through the square to a church where people were visiting the gold and glass casket of Señor Sepultado, the figure of the dead Christ, as if they were paying their last respects to a real person. Faith for me is so different, so much more abstract, that while this was strangely moving, it was as foreign as praying to Vishnu. Behind the church lay the ruins of what once was a huge cathedral that was destroyed in the earthquake of 1773, when the town was devastated and abandoned. Here the Blessed Sacrament was displayed in a portion of a cracked wall illuminated with lights and candles in dead branches. Crowds of people pushed in to venerate it. It was a stunning sight, so much so that I began to suspect it was as much about competitive set decoration as religious devotion.

On the street, Christ in a crimson robe, carrying the cross, towered over the crowd, swaying on an elaborate platform born on the shoulders of twenty men dressed in black. Under their feet an elaborate carpet with patterns of pine needles, roses, rose petals, statice, chrysanthemums, and colored sawdust that was shredded and smashed. Roman soldiers in red robes blew trumpets. Herod, Pilate, and the two thieves were followed by children carrying banners. A huge crowd clogged the cobblestone streets. Loudspeakers announced that cars would be towed if they were not moved. On every street townspeople hosed away the dead flowers to begin new carpets, putting the last petals in place minutes before the next procession trampled it. All the while a flute and drum funeral dirge floated on air hazy with incense and heavy with the smell of pine needles and roses.

April 22, 2000, Antigua, Guatemala

In the hotel courtyard a dolphin fountain arches water into one end of the blue and green tiled swimming spool. Purple bougainvillea blossoms float on the surface of the water. I am the only one here. I feel like I am in my own home, having just been served an impeccable Caesar salad on the upstairs balcony. After all the scenes of penance and Christ's suffering we have seen in the last two days, it seems a bit self-indulgent, particularly since poor Michael is upstairs sick in bed and poor Jack is in jail around the corner. I feel like I should be crawling over the cobblestones on my knees or whipping my back for all my past sins.

* * * * *

The day before had been exhausting, especially for Michael, who was battling the flu. The ceremony of the Crucifixion of Christ started an hour late. Meanwhile, thousands of people milled about: Indian women selling their wares on the church steps; food vendors; men selling balloons, cashews, cotton candy, windmill whirligigs, and little purple felt dolls dressed like the *cruceros* (cross or pall bearers). Groups of Indian families sat on the grass under the trees while crowds of people went in and out of the church to wash the Christ and pay their respect. I felt like I was in the middle of a biblical movie set. Three crosses were set up outside the church, two with figures of the thieves and one waiting for Christ. I wasn't at all sure what to expect.

Finally, Christ was brought out, attended by men in black robes and pointed hoods who hung him on the cross while very loud, funereal dirge music played and then switched to religious pop song style music. Over this you could hear the Good Friday "examination of conscience" going on in the square. Fortunately, this was not an actual nailing of Christ to the cross as is performed in some places, like the Philippines, but the emotion was high.

Later that night we stood on the street corner and watched another procession from the church of La Escuela de Cristo. Long rows of men in black robes and hoods poured down the street, followed by floats illustrating the Stations of the Cross and the Crucifixion. Behind them a huge silver float topped by Señor Sepultado's coffin slowly passed over the crumpled flower carpet. Then long rows of women in black— fat, thin, old, young—and children, dark skinned and light, carried a massive wooden float with the Virgin dressed in black, her crystal tears glowing in the spotlight. The drums boomed. The earth shook. The music wept as the heavy float wove back and forth, then went forward, wove back and forth again, went backward, then forward as if a metaphor for all our lives. At the end of the block the procession stopped for new women to move in and relieve the others.

· The whole town was black and smoking as the procession left the square to carry on through the town. Incense clouded the air, deep drumbeats echoed in my head, and my body was crushed in the crowd until I thought I would fall over. Slowly the crowd thinned and a strange quiet settled in. The music drifted away with the smell of incense. Exhausted, we went around the corner and luckily found a table in a semi empty and quiet restauran,t where we ate a meager fish dinner.

I said, "I guess I did become a pre-Vatican II convert to Catholicism for the 'performance' as well as the theology—the beauty of the mass, the liturgical music, the Latin, the theater—but this is something else."

"Right, but then there was Vatican II, the English Mass, and folk songs," Michael pointed out. "Tricked you."

"I know. It's all the same story, just a different score."

The next morning we walked to the Santo Domingo church for Easter Mass. There were no flowers. On a ruined wall of the church white fabric hung over the altar to the floor, forming a canopy over the altar, which was lit with candles. All the chairs were covered in white. A woman was kneeling at the altar leading the recitation of the rosary and a man was playing synthesized organ music as people slowly filled the chairs.

The sermon, as best as I could understand, seemed to downplay all the drama of the past days and emphasize how Christ lives through us every day in how we live our lives and love and care for other. There was a very gentle breeze stirring the drapery; the sun was shining but it was cool; a soft, quiet calm pervaded the scene. I felt a powerful sense of peace, "the peace that surpasses all understanding." After Mass we headed back to our hotel holding hands in silence, not wanting to break the mood.

Later I went for a walk along the quiet streets. A lady was sweeping her sidewalk, families were saying good-bye to relatives and packing up the car, a crumpled man slept in a doorway. Inside La Escuela de Cristo a few people were praying. Huge floats sat abandoned in the churchyard. An old woman rubbed her hand along the silver side of the float platform as if reliving the experiences of the previous days. The streets were empty. Blank walls of soft pinks and greens looked dazed in the sun, the cobblestone streets patterned with colored sawdust pressed in the crevices.

As I approached the Church of San Pedro, a small crowd was gathered around a continuous carpet of flowers that extended for a solid block directly to the door of the church. It was a very elaborate design of yellow and white roses, chrysanthemum petals, purple statice, mangos sliced in three sections to look like birds, images of the lamb of peace, rosaries, and baskets of yellow, white, and orange flowers. Mass was just ending. I couldn't believe that I had fallen upon the scene at exactly the right time and had exactly two exposures left on my last roll of film: one for the carpet and one for the procession. I took the carpet picture too early and really didn't get the best possible picture, but I waited for the last one. Just as the float with the risen Christ moved out of the doorway into the sun there was a place for me to kneel down and take one picture. The music swelled with joyous tambourines. Men and women accompanying the float were dressed in bright robes. Dancing and walking beside it were the poor, the retarded, and Indian families. This is the one procession where one does not have to pay to participate, since San Pedro is the church that ministers to the hospital of the poor.

A Mayan couple I had seen the night before were among the procession. Old, small, and bent over, walking slowly, step by step, hand in hand, they seemed to ignore everything around them, focused on their own spiritual journey. Later, in the trampled carpet, I found one perfect yellow rose, which I picked up and carried with me the rest of the way back to the hotel.

* * * * *

After a week in the world of Eternal Spring, we returned to our river home where the rainy season was starting to "steam." I kept busy with boat canvas projects while Michael was constantly rebuilding something; all the lockers stood open and tools were spread out on every surface that wasn't covered with sewing materials. The afternoons were spent cooling off in the pool, the evenings hanging out at the bar. Same people. Same conversations. I grew restless and yearned to return to the stimulus of urban life.

"Let's just wait out the hurricane season in Antigua. Remember all the Spanish schools we heard about? Maybe we could live with a family."

"What about Jack?"

"Look. I found the perfect place: La Escuela de San Jose el Viejo."
I read from the brochure: "Located in a flowery garden compound
with small individual casitas that you can rent for the duration of your
studies. Classes are designed to accommodate the specific needs and
interests of each student, who has their own individual instructor for
four to six hours every day."

After a few more beers, Michael softened. "Okay, why don't we
try it for a couple of weeks," and soon Jack was in the backseat of the
rental car, sitting on a throne of duffel bags like a little prince, and we
were off on a new adventure.

Being a compulsive student, I was in heaven. Michael was just
happy to be away from the strain of constant boat projects. Jack was
happy to sit under my chair during school time as long as there was
tennis ball time after class. The three of us settled into our tiny *casita*
with its tile floors, mounds of blankets, and miniscule kitchen. We
didn't see each other for most of the day during the week because we
were studying with our individual teachers in separate little open-air
pavilions. Every day I felt more fluent in the language because much
of the emphasis was conversational, and we had the added bonus that
daily life presented constant opportunities to practice.

Antigua is a picturesque, cultural town with interesting museums,
restaurants, ornate Spanish colonial churches, artful shops, and the
most vibrant, verdant, abundant, and visually stimulating market
I have ever seen. Hills of fresh fruit, vegetables, greens, and herbs
mounded up on tables, and tarps stretched to the horizon, artfully
interspersed with bouquets of calla lilies, roses, zinnias, and irises.
The vendor ladies themselves looked like bouquets of flowers in their
colorful *huipiles* (embroidered blouses). Just going to the market was
thrilling and photographing irresistible. Two weeks stretched to four.
Then six. Every couple of weeks I lobbied for a few more weeks.

When we weren't going to school, studying, marketing, or
swanning about town, we took off in our rental car. Up, up, up steep
hairpin turns; through patches of woolly fog where a sweater felt cozy
in the car; past vaporous pine forests and tiny villages, the land layered
in fields of cabbage and corn. No burned earth here as in the lowland

Montagua Valley, but neatly cultivated rows of brown dirt dotted with green sprouts. Everywhere along the road women swathed in yards of colorful fabric walked: often balancing piles of firewood or cloth bundles on their head, with a baby tied to their back and little children clutched in both hands. At a bend in the road, a lone woman and small child tended a herd of sheep in a green patch of ground at the foot of a steep hillside. Mud steps led down another hillside. A family waiting for a bus materialized out of the fog that drifted in and out through the mountain passes on the way down to Huehuetenango. Michael obligingly stopped the car so I could take photographs.

With the exception of a brief trip home for son Danny's wedding in July, this was our life for the next six months. It was one of the high points of our travels. Michael got a little bored with my academic intensity, but he did love a road trip, and we took many of them. Through our intimate relationships with our teachers we developed an understanding of the history and social problems of the country. Interestingly, my two teachers not only had different teaching styles and interests but also represented two distinct aspects of Guatemalan society.

Georgina, a product of the conservative Ladino culture, was a staunch evangelical Christian more interested in having conversations about politics and family life than verb tenses and grammar. We often shared family stories, and I learned a lot about her life caring for her sister's six children. Gesticulating with perfectly manicured hands and tears in her eyes, she recounted their story. "Their parents were shot in front of their eyes. What could I do? Of course I took them in." Earlier, her grandfather, who had been in the military, had left her his house, but part of it had been partitioned off to make homes for people who couldn't afford another place. So, while it was a big house, Georgina and the six children lived in very cramped quarters. Unmarried, she dedicated her life to raising these kids, who ranged in age from seven to nineteen.

Since both my son and her niece were each soon to get married, weddings were often a topic of discussion. Georgina was in charge of the plans. Even though the Ladino and Indian customs are different, they seem equally structured. "In Ladino weddings the bride and groom choose *padrinos* who support them, give advice, function as role models, and often help pay for the wedding. It's a big expensive celebration. But everyone in both families is involved in the many fiestas and events surrounding the wedding."

Madeli, my second teacher, was of Indian descent, small and intense. A born teacher who loved my enthusiasm about learning, she constantly pushed me to "get the grammar right." We also talked about weddings. In Indian weddings the *novios* (engaged couple) are engaged for a year, during which neither can even talk to a member of the opposite sex. I shook my head in disbelief.

"The bride to be makes a *tzute* for her mother-in-law. A *tzute* is a very elaborate rectangular width of cloth woven on a belt loom and joined to make a square so that it can be folded and placed on the head as a protection from the sun, thrown across the shoulders, or worn around the neck as a cape during festivals. The mother-in-law presents her daughter-in-law to be with an apron and she has to do all the cleanup after the wedding party." The rest of a married woman's life is all about bearing child after child, working in the field, taking produce and goods to market, weaving, making tortillas. Somehow Madeli escaped this fate but confessed with a sigh, "Rarely does anyone in the family learn how to read or write because as soon as they are old enough they have to work."

For the Indian newlyweds, land is a serious problem. With each new addition to the family the land gets divided up into smaller and smaller parcels. Sometimes all that is left is the side of a hill, which may wash away in the rainy season along with the tiny house on it. Often the newly married couple continues to live with parents because they have no land on which to build a house. This is not just true for the Indians, as Georgina's story testified; everyone was suffering hard economic times and escalating costs for housing.

Madeli was an example of how difficult it is even for educated people to make a living, and she spoke passionately and bitterly about the hopelessness of the Guatemalan political and social problems, where graft and corruption are a reality of everyday life. Georgina acknowledged the same problems but was more supportive of the government. Both of them worked hard, got paid very little, and struggled every day, just praying that the rains wouldn't "wash away the house."

* * * * *

While modern American weddings may be very different from Guatemalan ones, there was a good amount of preparation and ritual that we ourselves had been sorting out long distance for the past year. The emotional sorting out was a different thing.

June 17, 2000, Antigua, Guatemala

We are getting ready to take a break from Spanish school and fly home for Danny and Lauren's wedding in Nantucket, while Jack hangs out with Daphne and the gang at Mario's. Daphne assures me that it will be fine, but I can't help worrying. I also can't quite get my head around the idea that we are going to Nantucket for Danny's wedding. This life seems so normal that a wedding in Nantucket seems exotic. Maybe it is. Daniel, our free-spirited younger son, married is another hard concept. I know it will be wonderful to be part of such a happy family celebration. It just all seems so far away and unreal. I know, once there, I will be back in that reality and this will seem like an odd dream.

* * * * *

And this was true but, once again, after a three-week whirlwind trip home to Nantucket and Annapolis, we were back at Mario's Marina, scrubbing away the mold and patching the varnish on *Ithaca* like we had never been away.

While we were gone Old Hank died. It turns out he had been dead for several days before "young Hank" found him on the boat. Willy filled us in. "Old Hank had always said he was going to leave the boat to the kid, but a cousin from Chicago got wind of it all, came down here, put up a ruckus, and sold it to some guy from Columbia." That afternoon we all stood on the pier and watched *Seraphina* pull away from the marina and steam down the river. As I stood on the end of the pier with the rest of the marina crowd, I felt guilty that I had never made an attempt to talk to Hank, at least tell him how much I admired his paintings. Daphne said, "The funny thing is, Hank's still on board. We had his remains cremated and stashed in the bilge. He always wanted to go back to sea."

After a couple more months of Spanish school and land travel, threats of hurricanes in the Caribbean had passed and it was time for us to go back to sea as well.

October 15, 2000, Antigua, Guatemala

I am really sad to leave here—the captivating colors, the golden light, the flowers, the buildings, the vibrant patterns of the women's clothing against the pastel walls. Shimmering blue head wraps against the yellow wall of La Merced. There was so much I wanted to photograph but it always seems like we were in a hurry and I was caught between Michael and his capers, school and the weather, feeling like a kid being dragged by the hand through the candy store. Finding time to wander about by myself always seemed difficult. Maybe I didn't try hard enough.

I even fantasized about buying an old church down the street that was badly damaged by an earthquake and building a little house within the ruins, working with the poor, teaching English. What a nut. I am disappointed that I didn't do more drawing, and the photographs I have taken are all pretty ordinary tourist stuff and rather faded prints at that. I don't know if it's the film, the processing, or just bad exposures. The few times I have tried to muck about with pens and watercolor the results are, to use Georgina's expression, "horreeebley". . . . I seem to have lost all ability with a brush. It's a funny thing, this urge to "capture" the thing we love or find beautiful, to make it last forever, to paint it, photograph it, describe it in words. It is that intense "seeing" that gives such joy. Even if the results are truly awful, the process never ceases to be compelling.

* * * * *

Perhaps I didn't realize it at the time, but much of this compulsive journal writing was just verbal photographing. Nonetheless, it was time to move on, to say good-bye to the magnificent world of the Maya, and, following a very zigzag route south toward Cartagena, Columbia, and west to Panama, head across the Pacific—our first major ocean passage. But first we had to get around Cabo Gracias a Dios, the easternmost tip of the Honduran/Nicaraguan coast that juts out into the Caribbean Sea like an angry fist, and it was.

Sayonara Shipmate

O N NOVEMBER 5, 2000, WE CROSSED THE infamous "bar" of the Rio Dulce for the last time and headed east. We could still have turned north, gone home, or just cruised the Caribbean; but the call of the "Wild Blue Yonder" had sung her siren song and now it seemed inevitable that we would head south to Columbia, the San Blas Islands, the Panama Canal, and into the Pacific.

Inevitable as the decision may have been, easy it was not. What about Jack? A Pacific crossing entailed months at sea and landfalls unfriendly to foreign dogs, who could be shot if brought ashore. In New Zealand he would have to be quarantined for six months. Nothing was good about this scenario. We both knew having him on board was often not safe for him or us, but we tried not to think about it. Realistically, we had to accept the fact that it was time for Jack to retire and return to a leisurely life ashore. "The Little Prince" would be the perfect practice baby for newlyweds Danny and Lauren. All did not work out quite as smoothly as we envisioned, but more about that later. At this point in the story we are just trying to get around Cabo Gracias a Dios.

The overnight passage from Rio Dulce to East End Harbor on Útila in the Bay Islands off the coast of Honduras started out calm. Then the wind on our nose picked up. Raising the main stabilized us a bit in the choppy seas; it was still a rough beat, however, and hard to get used to life out in the open ocean after such a long hiatus. At 8:30 the next morning we made landfall, headed toward a white church steeple on shore, and anchored in a mellow bay. It had been a short but difficult passage. During the night the alternator had failed, putting the batteries and electrical system at stake. Then the water maker stopped working. Michael suspected the pump. So straightaway we had problems.

After checking in, we walked around the typically grubby Caribbean town looking for lunch. It was blazing hot and humid. Lunch was more than disappointing: hideous tacos in a hippie restaurant with no food—not even iced tea—because the boat hadn't come in. I was grumpy. Later we stopped in at the only bar with a television; it was tuned to the election returns but it was hard to hear over the noise, and the king of the "clicker" insisted on channel surfing just when some late-breaking results were about to be revealed. As far as we knew, we still didn't have a president.

November 9, 2000, Útila, Bay Islands

Yesterday we finally got the alternator going and the water pump fixed, but we broke the main hatch cover when we dropped the dinghy down on it by accident. Michael, who never swears, let fly some pretty coarse language. I said, "Not very nice for an officer and a gentleman." That was the wrong thing to say.

The ups and downs of the past couple of days, like the sea itself, are such an example of what this life is like: one moment magical, the bow wave like a horse's mane spewing diamonds over the black smooth sea with every rise and fall of the bow. Then the rocking turns to pounding and a crazy horse flings mad frothing water crashing over the deck. Maybe this is where the phrase "sailing over the bounding main" came from. The challenge is to just get through each day without killing each other, crying, or giving up— not just surviving the weather but surviving the inner storms and tumults, being kind and understanding and unselfish, maintaining a calm core of faith, a quiet inner room where all the furniture is safely nailed down in the right place no matter how violent the storm.

* * * * *

From Cayos Cochinos in the Bay Islands we motored across a flat hot sea and up a narrow jungle-like river to a new marina in La Ceiba, Honduras, recently opened by a young German couple, Tony and Rita. Jack immediately jumped off the boat just as I saw the spider monkey tied to a tree hanging over the pier. The monkey, completely fearless, looked like he wanted to play. Jack was puzzled. He knew it wasn't a cat, but what was it?

Then there was Lola the parrot, who nonchalantly waddled down the walkway toward us to supervise Michael while he hooked up the electricity. Again, Jack was dumbfounded, but by this time he was firmly secured to the boat. Joining the ensemble were a lovely, friendly white cat—whom Jack luckily had not yet discovered—a big Rottweiler, and a little brown island dog. According to Rita, they all lived and played happily together. The parrot rode around on the Rottweiler's back and the monkey pulled the brown dog's ears. Oh! And there were also rabbits, fortunately in a cage in the backyard.

It turned out we were stuck in the marina for the next couple of days because of weather. Life in the "Peaceable Kingdom" was a challenge because all the other animals were so curious about Jack the wild Labrador. The monkey, the parrot, the cat, and the brown dog all kept coming down to the boat as if they wanted to come aboard. The monkey actually did. I was putting away the groceries and heard a scratching noise on the cabin top. Jack started barking furiously. Michael broke a bottle of wine in the table storage, and I stepped in Jack's water bowl, spewing water everywhere. As I reached for Jack, Michael scrambled on deck to get the monkey, who was sitting with wide-eyed fascination at all the confusion he had caused.

Later the cat, who had been watching from a safe distance on the pier, decided to come aboard. She had one paw on the deck when Jack saw her and lunged. Luckily, he was tied onto the man overboard deck lines (sailors actually call them "jack lines") and couldn't reach her. She bounded off and we never saw her again. Then Buddy the Rottweiler, a handsome young boy with sweet face and upturned nose, ambled down out of curiosity. Ignoring Jack's defensive barking, he walked calmly up and down the pier next to the boat as if to say, "Wat da madder wit you, mon? Life be cool." Lola the parrot would also waddle down unexpectedly, completely unaware that Jack was a bird dog.

The weather kept us in the marina until Thanksgiving, and we were grateful when we finally got out of there without somebody being Jack's turkey dinner. The day after Thanksgiving we headed for West End, Roatan, in the Bay Islands, where we spent three days getting our act together for the passage to Cartagena, on Colombia's northwest coast.

* * * * *

December 3, 2000, at sea, bound for Cartagena, Columbia

Still on a beam reach. Wind up this afternoon. Doing 7 knots in 25 knots of wind. Crossed latitude 15 degrees north about 1800, finally passing Cabo Gracias a Dios. Now we know why it is called "Cape Thanks to God."

Finally calm enough to write. Sun slanting across the bobbing bow, blue sky with hopeful "puffies" instead of dark storm clouds, gentle undulating seas, and all is right with the world. The boat is rocking along at 5 knots, and the autopilot whirring comfortingly.

We have not had many days this mellow. It is such a welcome respite from the pounding, rail in the water battles with thunderstorms, strong unpredictable winds, and rough seas we have had almost constantly since we left Roatan. Our plot east across the northern coast of Honduras looks like a drunk was at the helm as we battled for every inch of "easting," sometimes going backward, losing half of what we had gained hours before, just to get a better angle on the wind and avoid the reefs.

Two nights ago we did have a nice break when the wind died down a bit, the boat leveled out, and we actually were able to have a dinner together at the table with place mats, knives and forks, even a little salad on real plates instead of eating noodle soup out of a plastic cup, bracing ourselves against a bulkhead while the boat heaved and pounded. It is hardest on Jack.

* * * * *

The next day we were becalmed most of the afternoon so I took the opportunity to do some boat cleaning while we drifted. Mildew and dog hair were driving me crazy. I opened up the boat for a few hours of airing out and washed down the interior with Clorox and water. Even washed myself. A real shower and clean hair always seemed the height of luxury on a tough passage.

Jack was such a trooper. By now he would brave the bow once a day to pee and poop almost on command. But most of the time he had to be with me constantly unless Michael was napping, and then he would curl up next to him in the narrow space between the table and the bunk. Once in a while, when he got bored, he would drop his tennis ball on my foot and bark—the signal for the "go back for a pass" game, even though he could barely keep his footing on the rolling and pitching cabin sole.

When I would say "Come on, Jack, let's go to the grooming station and get brushed," he would jump up on the helmsman's seat behind the wheel where I would brush him so all the hair would fly off the stern while he leaned against me to keep his balance—so willing, although clearly not happy. The thought of leaving him home in January killed me, but our passage in the previous few days finally proved to me how unfair it was to subject him to such discomfort and danger for weeks at a time.

It had been a hard passage for all of us: navigating was difficult, and the loss of sleep was draining, but the biggest problem had been the weather: constant rain, erratic thunderstorms, wind, no wind, made it impossible to stay dry for more than two hours at a time. My feet were rotting from constantly being wet. The frequent wind shifts made it hard to hold a course, and the engine overheating meant we could use the engine for only an hour every day to charge the batteries. Plus, we were running low on fuel. A lot of worries kept everyone on edge.

* * * * *

On December 7th, we finally motored through the narrow "cut" in the old city walls of Cartagena and tied up at the city pier. Jack was off the boat and peeing on a palm tree before a single line was secured. As usual, we had broken gear to fix, parts to source, piles of moldy laundry, no fresh food, and a low liquor light. We had come to the right place. Cartagena was a delightful picturesque and well-stocked city. We got a map and started walking.

After the immediate needs were addressed, we set to work arranging the logistics of our trip home for Christmas, this time with Jack. After many glasses of wine and tearful conversations, I had finally acquiesced. Jack had to go home.

"I know, but I just can't stand it," I cried into my wineglass. Michael squeezed my hand. "It's not like we're losing him. He'll still be in the family. He'll be Danny and Lauren's practice baby. We can see him whenever we go home. He'll be safe. He'll be happy. And we'll be safe." He put his arm around me and held me for a long time. Jack licked my knee.

After searching all over town, we finally located a large enough travel cage for Jack, then made a special trip to the airport with the cage to ensure that there would be no problem on the day of departure. We were emphatically assured that there would be no problem. When we checked in the next day, we were equally emphatically assured that there was a BIG problem. Jack could not fly with us because the cage was too large. Emotions and voices rose exponentially as we confronted a series of "officials" and the time to departure drew near. In desperation, I broke down in tears and cried out in Spanish, "I can't leave my best friend." Latins hate to see a lady cry. Sheepishly they relented. Jack curled up in his cage and was wheeled away with the baggage. Whew. We ran to the departure gate.

Once on board the plane we looked at each other, mentally slapping our foreheads. Of course. They wanted a *propina*. All could have been resolved so easily if we had just come through with a few extra pesos to the right person. In the emotion of the moment we lost sight of one of the first rules of travel: the discrete palming of cash to the "guy in charge" works miracles. Over the years, we had many subsequent opportunities to remember this lesson.

Once again our visit home was full of hellos and good-byes, joy and sadness. Hello to our new grandson Dallas, who was born on January 26, 2001, and good-bye to our dearest sailing buddy, Jack. In the blink of an eye, we were back in Cartagena, or "motor city" as we called it, having had five motors repaired there. The charm of the old city helped stave off the gloom of missing family and friends. Wandering along its stage set streets, colonial buildings, and balconies dripping bougainvillea, we sampled a different restaurant every night, took moonlit carriage rides, and hung out in colorful bars. I battled my internal gloom by focusing on the future, reading, working on the boat, and getting ready for the next big challenge: a Pacific Ocean passage. Next stop the San Blas Islands and the Panama Canal.

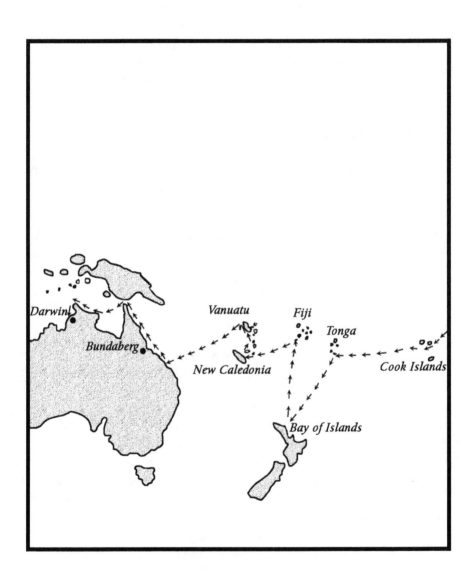

Darwin

Bundaberg

Vanuatu

Fiji

Tonga

New Caledonia

Cook Islands

Bay of Islands

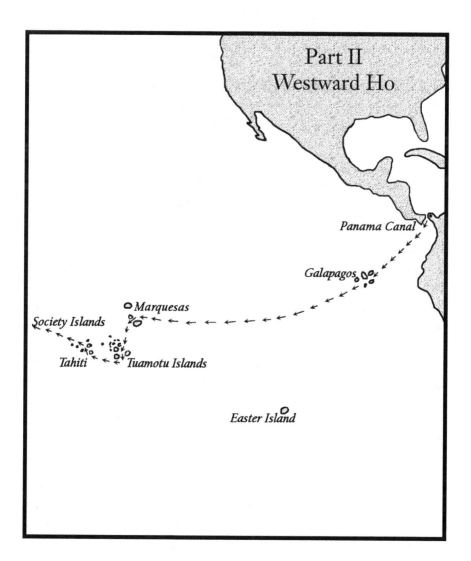

Part II
Westward Ho

Panama Canal

Galapagos

Marquesas

Society Islands

Tahiti   Tuamotu Islands

Easter Island

Westward Ho!

AFTER A STOP IN THE SAN BLAS ISLANDS, WHERE we bought many more *molas* (local Indian textiles) than we intended to, we headed to Colon at the head of the Panama Canal. On March 19th, Michael's sixty-first birthday, we passed through the east entrance of the Colon breakwater, threaded through hundreds of big ships, and anchored in "the flats" to await our measurement and assigned time to make the Canal passage.

The ritual of the Canal passage takes time and money. Each sailboat requires four line handlers, with four very long lines to keep the boat centered in the locks, as well as four very ugly black tires which you are required to hang off the side of your pristine white hull—all of which the yacht owner has to source and rent. Other cruisers are usually anxious to act as line handlers just to get a sense of the experience and problems before they have to bring their own boat through, so we had no problem finding experienced and congenial sailors for the job. The fee to make the transit is based on your boat's length. It takes a while to get all this organized, and then you have to wait for your assigned time. Colon is not a place where you want to spend a lot of time, however, so we were happy when our number came up ten days later.

The Panama Canal, a 48-mile-long waterway across the Isthmus of Panama, links the Atlantic and Pacific Ocean with a system of locks, rivers, artificial lakes, and dams. On the Atlantic side, the three-stage Gatun Locks lift ships 85 feet above sea level into the 15-mile-long Gatun Lake, which flows into the 5-mile-long Chagres River where the Pedro Miguel Lock begins the first part of the descent by lowering ships into the Miraflores Lake. Then the Miraflores Locks deliver ships down to Balboa Harbor on the Pacific side. The canal took almost fifty years to complete, a story brilliantly recounted in David McCullough's award-winning *The Path Between the Seas.*

Thinking back, I still shiver with amazement. Who would have thought that *Ithaca* would traverse this iconic waterway and travel to the other side of the world? Aside from a few nervous moments in the last Gatun Lock, when the captain of the freighter in front of us created a huge wake by starting his engines, all went smoothly. After the Pedro Miguel Lock, we stopped for a couple of days in Miraflores Lake at the famous, now defunct, Pedro Miguel Yacht Club, where we waited for son Pete to fly down and join us for the last locks.

Early on the morning of April 2, 2001, with Pete on board, we motored out of the Pedro Miguel marina and by 11:00 had passed through the Miraflores Locks and under the Bridge of the Americas. We were through the Panama Canal. But don't open the champagne yet. Just as we passed under the bridge, all teary-eyed and sentimental, the engine-overheating alarm blared. The water pump had died. Pete saved the day by pouring water into the heat exchanger while we slowly motored to our mooring at the Balboa Yacht Club. By 1:30 we were popping the bubbly and thrilled to be celebrating this important milestone with our son.

Does it seem like this boat was always broken? It did to us many times. We were now through the Panama Canal, though, and there was no turning back. After installing a new water pump, we spent a few relaxing days exploring Panama City with Pete, who through snapshots and stories brought a bit of Annapolis to Panama. Jack seemed to be fitting into his new environment in Annapolis and baby Dallas was thriving.

It was here, however, that I discovered something about my son I never knew: his absolute inability to shop, which he probably inherited from his mother. After a day of meandering we stopped at a giant tourist mall so he could pick out a gift for his wife, Tracy. Two hours later he still hadn't decided. I identified completely with his predicament. Finally, he settled on a small woven Panamanian basket. I don't know if she ever realized how much love and anxiety went into choosing that squash-shaped basket decorated with yellow birds or how carefully he wrapped it so it wouldn't get bent in his backpack when he left.

Then, in what seemed like a flash, Pete was gone and we were headed west, into flat, slightly rolly seas, and then south, our destination the Galapagos Islands off the coast of Ecuador. This would be a long good-bye, but we pretended it would only be a few weeks.

* * * * *

April 12, 2001, at sea, bound for Galapagos Islands

Today we broke out of the doldrums with some solid wind. An 8-knot breeze ruffles the sea surface and pushes us along like a leaf. A squashed grape moon illuminates the water and turns the sea a steely, charcoal blue. Bow waves beat out a soft, rhythmic swish swish swish. The autopilot tick tick ticks, making small course corrections. The halyards creak and click. The turnbuckles squeak as the genoa cracks in a gust of wind then shutters, straining against the starboard sheet like a racehorse against its reins. A silent bird curled in the fold of canvas curtain under the bimini tucks her head under her wing and goes to sleep, while I snuggle down in the lee of the dodger with a book. Lulled by the endless motion of the sea and the gentle rocking of the boat, I drift off into the velvet arms of a dream.

* * * * *

One of the many things I loved about being at sea for endless days at a time was the luxury of being swept away by a book. We were sailing to the Galapagos and I was reading *The Beak of the Finch,* Peter and Rosemary Grant's book about twenty years of research on Galapagos finches. It made me think about the poetry in science—life in constant flux, like the sea itself. I mused in my journal:

It seems that the whole process of evolution and natural selection is not so much about survival of the fittest but survival of the most expedient, the most efficacious at the time. Life is really more a question of relativity, how everything is related to everything else in the vast cosmos. There is indeed a 'special providence in the fall of a sparrow.' This vast net of connections, continually woven and unwoven like Penelope's tapestry, does not deny a

God but glorifies His creation, ever renewing and refining itself in a world without end, amen."

The Path Between the Seas presented evidence of man's hubris, the need to mold nature to his will, which is itself a constant, pressing evolutionary urge—to seek out new "niches," battle the ever-changing environment to survive, like the finches on Daphne Major. Different skills need to evolve at different times. Cataclysmic events will happen, but in the end, "the canal will be built" to quote Ferdinand de Lesseps, although, metaphorically, thousands of finches fall in the process. There was always so much to think about on that ever vanishing and renewing, breathing blue field of peaks and valleys.

April 14, 2001, under way to the Galapagos

Breeze up to 10 knots out of the south. Steering 200—engine off—all quiet, except for ripples slapping the hull. Sun on my back, cool gentle wind on my face, blue dome of sky overhead, little "puffies" on the horizon—I am at the center of a universe of blue and white. Then "Click." The autopilot acting up again and entropy enters paradise. But we are so perfectly trimmed we're steady on course without a "pilot." At least for a while, Ithaca is sailing herself.

*   *   *   *   *

On April 20, 2001, we crossed the Equator—five times in fact! The first several times because we couldn't get the video camera to work; once to douse Michael with champagne, as he wasn't yet a shellback; and lastly for me to swim from the Northern Hemisphere to the Southern. Then we heard the radio squawk: "*Ithaca. Ithaca.* This is *Nimbus.*"

"*Nimbus. Ithaca* here. How's it going shipmate?"

"Great, except I could sure use a little of that fuel you're burning up going back and forth over the Equator. We're running on fumes."

"No problem. We'll be right over."

Our Kiwi friends, Greg and Linda, were completing a circumnavigation in a 25-foot sloop with very little fuel capacity.

"We're a sailboat, mate. We don't motor, but we're running out of rum and it looks like we'll be stuck out here for days." So, back we went again for a mid-ocean rendezvous, where we threw over a line and passed our extra fuel to our friends. When we made landfall, they were the first to buy us a drink.

* * * * *

At sunrise on April 22, 2001, what looked like a strange illuminated triangular cloud on the horizon materialized into a huge rock, called Kicker Rock. In fact, it looked something like a big boot, three miles off the coast of San Cristobal Island in the Galapagos, along whose long, low, dark shape we had been cruising. As the light brightened, I could see one of the volcanoes of San Cristobal, a peaked arrowhead against the dawn sky. Slowly the gray clouds turned a blue-gray into pink as one towering cumulus vaulted the sky in front of the rising sun like a column of pale fire.

The Galapagos Islands, precariously perched on the Nazca tectonic plate that straddles the Equator 500 nautical miles off the coast of Ecuador, have been in constant flux for millennia. The first islands bubbled up from the Earth's molten core 80 to 90 million years ago. Some have disappeared over the eons, and others, like Isabella and Fernandina, are still being formed. To date there are eighteen main islands, three smaller ones, and 107 rocks and islets, many of which are protected preserves. Until 1969 the only way to visit was by private or chartered yacht. Now private yacht anchorage is restricted to four sites, and most visitors arrive by air.

We made landfall at Puerto Baquerizo Moreno on the southeastern tip of San Cristóbal, the most easterly of the islands. Puerto Baquerizo is a fishing village, and most of the boats in the crowded harbor of Wreck Bay were fishing boats, many of which had been commandeered by lazy sea lions who luxuriously lolled on abandoned bows and decks like summer sunseekers. We dropped anchor at the head of the harbor, inflated the dinghy, and had just settled down for a celebratory beer when we were greeted by two young sea lions who swam around the boat snorting and puffing, playing with the fenders, banging against the hull, and pushing each other on and off the dinghy like two kids. "We'd better winch the dinghy on deck to keep it from becoming the teenagers' swim platform," Michael wisely suggested.

Ashore we found a small fishing village transitioning into a tourist town, with a new airport, a nature center, and a handful of predictable tourist T-shirt shops along a dusty main street undergoing beautification. But the townspeople seemed standoffish and unfriendly, as if we were a burden they must bear for economic survival. The conflict among the fisherfolk, the environmentalists, and the tourists became more evident with every passing day. Nevertheless, we were happy to find a brand-new cyber café, an ATM—which, to our surprise, dispensed dollars—and some lovely fresh broccoli on our initial wandering about. Sadly, we discovered there were only a limited number of walks you could do on your own. You had to sign up for a tour for almost everything and could not see some of the best attractions on the other islands without taking a government approved boat.

One day we found a little grotto surrounded by rocky cliffs and went snorkeling. Out of the murky blue came three sea lions who swam around us in circles. One light brown one with huge blue eyes swam alongside me blowing bubbles, then hung upside down in front of me staring quizzically as if trying to figure out what kind of creature I was. I popped my head up and yelled to Michael, "Did you see my new best friend?"

"Yes, did you see my girlfriend with the big eyes and long eyelashes?"

Later we had a picnic on the rocks while sea lions snoozed nearby. Michael strolled over and lay down next to a big bull as if he was taking a nap too. Thankfully the big guy never even opened his eyes, but I couldn't resist a quick photo. Frigate birds swooped down from the cliff overhead and a lazy pelican perched on a black rock, head hunched down into his wings for his afternoon siesta. We were in our own little patch of Galapagos paradise.

Booking space on a small tour boat for a three-day trip to some of the outer islands was an unexpected treat. As much as I'm not into tours,

I have to admit it was fun. First of all, it was a great relief not to have to worry about the anchor dragging or navigating through unfamiliar, congested reefs. Or cooking, for that matter. Accommodations were small but comfortable. The head worked. The food was good, and the passengers were an interesting mix of European and Australian backpackers, a Dutch photographer and an Irishman, a cuddling Ecuadorian couple, and a handful of Spanish-speaking people. Best of all, our Ecuadorian guide was knowledgeable, was enthusiastic, and spoke very clear English.

We hiked to the top of a crater on Bartolome Island, snorkeled on a beach below Pinnacle Rock, saw giant turtles, flamingos, and bright red Sally Lightfoot Crabs on the black lava rocks sticking out of turquoise water. In afternoon sunlight, a beach crisscrossed with broad tracks in the sand revealed where turtles had come ashore to lay their eggs. Huge frigate birds swooped overhead, waiting for the little turtles to hatch and make their dash to the water, when they would be fair game and gobbled up by the birds or feral cats. More survival of the fittest.

Acres of iguanas were humped like dark logs on the beach; baby sea lions huddled in sea lion kindergartens; solo males lounged in their bachelor "pads" while big beach masters defended their harems—all so close by it seemed that the animals and birds were oblivious to our presence. Frigates, boobies, and gulls swooped through the white spray against black rocks, the frigates sinisterly nesting with blue-footed boobies to steal their food. Hundreds of the males perched on bushes with their big red pouches inflated to attract the females, seducing them with twigs to build their nests.

Colorful and fierce, the frigate birds are the real pirates of the Pacific. They will grab the elegant red-billed tropic bird by its long tail and shake it upside down until it throws up its fish, then swoop down to catch it as a midday snack. That's how the "fittest" get to be the "fittest."

A week later we were anchored in Villamil, on the island of Isla Isabela, waiting for the fuel barge . . . for days. When a good-sized ship entered the harbor and materialized into a gray navy ship instead of the fuel ship, you could practically hear the whole anchorage groan. Hordes of townspeople gathered on the town piers, suggesting that something big was up. We had heard that three fishermen had been missing for five days, and all the fuel on the island had been used up in searching for them. Then two days later we heard that they had been found 200 miles south of Villamil, where they had drifted in an open boat for twelve days after their engine quit.

An American plane, probably a drug plane, had found them, and they had been picked up by an Ecuadorian fishing boat. All three men—ages thirteen, twenty-three, and thirty—were alive and well. The navy ship brought them back to Isabela and off-loaded them into a launch with two naval officers in white. They went right by our boat but did not wave. Apparently they had been illegally fishing for shark fins and sea cucumber. They were taken away in a military car, heads hung low. This kind of conflict between the fishermen and the conservationists was ongoing.

Eventually, the long-awaited fuel ship arrived and *Ithaca* greedily drank every drop of diesel she could swallow. The next passage to the Marquesas Islands, 2,967 miles to the west, was going to be a long one.

Transiting with No Transmission

MAY 12, 2001, AT SEA, 2,967 MILES TO THE MARQUESAS

Midday. Motoring. Main flapping. Stormy petrels dot the flat, blue-gray water searching for fish. A whale breaches to port. Crash. An explosion of spray and white frothy lace spreads over the silent sea. All is calm again except for a nagging worry.

Weighing anchor yesterday, we had difficulty shifting into forward. The culprit, a broken gear cable which M tried to fix all day to no avail. Eventually he bypassed the cable, climbed down into the engine compartment, and manually switched gears. Now we are stuck in forward and have no backward gear. Oh well, we only want to go forward anyway, right? Anxious to move on to the Marquesas, despite our better judgment, we left just as a sea lion head popped up dripping whiskers and big eyes as if to say, "Oh no, you're not really going?" Well, we are—sort of—slogging along with no wind.

* * * * *

Five days later we were rolling in swells bigger than 6 feet off the port quarter and 15–20 knots of wind out of the S–SE. *Ithaca* was averaging 7 knots. Amazing. The day before, we did 167 miles in twenty-four hours, our best speed ever. We reefed the main so Hans, the wind vane steerer, could handle the seas better, but it was still very lumpy and hard to do much of anything but basic cooking, cleaning, resting, and reading. Even writing in my journal was a challenge.

Our routine at sea was always the same. I stood watch from 6:00 to 9:00 a.m. while Michael slept. When he got up, we listened for about an hour to the Flying Fish Net on the single sideband radio, where other boats called in and gave their positions, weather, and general information. After the Net, I usually showered, tidied up the boat, did a small boat project or two, maybe made bread, maybe napped, then made lunch and went back on watch in the afternoon while Michael napped. Usually we would have a beer around 5:00 or 5:30 and dinner around 7:00. Michael took the evening watch from 9:00 until midnight while I slept, then I took the midwatch from 12:00 to 3:00 a.m., and slept again from 3:00 to 6:00 a.m. After a while it just seemed like a normal way to live. It suited our sleep preferences, he naturally being a late night guy and me being an early riser. But, I always felt a little guilty because Michael basically did two night watches and, in reality, I did only one.

When I wasn't doing anything else, I was reading. Now it was Melville's *Typee*, about his passage from the Galapagos to the Marquesas on a whaling ship in the 1840s. Now THAT was adventure. When he landed, three different warring tribes confronted him, one of which was cannibals. What strange new things would confront us—*if* we ever got there.

We were still making incredible progress at 7 knots of boat speed, averaging 170 to 180 miles a day. Great speed, but rough, with big foaming swells in a following sea. One day I had just taken the last two loaves of bread out of the oven when a huge "rogue wave" poured into the cockpit, down the companionway, and in through the portholes. Michael was soaked.

"Damn. That just went right down my neck."

"Your neck? Look at my poor bread that took me all morning to bake!"

Salt water had poured over the stove and drenched the loaves. I almost cried. Making bread in such rough conditions had been arduous, and I was exhausted. Fortunately, the first two loaves stayed dry, and, after I put the two wet ones back in the warm oven for a while, they and my spirits revived. But I still complained in my journal.

May 18, 2001, at sea, Galapagos to Marquesas

I have not been accomplishing anything so far on this trip except reading, trying to stay rested, and making bread yesterday. Just getting through the day, keeping the boat tidy, fixing meals, and standing watch has consumed all my energy. By now I had planned to know at least two songs on the harmonica, be well into my "teach yourself French" book, and have all the brass polished down below.

* * * * *

By May 21ˢᵗ we were in the doldrums. Squalls blackened the horizon, but no wind. The genoa flapped and slapped like it would rip the forestay off the bow. Periodically it billowed out and drove us along at a steady 5 knots, but so intermittently that it was hardly worth the discomfort.

After the third sleepless night, I suggested we start the engine. Suddenly, we had no forward gear. After manually switching into forward when we left the Galapagos, we had forgotten to manually switch back to neutral when we turned the engine off a day later, so the constantly spinning propeller had burned up the clutch plates. Very disheartening. We could still use the engine to charge our batteries, but we had no transmission. After thinking this was going to be a record trip in 20 days, it was going to be a lot longer. Michael was disconsolate, anticipating that when and if we got to Nuku Hiva we would be stuck there for months, lacking any means of repair or access to parts. I had faith something would happen. But I couldn't believe our passage to the Marquesas could be so sabotaged.

The days were tedious, hot, and frustrating, filled with endless sail tweaks in the hope of moving the boat half a knot more in the small puffs of air. We did have a minor bit of good luck when we finally caught a fish on the "Rapello" lure—a small wahoo. An ugly fish, but great tasting. I did laundry, cleaned, and made bread but still never got around to polishing the brass, learning my list of French irregular verbs, or progressing much on the harmonica. Then, a break.

May 29, 2001, at sea, 700 miles to go to Marquesas

15–20 knots of wind finally filled in a few days ago and Ithaca is surfing on big rollers chasing our stern making 5–6 knots of boat speed. By my count, 6 more days to Nuku Hiva. Then the fun begins, getting into the anchorage and securely anchored with no engine.

Last night we watched a home movie of the kids playing ball in the backyard, so mesmerized by those adorable faces we almost forgot we were in the middle of the South Pacific, silently sliding along a silver shaft of moonlight, the Milky Way arched over the mast, the Southern Cross tilting sideways off the port beam and the Big Dipper off to starboard spilling the North Star into the dark horizon.

French study has been sporadic, as it is very hard to read or concentrate when it is tough and rolly. Most watches I catnap a bit or read Steve Callahan's harrowing tale of being shipwrecked and "Adrift" for seventy-six days. His tenacity to survive, his skillful and ingenious problem solving and improvisations are remarkable. His poetic sense of being alone with, but at the same time doing constant battle with, his environment is a duality we experience daily on a much diluted level, of course. Being at sea is like a love affair with a schizophrenic—mellow and romantic one moment, treacherous the next.

* * * * *

We were counting the days and hours until we made landfall, hoping for Sunday, but two days of calms delayed us a day. The closer we got to landfall the more nervous we became. Since we would be completely under sail, we worried that calms close in could leave us drifting uncontrollably, but too much wind could blow down on a lee shore before we got anchored. It was time for prayer.

The past three weeks had taught us to live with the unknown: one minute in awe of a "biblical sunset" or quietly drifting on a beam of moonlight, staring at a velvet infinity of stars; the next moment battling frustration and exhaustion, beating to windward in a drenching downpour at 2:00 a.m., blinded by rain, fogged glasses, and darkness, unable to see anything but, in the glow of the compass, that you are headed backward. A heartbeat later you could be standing behind the wheel trying to coax a knot out of the fickle zephyrs that tease you from all directions, while sails flap and the wind vane on top of the mast goes around in circles. More than anything else, sailing demands patience and endurance.

Not only was I nervous about anchoring in a strange harbor under sail, I also always felt a tinge of regret approaching port. I love the simplicity of life at sea, the peacefulness, the ritual of days, watches, falling asleep to the sound of the boat creaking, water swishing—yes, even the rocking and always the endless and ever changing companionship of the sea. Once in port the pace of life picks up, with long lists of fix-it projects, days spent in sourcing marine parts or on major re-provisioning excursions, plus the busy social life of an often-crowded anchorage.

Around midnight a dark shadow materialized on the horizon—landfall. Gradually, a gold setting moon revealed the jagged outline of Nuku Hiva. As dawn brightened, soft green and brown contours gave shape to the shadows. Sailing wing and wing, *Ithaca* lurched like a plodding elephant over the 6-foot swells. Approaching the island my anxiety meter rose and fell with the fickle wind. Fearing we would be blown down onto the looming cliffs before I saw the harbor entrance, I held course with a pounding heart then tacked close in and *Ithaca* veered comfortably out of harm's way.

By 8:00 a.m. Michael was up and so was the wind: 13 knots now stirred up a rough sea. We took in the yankee, the smaller of the two headsails, came about on a starboard tack, and headed toward the narrow cut into the harbor where there was less wind in the lee of the surrounding cliffs. Bright sun, sparkling water, towering walls of velvet green, and a whole school of dolphins frolicking and leaping all around us was cinematographic, but I was way too nervous to get out the video camera.

The outer harbor, being more than 100 feet deep, was too deep to anchor, and strong winds funneling down the narrow valleys between the cliffs made it impossible to sail into the anchorage where more reasonable depths at 40 feet were to be found. Our only option was to launch the inflatable dinghy and use the outboard engine for power, not a slight task in the unpredictable winds and currents. The inflatable was stowed on deck under the less stable sailing dinghy. So we had to drop the main, off-load the sailing dinghy, then blow up the rubber dinghy on deck, launch it, and lower the outboard engine before getting blown down on the beach.

Finally, with the inflatable tied abeam fore and aft, Michael steered the dinghy and powered us into the anchorage while I kept Ithaca pointed into the wind. Intermittent gusts threatened to blow us down on nearby boats, but luckily the anchorage was not too crowded and we found a spot to drop the anchor on the first pass.

Once convinced the anchor was holding, we broke out our last remaining beers and celebrated our arrival after 23 days and 3 hours— not bad time considering we had sailed all the way. Totally exhausted we munched on a meager lunch of cheese and plantain chips and then flopped on our bunks for several hours, enjoying the gentle rocking of the boat, such a relief after all the anxiety and feeling like two clowns in a barrel for so many days.

That afternoon we got cleaned up and went into town expecting to buy fresh veggies and French baguettes and to restock our beer supply, but everything was closed. Only the Catholic church was open, as if waiting for us to come ashore and thank God for a safe passage before we did anything else. It was an old church in the center of the harbor decorated with wooden carvings and stone tikis. A Polynesian woman sat all alone in the front pew singing and praying softly. Everything was quiet outside except for birds twittering and leaves rustling in the breeze. We felt as if we had been blown ashore in a little leaf and rested safely in the warm sand after a terrible storm at sea—calm, thankful, with a genuine feeling of awe and gratitude for God's grace.

The island looked magical in the mist, immense green jagged cliffs shooting up all around the horseshoe harbor of deep forest green water. Hibiscus, flame trees, poinciana, and white flowers like frangipani bloomed everywhere. A green park arched around the breakwater where remnants of mossy stone carvings and tikis lay tumbled in the grass. The dirt streets were empty. A handful of men played bocce ball in the parking lot, while a group of ladies seated on a white blanket under a tree played bingo. Later we read that it was Whit Monday, the day after Pentecost Sunday, which is a holiday in French Polynesia. That night a ferocious series of squalls ripped our awning and kept us awake most of the night worrying that our anchor would drag and we'd be tossed about as if we were back at sea. So much for tranquil paradise. In the morning the water was the color of café con leche and the surrounding cliffs dripped with waterfalls like icicles on a Christmas tree.

Two days later we found Raoul, our guardian angel in the form of a gallant young French mechanic who lived on a small sailboat in the harbor with a toddler and a very pregnant wife. Raoul removed the transmission and took it back to his boat, which was also his workshop, where he was able to reverse the gear plates and make it functional until we could get to New Zealand to install a new one. After installing a new gearshift cable, which we had to order from Papeete, Tahiti, we were on our way again, exploring the Nuku Hiva's deep mysterious bays, mountaintops, and the world's third highest waterfall.

On June 24th we bid *adieu* to Nuku Hiva and continued south through the rest of the Marquesan chain to Ua Pua, Tahuata, and Fata Hiva. From there it was a seven-day passage to Rangiroa in the Tuamotu Group. By July 12th we had anchored in Papeete Harbor, Tahiti.

Romance in Paradise

I N MOST FANTASIES FRENCH POLYNESIA IS
Tahiti. Thanks to Gauguin, serious romantics think of it as
a land of languorous ladies with bare breasts under purple
shaded palm trees, sirens beckoning the wayward sailor to a green
tropical Eden where life can be lived in primitive but sybaritic
simplicity. Sadly, we never found this place.

In actuality, French Polynesia encompasses 118 diverse islands and
atolls scattered over 1,500 miles of the Pacific Ocean, organized into
five very different island groups: the Marquesas; the Society Islands,
of which Tahiti and Bora Bora are part; the Tuamotu archipelago of
78 low-lying coral atolls; and the remote and unpopulated Austral and
Gambier Islands farther south. According to Wikipedia, the French
Polynesia we know today was one of the last places on Earth to be
settled by humans during the Great Polynesian Migration in 1500
B.C. And the Marquesas, discovered in 200 B.C., were the last among
them to be settled, which probably accounts for their still remote and
magical character.

Tahiti, on the other hand, reminded me more of a tropical Los
Angeles than an island paradise—polluted water, mountains sheared
of vegetation, ribbons of asphalt, traffic and exhaust fumes instead
of flowers. It was a jolt to me, especially, as I had been there in the
'50s as a sixteen-year-old traveling with my family on one of the
first commercial cruises to the South Pacific. Back then, Papeete,
the capital, had one paved road, and strolling along the dirt paths
with a handsome Mormon missionary had been a storybook romance
I never forgot. Now trucks spewed dark smoke, horns blared, and
the walk to the Port Captain's office past a gussied up and "touristy"

waterfront was more like Baltimore's Inner Harbor than the Papeete of old.

Fortuitously, however, our arrival coincided with the week of Bastille Day celebrations, a five-day festival of Polynesian music and dance where groups from all the islands beat drums, swung hips, and flung fiery torches in blurringly fast and furious competition. No "Lovely Hula Hands" here: this dancing was electrified, and the cadence of the music, the insistent drums, and the dense harmonic singing became the soundtrack of the rest of our voyage across the Pacific.

Here, also, we had some very special visitors—Danny and Lauren, who were celebrating their first anniversary courtesy of American Airlines, which a year earlier had sabotaged their honeymoon not once but twice with broken airplanes. Now, imagine this: young wife with her new husband comes to Tahiti for their second, but really first, honeymoon. Young wife barely knows her new in-laws, who are always off on their sailboat somewhere, and, in fact, knows their dog better than them and is not too keen on him. She brings an assortment of outfits anticipating a "South Pacific cruise." Young husband brings a bathing suit, a surfboard, and an extra pair of shorts. There are no separate cabins on this cruise ship. Their accommodations in the forward V berth can only be closed off by opening the head door, which does not ensure privacy and bangs closed whenever there is the slightest wake or ripple of wave. Cheerfully she steps aboard this 38-foot raft that will be her home for the next two weeks.

Our first night together we set sail for Moorea, a jagged mystical island on the horizon often mistaken for Michener's fictional Bali Hai. A full moon rises over the horizon. Nothing could be more romantic. Right? Wrong! Michael is on watch about 1:00 a.m. Seas off the port quarter have picked up and the boat rolls briskly from side to side. Lauren, swathed in a sleeping bag, stumbles up the companionway into the cockpit. Even in the moonlight she is green. Michael gets her a pillow and tries to make her as comfortable as possible, but it is obvious she does not feel well. Never once during the whole two weeks, however, did she ever complain. Even though she slept out on the deck almost every night.

During the day Lauren, Danny, and the surfboard would motor out in the inflatable dinghy to the nearest reef break, where he would disappear into the surf and she would sit on the beach reading a book. When the surf wasn't up, they headed for a beach resort and a little more civilized vacationing. Trying to keep our sea time to a minimum we made short hops around Moorea's lovely bays and hopscotched over to the island of Huahine. One day, on a bike ride around the island, we stopped at a pearl farm and Danny bought Lauren a sumptuous black pearl on a silver chain that she wears to this day. Who says romance is dead? For them now, after fifteen years of marriage and two children, it is clearly still very much alive. Anyone who can survive seasickness without complaining can survive just about anything.

By the time we parted at the ferry dock in Huahine, we had become so used to having Danny and Lauren aboard that *Ithaca* felt empty, lacking something important, after they left. They had brought "home" to us, and for days afterward we moped around missing the laughter, stories, and love. Even the thought of our next adventure to Easter Island didn't quite quell the longing for family.

9/11

E ASTER ISLAND IS NOT A COMFORTABLE destination for sailors. Its only harbor is untenable, deep and so famously rough that few sailing yachts venture this far off the Pacific trade wind route. The need to renew our French Polynesia visas, however, gave us the perfect excuse to fly the short distance by air from Tahiti. After five days, we returned to the boat in Motu Tautau, Taha'a, on September 11, 2001.

It was our anniversary, but all thought of celebration was forgotten when we learned on the Net about the terrorist attacks in New York and Washington. We called home immediately and were able to get through to daughter-in-law Tracy, who told us about the Pentagon being hit. "What about Tom (Michael's brother)?" She didn't know. Later we learned from Pete that Tom walked out of the building and was home safe, as was everyone else in our family, although Tracy had lost a good friend in one of the towers. We listened to what English news we could find on the single sideband radio and got little bits of information and pictures from the television news at the airport bar and marina restaurant, where we had gone for our anniversary dinner the previous night.

Unfortunately, the French news broadcaster spoke too fast for me to follow it very well, but the images we saw were shocking enough: the second airplane hitting the World Trade Center and its subsequent collapse, masses of firefighters and police being rushed to hospitals, and pandemonium on the streets. All air traffic had been canceled, and President Bush had declared a state of war. It was so frustrating to be so far away from home and not be able to really find out the details of what had happened. Michael, ready to don his flight suit and launch off the carrier, said, "We should go home." I countered: "What good would that do? Let's wait till we know more."

We did get some BBC frequencies from a fellow cruiser, but it was so depressing we turned it off and watched an old video of the kids at the beach, which always made us laugh.

A week later we were in Hurepiti Bay, Taha'a. The weather reflected our mood: overcast and drizzly. At the local Internet café we were shocked to learn that our dear friends Buddy and Dee Flagg had been on the airplane that crashed into the Pentagon. What a terrible irony that he, a rear admiral in the US Navy Reserve and an F8 pilot, should die at the hands of a fanatical terrorist.

We walked around in a stunned daze for the rest of the day then called home, talked to Pete and Alexis, whose six-year-old vivaciousness made me cry. She was going to be a unicorn for Halloween. Later we had lunch in a very "decorated" Chinese Polynesian restaurant where we sat by the window watching the rain, just too sad to talk. Alexis had said, "Da, you have to come home because my picture doesn't talk anymore"—the picture that Buddy and Dee took of us when we all went sailing during Michael's class reunion weekend. We had sent it with a message to Michael's mother and then given it to Alexis with a new message after Margaret died.

But our lives, like everyone else's, went on.

A Sea Change: Taha'a to Tonga

F ROM TAHA'A WE SPENT A RELAXING WEEK IN the Lagoon at Bora Bora, snorkeling with giant manta rays and consuming many last ceremonial drinks to toast the demise of the notorious Bora Bora Yacht Club, before moving on to Rarotonga and the Cook Islands, 535 miles westward. Through rainsqualls and rolly seas, we plodded on to the small independent island country of Niue, where on a blue infused morning we were greeted by a pod of whales cavorting through the mooring field. Later we discovered that, once more, we were getting there just in time for the party, as Niue was having a Centennial Celebration to commemorate 100 years of independence from New Zealand. There were feasts, dancing, parades, and all kinds of cultural events. AND, it was my sixty-first birthday! Although, judging from the entry in my journal, I was none too happy about it.

October 17, 2001, Alofi Harbor, Niue

Today I am 61 years old. How can that be? It utterly amazes me, until I look in the mirror. Still, with the kindness of blindness, I suppose I don't look as bad as I used to think 60 would look. Or, I just refuse to accept it. It's not so much the aging that is depressing as the loss of time. The loss of time to do things like master a musical instrument or a foreign language— write a book. However, I still am naive enough to harbor a hope that I will accomplish that goal, if not sail up the Yangtze River or down the Amazon. We will be lucky to get to the Mediterranean at this rate.

Naturally, many things pass out of the realm of possibility as one ages, but at least I still have the luxury of choices, however narrowed by this major commitment of "sailing around the world"—an effort which obviously will consume the remainder of my vital years and preclude other possibilities of pursuing a serious life in Art. A loss I sometimes regret desperately. But as

I repeat mantra-like to myself when I am in a slump, a real artist makes art no matter the circumstances, lifestyle, or lack of materials. It is almost a biological necessity.

Just finished reading Margaret Atwood's Blind Assassin which touched me in so many ways—the relationship of the sisters, the narrative of the old woman writing the story of her life on a rickety table on the back porch, watching the last season of her life empty out—wanting to leave a mark, clear it up, get it straight, tell it like it is—or was. How I understand, empathize, ache to do the same. Like a mute crying to say one clear word: look world, look at this, can you believe it, the wonder, the horror, the happiness, the isolation, the extreme loneliness of "I."

The trick is to be fully engaged in life's miracles—real or not. What else is there? What have we left? Like reading a good book to the very last page where hopefully it is finally revealed what the whole damn thing has been about, even though you thought you knew at various points along the way. You were wrong wrong wrong and now finally you see, accept, close the cover, and breath a sigh. That was a really good book. Sad, strange, misguided at times, but not much missed, good and bad. A hell of a story.

* * * * *

Oh dear. That dreadful black mood soon passed, however, as always, and I was "on the jazz" again as we left Niue on October 27th.

After a rolly three-day sail, missing Sunday entirely when we crossed the International Date Line, green cliffs loomed through squally showers signaling the entrance to "Harbor of Refuge" port in the capital city of Neiafu, Vava'u, Tonga, where we came alongside a rickety wharf to wait for Customs and Immigration officials.

Neiafu is a picturesque town whose old wooden buildings give a flavor of the South Pacific of years ago. It has none of the sensuous, colorful feeling of other Polynesian islands, however. Many of the women wear black with elaborate woven mats around their middles. The men wear either black or blue lavalavas (sarong-like wraps) with shorter mats around their waists—sometimes coarse, sometimes as delicate as embroidery. It is a very conservative society where it is inappropriate to hold hands on the street, the dancing is discreet, and no midriffs are bared or hips shaken, although fidelity in marriage is not necessarily the norm. Curiously, though, like Isla Mujeres or Mario's Marina in the Rio Dulce, it is a "cruiser hangout" where yachts and their crew have semi-permanently anchored themselves to the bottom.

The next day, All Souls' Day, we went to Mass in a cemetery and were treated as special guests. A teenaged boy disappeared into a nearby house and carted out a small bench for us to sit on, while most families sat on mats on the ground or on the graves they had decorated with quilts, tapa cloth, and plastic flowers. There was a large blue-and-white crucifix at the highest point of the cemetery next to an altar under a tent bedecked with lace tied with pink ribbons. Two thin eight-year-old girls were arranging red, orange, and yellow plastic flowers on the top of one grave, decorating the surrounding low stones with live greens, patting and smoothing the site as they would their mother's bed. One was wearing a dress of vibrant orange and yellow flowers, which blended in with the flowers on the grave. The other was in a blue dress, both girls a stark contrast to so much black in the bright sunshine. During Mass they sat at the foot of the grave playing "pick up stones" like playful guardian angels that would have been carved in stone in another culture.

The choir sat in front of the altar: women dressed in black with traditional mats of various styles around their commodious middles. Men in similar garb sat behind them. The choirmaster stood on a low bench in front of them, wearing a short-sleeve black shirt, a black lavalava, and a short woven mat tied with brown coconut fiber rope around his waist. The all-enveloping music vibrated the surface of my skin like mild electric shock waves of intricate harmony and delicate syncopation—unexpected turns and stops. Low voices of the men harmonized within themselves and against the female voices—high sopranos, mezzos, altos, weaving in and out, all guided with great care and pride by the man standing on the precarious bench mouthing the words and directing each section.

I just ached to take photographs but resisted, as I felt conspicuous enough. There are so many taboos in this culture—no one even shakes hands at the "sign of peace," which I realized just in time to whisper to Michael not to hug me. Photographing during Mass or at the cemetery at all would have undoubtedly been very bad form.

After Mass, the last harmonic chord drifted off over the hillside and the far palm trees as the sun turned its low golden spotlight on the scene. Everyone gathered up their stools, rolled up their sitting mats, patted the graves, and meandered back down the hill to waiting pickup trucks for the ride home. We walked up to the hillside restaurant that overlooked the cemetery and both harbors where we ate a pizza, still under the magical spell of the experience.

Briefly I reconsidered my wish to be cremated. It was such a nice thought to imagine my family gathered around my grave once a year, caressing and smoothing me, praying and singing such beautiful music. But then what right do I have to be so selfish at such a time when it would be they who would need the caressing and smoothing, the prayers and the music. That led to a surprisingly dark fleeting thought. What if we never got home at all . . .

But, as luck would have it, our last long passage of the year, 1,069 nautical miles to Opua, New Zealand, was fairly benign, broken up by a three-day stop at Minerva Reef while we waited for a nasty low to move through south of us. Minerva Reef, a circular reef surrounding a patch of shallow water in the middle of the ocean, is like a mirage at sea.

Approaching it you see nothing but sticks, sailboat masts (if there are any), anchored in the middle of the reef. At high tide the reef itself is completely covered with water, and you feel as if you are anchored in the middle of the Pacific Ocean, a very bizarre sensation. Slowly the reef filled up with boats and a little community developed as we all shared our weather information, food, beer, and boat bits for fix-it projects. I repaired a rip in the bimini and made bread while Michael replaced the water maker pump.

Two days later we motored through the narrow reef cut, raised our sails, and headed for New Zealand, arriving in Opus six days later at seven in the evening, just on the edge of a predicted patch of bad weather. The air was vaporous and visibility bad as we followed *Wandering Dream*'s yellow spinnaker into the Bay of Islands Harbor.

When we passed the huddled white houses of Russell, hundreds of sailboats loomed out of the fog, racing in different directions all around us, reminiscent of Wednesday night races in Annapolis.

We inched our way through the congestion to the Customs dock, where our buddies on *Quixotic* gave us a big cheer. Then a friend on *Born Free* took our lines and we manoeuvred alongside the pier against the wind and current to await the officials. It was the day before Thanksgiving, and we certainly were.

Customs men worked overtime to get us all checked in ahead of the storm. Even the health official took just a few things, forgoing the food locker "strip search" many cruisers had anticipated. Paperwork completed, we moved to a permanent slip and hurriedly got ourselves secured before dark.

Only then, exhausted and relieved, did we open our bottle of Daniel le Brun champagne and toast our arrival. Sometimes we forgot how special this experience was because we inhabited a crazy community of adventurers who were all doing the same thing. But there were moments when the reality of our accomplishment hit home and we were amazed at where we were and how far we had come.

That night was such a moment. After our private party, we went up to the yacht club and joined all our friends. Some, like us, had just arrived; others had been in a day or two or even a week earlier. But everyone was feeling the same exhilaration, relief, and excitement of having arrived at an important milestone in their sailing careers. For some, like the skipper of *Kon Tiki*, it was the completion of a circumnavigation. For others, like the British sailors, it was the halfway mark. Everyone—some more easily than others—had survived the dreaded and storied "passage from Hell" from Tonga to New Zealand, with its unpredictable perils and weather patterns.

We had been unusually lucky the whole trip. Our passage included some of the best sailing we had done all year during a string of beautiful sunny days and sparkling blue seas, provided by a huge high that hung over us like a guardian angel. Only the last day slowly gave way to the encroaching monstrous low from Australia and the Tasman Sea. Light winds at times forced us to use the "iron spinnaker" (the engine) as we raced against the deteriorating weather; but, unlike many boats that were utterly becalmed for days at latitude 30 degrees or caught in 40-knot winds, we had a dream passage.

As someone stood up, raised his glass, and gave a toast—"Thanks to all our friends who helped us along the way with Net check-ins and weather reports"—I said to myself, "Thank you, thank you, thank you, God." Even though I joked about "Net Nutties," some people were especially giving of their time and expertise and really helped to make it a lot easier for all of us. Everyone stood up, held their drink high. "And here's to any poor sailors who are still out there in the storm." Group chorus: "Amen."

The Land Down Under

"DOWN UNDER." I'M NOT SURE IF IT IS ONE word or two, but I do know it is an upside-down world where Christmas is in summer, snow falls when sunflowers bloom, and, if you're smart, you can avoid winter altogether by going north in June. From November 2001 to August 2004, with the exception of the occasional trip home for Christmas, we did just that, cruising the waters of New Zealand and Australia. We hadn't intended to go as far "down" as New Zealand, but when a couple of Kiwi circumnavigators gave us a Kiwi courtesy flag as a thank-you for being their line handlers through the Panama Canal, we had no choice. In fact, on a South Island road trip, we went all the way to Stewart Island, about as far "down" as you could go short of Antarctica. We spent an unplanned eighteen months in New Zealand, partly trapped in an eight-month, ever escalating boat refit, but mostly seduced by the land and its people. In many ways it is one of our favorite stops.

Knowing we were in for a long and messy refit process we put the boat on the hard, bought a car at the car auctions in Auckland, then found a garage apartment in the village of Opua, in the Bay of Islands region of the North Island, and moved off the boat. The owners, Robert and Elizabeth, who lived above us, became our surrogate family. Robert, a burly, gumboot-wearing, ex-rugby player who was as proud of his *pipi* (small clam) fritters as his lamb on the "barbie," always treated us with amused bewilderment, completely mystified by our gypsy life. While Elizabeth, a graying grandmother whose prize roses were as precious to her as her five grandchildren, included us in every family event and randomly fed us like stray kittens when we were clearly too bone tired to cook. Other times we survived on roasted chickens from the village grocery store, where the checkout girl knew us by name, as did the post mistress, the liquor shop vendors, and the boys at the marine store. In fact, everyone in town knew us and commiserated with us over our broken-boat stories.

Every week for eight months we worked on *Ithaca* side by side with carpenters, painters, fiberglass experts, electricians, and engine mechanics who were the best in the marine business. They taught us, teased us, laughed with us, and teared up when we left. They were our best friends, and their pride in *Ithaca* as she "splashed down" the last day paralleled ours.

Every Sunday we drove out of town to a small village where there was a tiny white clapboard Catholic church—covered in green mold. Father Albert, with his round face and rimless glasses, always reminded me of a surprised frog, astonished to find himself disguised as a priest. I grew to suspect that his curious facial expressions and bewildered pauses as he searched for the right word were actually a ruse to make us listen for the moment when he would utter, with utmost clarity and simplicity, the importance of integrity, justice, peace, and the priority of love. A message we needed reaffirmed at least once a week as mounting bills, broken gear, and unexpected boat problems stressed our relationship to the point where just getting through dinner without someone throwing a carving knife was an act of charity.

One of my roles on the boat has always been, unsurprisingly, "Chief of Comfort and Beauty." That translated to keeping *Ithaca* dry, warm, clean, waxed, polished, and varnished. Thus, during our eight-month refit we took every stick and panel of teak that could be unscrewed off the boat and carted it to an abandoned sail loft which became my "studio" where I spent the dank rainy season stripping, sanding, and varnishing. Our boatbuilder, Ian Wood, was amazed at my tenacity, even if his favorite expression was, "Well, you're not gonna do it that whay, are ya?" I would stand, perplexed, with the screwdriver or hammer or sandpaper in my hand, and say, "Well, I was . . ." and he would laugh like it was all just a joke or patiently show me a better way.

I was just as amazed by his perfectionism. Every piece of wood he touched on *Ithaca* was perfectly fitted and sanded no matter whether it would ever be seen again or not. When the day finally came that our nautical home hung in the travel lift, reborn and ready for launch, we gathered all the workers together for a party. Everyone signed their name on the bottom of a cabin drawer next to the names of the men who originally built the boat in Bristol, Rhode Island. There were lots of toasts, jokes, and jibes.

Toward the end of the afternoon I stood up and spoke about the building of the Transcontinental Railway and its appropriateness to the occasion. "Two teams from opposite sides of the country—in our case, opposite sides of the world—worked toward the completion of a heroic task. When both sides met at Promontory Point, Utah, the last nail they drove in was a golden spike. Since we have already driven in the last nail, Ian, I want you and the whole team to have this golden spike in commemoration of the completion of a heroic task: the refit of our beloved boat, *Ithaca*." I handed Ian a long spike I had sprayed gold. He bowed, held it up over his head, and everyone cheered. A couple of days later, when we had left the yard and were headed south, I found the golden spike in the back of the nav desk with a note attached. "WE did it. Good Luck. IW."

* * * * *

After eight months of refit, the weather window for going back up into the Pacific and continuing to Australia had closed, so we moved to Tauranga, in North Island's Bay of Plenty region, and stayed in New Zealand for another ten months. Traveling the length and breadth of the country, we explored every road, path, lane, mountain peak, and valley. We bought camping gear and hiked the famous Milford trail, kayaked the Abel Tasman, tackled the "white water" of the Whanganui River, became experts at setting up our tent in the rain and starting a fire with soggy sticks, helped shear sheep on farm stays, became rugby fans, walked across glaciers and through dripping rainforests, and soaked up the culture in Wellington and the sulfurous fumes of thermal waterfalls in Rotorua.

Everywhere we fell in love with down-to-earth, friendly, hardworking, unpretentious Kiwis and their magical land. I had become a travel addict. Almost every page of my Lonely Planet guidebook was densely underlined and starred. At a little café in Wellington, Michael and I had the inevitable conversation: I wanted to stay in an isolated campsite in the Victoria Mountains. He didn't. "No. It's time to get back to the boat. We're running out of money and I'm tired." He was right, of course. I was being a spoiled brat.

April 5, 2002, Tauranga, New Zealand

Two months on the road and it is nice to be back on the boat, not having to worry where we are going to spend the next night, but there are still so many places we didn't see and things we missed along the way. We did, however, cover a good bit of the landscape, drank fabulous New Zealand wine, and met many enchanting people. But it is the wilderness that really speaks to me. Each place I wanted to pitch my tent and stay. I longed to be out in it, not just driving by. My favorite times were the hiking up a hard hill, breathless and sweaty, stopping finally to catch my breath and listen to the birds, study the millions of mosses and ferns or distant vistas from a mountaintop beneath my boots. Such a feeling of physical and mental well-being must be why men climb mountains. The peace within matches the peace without—one climbs not because "it is there" but because YOU are there.

For such a "touristed" country it is amazingly easy to lose yourself here and feel you are the only person in the wild. It is not surprising this should appeal to me, since I love being at sea or in an isolated anchorage, a relatively rare occurrence in our experience . . .

Trying to sum up the past couple of months, much less the last year, as I come to the last pages of this journal, I wish I could say I've grown in proportion to the vastness I've experienced, but I'm just as mean, cranky, and selfish as I was last year, given my continuing poutiness with M's lack of enthusiasm for my personal passions and curiosities. I am a hermit and an interior person. He is the social, civilized one who doesn't really like to stress himself physically or live in a tent. He doesn't get caught up in things the way I do. Maybe I need this balance in my life; otherwise, I would probably be living in a hut in the bush in the wilderness of Westland by now. He is my reality touchstone. A hard role to play. I need to see it from that perspective and be grateful not resentful.

*   *   *   *   *

July, being winter Down Under and summer Stateside, was a good time to make our yearly trip home. Increasingly, grandchildren were growing and barely remembering us. Families were busy and bemused by our adventures but limitedly interested in the details. Not only did we live in two different hemispheres; we lived in two different worlds! While my sister, still incommunicado, lived, I supposed, in outer space or someplace where there was no mail delivery since she never acknowledged my correspondence.

The saddest discovery was that our dog and the newlyweds were not such a good fit after all. It seemed Danny, when push came to shove, chose Lauren over Jack, understandably. This was a big problem. We made posters and put them up on every vet and pet store bulletin board for a forty-mile radius around Annapolis. We pleaded with family members and called friends, but his next home would have to be a special place. The "little prince" was a twelve-year-old "sea dog" who didn't like to share. He didn't really like children any more than he liked cats, nor was he comfortable with other dogs in the household. He had always been the sole adored one in a family. Things were looking bleak and the marina bill in Tauranga was mounting up.

"Someone has to get back to the boat," Michael pointed out realistically. I broke down and yelled through my tears, "I am not dumping him at the SPCA."

"I know. We'll work it out. Don't worry. Why don't you just stay here with Jack until you can find him a good home." I hugged him through my tears. "Thank you."

So Michael returned to the boat while Jack and I rented a small place and searched for a suitable solution. It took three months, but eventually an older couple who lived on the water in Oxford, Maryland, came to the rescue and scooped him up before I had a chance to think of a reason for them not to. Jack jumped into the back of their SUV, tail wagging, and never looked back. I sat on the couch and sobbed. By the weekend I was on a plane back down to Down Under, a loving husband, a beautiful boat, and a storybook life of adventure. Over the years we kept in touch with Jack via postcards and visits until he died many years later, having served as the unofficial "Mayor of Oxford" longer than any other Labrador in memory.

October 13, 2002, Opua, New Zealand

It is good to be back on the boat even though M is full of cruiser talk and I'm still in an emotional no-man's-land, bone tired and sad, feeling stretched like a piece of taffy by two completely different modes of being. I know I will get back "on the jazz," but as I get older it is harder to bounce back into it.

* * * * *

For the next six months we cruised the North Island and absorbed everything Kiwi. I bounced back, but by May 2003 our time in New Zealand was winding down. We returned to Opua for a few last-minute repairs; loaded up with charts and duty-free booze; and prepared for the passage to Fiji. Our good friend Ian Wood shoved us off the pier and we motored across a glassy Bay of Islands full of clouds and green hills. Midget blue penguins bobbed and dove around the bow as if to say good-bye. Everything was fixed, including the whisker pole that we had broken the day before. One main salon light was not working, but there always has to be something.

There are so many things I loved about this amazing country. It was hard to think of never coming back. Most especially to the towering mountains folding into each other like petals of a huge purple rose; the dripping bush, the rushing water; the vines and mosses and ferns; the bell bird's call and the clownish tui (or parson bird); the cooing pigeons under a towering canopy of green beech, rimu, and kakailrt; the pebbled shores of flat and multicolored stone; steep cliffs and steaming surf . . .

The vast Otago plains and deep fjords of the South Island; the open, uninhabited spaces; the white dots of sheep on velvety green hills; the Kauri Villas, the rose gardens; the blokes in shorts and gumboots; the dogs working stock across the road; the rugby, funny ads, and junky fashions; the accents—the rolling Scottish brogue, the Maori "eeh" at the end of every sentence, and "cheers" and "sweet as," "rugged up," "jerseys" and "jumpers," and "biscuits" (for cookies); the Kawakawa toilets and Kerikeri hedges; the changing light, weather, wild winds, and foggy calms. . . I love New Zealand because it is small and faraway and can afford its principles: anti-war, anti-nuclear, anti-GM, and magnanimity to its native Maori, with the crazy goodwill of the Waitangi Treaty waving a flag against human greed.

Most of all, I love the special people, proud of their country and their work: Ian, Robert A and "baby Rob," Jim and Evelyn, Zona and Cal, David and Elizabeth, Father Chris and Father Albert, Flo and the church ladies, the Farm Stay and Bed and Breakfast people, "Jack" at the "Hibourn" in Otago. People we knew for a couple of days or people we knew for a year—all friendly, helpful, open, funny—"Good on ya," "yous mates." I hope to see you again. *Whakatane* ("It'll be fine.").

Sailing to Savusavu

THE TEN-DAY PASSAGE TO SAVUSAVU, FIJI, WAS not a "cakewalk" as advertised. The weather was unpredictable, the sea rough, and numerous gear failures depressing. Much of the time the genoa flapped and strained to starboard in arbitrary wind and big swells, making it hard for Hans to hold a steady course and causing *Ithaca* to roll erratically. Then the head stopped working, the boom bale broke, and the alternator stopped charging the batteries so that the belt had to be constantly adjusted, not an easy task when the tool bag kept sliding across the cabin sole. Finally the wind speed indicator stuck at 00—all very frustrating after having just left New Zealand after an eight-month total refit.

Over time the seas subsided. Gradually we shed layers of sweaters for long-sleeve T-shirts, and, by the fifth day, it was calm enough to drown our sorrows with Manhattans in the cockpit and celebrate our halfway point. As *Ithaca* swished through the dark universe of stars, it felt like we were in a spaceship flying to the moon. I put my head on Michael's shoulder. He held my hand. We talked about how hard it is to believe in what you can't see, to have faith and trust what you know and pray for the strength to deal with the rest. "Yes, I believe, God, but help my unbelief."

June 1, 2003, at sea, 237 nm to Savusavu

This morning, as the sun rises bright orange over the starboard rail, a lone seagull cruises and dips in the sunlight to port, white flashing over the blue waves. He must be the relief bird for the brown noddy who has been gliding and carving graceful arches in our wake almost every day for the past week. I watched, mesmerized, thinking of mother as I always do when I see seabirds.

Whoever coined the phrase "dark night of the soul" must have had the mid-watch in mind. Black, Black, Black. Five days later the boat was heaving and pounding through the dark like a runaway horse. Suspicious sounds—creaking, rubbing, growling, whining; the wind roaring through the rigging; the genoa and the main rattling—plagued my imagination. I sat in the nav seat, eyes scanning from GPS, to radar, to barometer, and back to the GPS checking for speed, distance to go, and heading, while Hans steered the helm, erratically from 340 to 035 as the boat rose up on a wave, crashed, and slid down again, laying the port rail even more deeply down in the water. The deck was awash with foam and the port light above my head looked like an aquarium.

Periodically I ventured topside to look for traffic, adjust Hans, or take over if he was faltering and confused. I huddled under the dodger, feet braced against the companionway, watching the wind direction needle and wind speed, which still read an aggravating 00 but I knew it had to be 35 knots. In reality, it was probably 25. The boat speed varied between 2 knots in calms up to 7 or 8 knots in squalls. At one point I saw a heart-stopping 11 knots flash on the GPS.

It was imperative to hold a steady course, "pointed up," to miss the reef off the head of Koro Island and get to the pass by dawn so we could make Savusavu before dark. My job was to make sure we stayed on our rhumb line, which necessitated constantly adjusting and encouraging Hans, who was temperamental under stress. Gradually I made my peace with him, repeatedly returning to the wheel when he "lost it" to subtly adjust course and gently coax cooperation. The more I worked at it, the more I learned and the more confidence I gained.

Friday, June 5, 2003, at sea, bound for Fiji

Finally, running up the Koro Island pass I feel more comfortable and in charge while M tries to get some sleep on our soggy port bunk. I am in the cockpit. It is early morning. I'm holding onto the dodger rail, anxious about our course, the increasing wind speed, and if Hans can keep us off the wind as the approaching squall churns up the water and speeds toward us. Suddenly from under the starboard bow a big white seabird sails calmly into my field of view, and I feel instantly more relaxed. It seems as if we have been watched over by guardian birds this whole trip.

* * * * *

Michael got up for his watch and saw we were in the pass. "Good job, Mertis, avoiding that reef in this weather. Thanks for letting me sleep." (Mertis being the name granddaughter Alexis selected for me when "Marguerite" proved too much of a mouthful.)

I tossed off a "no problem" and crawled into the warm, soggy pilot birth, relieved to be off watch at last. When I awoke, hazy watercolor hills stretched low on the horizon. Land. A flotilla of seabirds joined us, sweeping and diving in our wake, but the wind and rough seas persevered till the very end. Finally we rounded the light marking the reef at the mouth of the entrance to Savusavu, a big orange island freighter hot on our tail. Once inside, the boat leveled out for the first time in five days and slowly the wind calmed as we steamed into the lee of the green hills.

We were in a different world. I stripped off my "foulie" and let that old tropical, indolent, and slightly decadent air caress me with its lazy fingers. Moist light softened the hillsides clumped with palm trees and dotted with small palapas.

Upriver, off the Copra Shed Marina, we picked up a mooring in front of the town. Shops were turning on their lights as the sun sunk. We made a drink, "commenced yachting," and congratulated ourselves on surviving a challenging passage.

Then I opened a port locker and discovered it was full of water—the source of the leak over our port pilot berth. "We'll deal with that tomorrow. I barely have enough energy to shower." Michael grilled a steak. I made a salad from canned veggies, and we sipped a nice red wine by candlelight, happy to be finally sitting upright and still for a normal meal. Most of all grateful to sleep in our forward bunk, about the only dry place on the boat.

Kava Crazy

FIJI, ALSO KNOWN AS THE CANNIBAL ISLANDS, was a violent place of inter-tribal warfare and human sacrifice until the London Missionary Society arrived in 1830 and subdued its more brutal practices, sadly also smothering many vibrant rituals such as body decoration and elaborate hair dressing. The first European visitor was the Dutch explorer Abel Tasman, who discovered the islands in 1643. Then Captain James Cook visited in 1774, but it was Captain William Bligh who made it famous in *Mutiny on the Bounty*. By the time *Ithaca* arrived, no bodies were brewing in caldrons nor were any arrows flying through the air, but many curious superstitions and rituals remained, some clearly holdovers from missionary times, others reaching back to tribal roots.

For instance, a person must always stoop when entering a *bure* (thatched hut) and leave his/her shoes at the door. You must always sit cross-legged on the pandanus mat and keep your head lower that your host's. You must keep your shoulders covered and never sling anything over them like a camera or backpack. Never wear a hat, cap, or sunglasses when meeting people. Men should be clean shaven. Women should always wear long skirts and never hold hands in public. We tried our best to comply.

The most ubiquitous ritual was the *yaqona* (Fijian) or *kava* (Tongan) drinking ceremony. The present-day milder, more sociable version of the ceremony introduced by the Tongans, escaped obliteration because the missionaries thought it less threatening to Christianity than was the original priestly practice. It remains a significant aspect of the culture used by the Fijians to welcome and bond with visitors, augment storytelling, promote their culture, or just hang out. Our first experience of this ritual occurred when we were invited to a *lovo*, where food is cooked in pit ovens and traditional values and culture are passed on through dance performances and singing that help keep local legends alive. The feast always started with a kava ceremony, as do most social events. In fact, it was common courtesy to always bring *sevusevu* (a gift) of kava to share with the village chief upon one's initial visit. Little did we realize how often we would have the dubious opportunity to experience this rite as we sailed through the Western Pacific.

Initially we were a bit nervous not knowing what to expect, but, following clues from the assembled guests, we sat down cross-legged in a circle facing the chief. A large wooden bowl called a *tanoa* was placed in front of him, with a cord that led to a white cowry shell representing a link to the spirits and symbolizing divine fertility. I sat next to Michael because I was an invited guest, but traditionally, I should have sat with the rest of the women behind the men and only taken the kava after the men and guests had. I knew that it was very bad karma to turn your back on the *tanoa* or step over the cord, so I made careful note of its location to avoid tripping over it in the dark, causing havoc in the heavens.

The chief muttered an incantation then put the wrapped, dried pepper plant root in the bowl and mixed it with water. Taking half a coconut shell, called a *bilo*, and dipping it into what now looked like a bowl of muddy water, he handed it to the man sitting on his left. The man clapped once over his extended stomach and said "*bula*," meaning "cheers" or, literally, "life," then drank it down in one gulp and clapped three times in gratification. Yuck. Two more men, and then it was Michael's turn. He clapped, said "*bula*," and clapped three times. The chief filled the *bilo* and handed it to me. I looked down at the vile-looking brew, tried not to grimace, and gulped it down. Yes, it tasted like muddy water too.

Fortunately, guests were only required to participate once, but tradition required that the entire bowl had to be consumed before anyone left the circle. Maybe I should have drunk more to sooth my arthritic knees as the *bilo* made several rounds of the circle and everyone got very talkative or dropped their chins on the chests.

According to the Lonely Planet guidebook, kava is a mild narcotic and has been used as a diuretic and stress reliever for pharmaceutical purposes. "After a few drinks you may feel a slight numbness of the lips. Long sessions with strong mixes will probably make you drowsy. Some heavy drinkers develop 'kanikani' or scaly skin and heavy use can lead to impotence." Frankly, I'd rather have a double martini. Kava became a big part of our travels, however, until we reached Australia where, fortunately, the national brew is a bit more palatable.

After the initial kava ceremony, we were presented with mounds of food: lots of rooty stuff which looked like yams and different versions of taro: chicken or chunks of mutton wrapped in taro leaves, taro cake, and a mucilage blob with sugar on the top made with taro and coconut cream. All of which we dealt with as gracefully as possible while our hosts sang and drank kava, it being a tradition that the guests eat first and the hosts take the leftovers.

I tried to make small talk with the ladies sitting around watching me eat, but it felt very awkward. Most of the ladies squirmed and chatted among themselves, tended to their babies, or busily replenished the ample food supply. One small dark lady with a missing front tooth said, "I am Litia," then she patted my arm and pointed to a thin shy child. "This is my daughter. She is going to school for the first time next year. She will have to be away from home all week. She is very scared." The child looked at her brown toes scrunching the sand. Litia smiled down at her and took her hand.

After we had consumed about as much food as we could, Michael and I made our apologies. We were "very tired from our walk." Heaping plates of food were foisted on us when we left, which when eaten in the dark was okay, but looked grim when we got back to the boat. As we left, Litia looked up at me with earnest eyes and said: "The children are doing a dance performance for Parent's Day tomorrow. I will wait for you on the beach." We had planned to leave the next morning but how could I say no to her.

As usual, we got the special seats, which were on a green hill overlooking the bay. After the performance everyone had to have a bowl of kava. Then I found my friend Litia waiting for me, as she had promised, her small hands clutching a large bag of fresh veggies. She and her family had so little and I had nothing to give her in return so I took some photos of her daughter, which I later mailed to her address, never knowing if she received them.

* * * * *

Located in the southwest part of the Pacific Ocean, 1,317 miles from New Zealand and 1,963 miles from Australia, the now independent country of Fiji consists of 322 islands, 100 of which are inhabited, the largest populations being on the three main islands: Viti Levu (big Fiji), Vanua Levu (big land) and Taveuni, the smallest. All are volcanic islands with rugged interiors, remote villages, pristine coral reefs, waterfalls, and tropical forests. We spent two months cruising through this exotic island group, anchoring in remote bays, exploring small islands, and meeting a variety of people: international cruisers, market ladies, teachers, hustlers, and hikers. We explored the interior on road trips, went on waterfall walks in the *wap waps* (Fijian for outback), and city walkabouts . . .

One of my favorite adventures was our last day in Suva when we rented a car and went on a quest to find the "pottery village," pottery being one of my many dilettantish passions. After an hour's ride in a rickety skiff on a narrow brown river, we scrambled up a muddy bank and were introduced to the "headman" who took us to his house where we rather awkwardly presented the required gift of kava. Then a group of ladies gathered around us on the floor and we chatted about where we were from and why I wanted to see the pottery making.

Eventually, we were taken to the meeting house, a large empty hall with mats on the floor, where the ladies hesitantly displayed things that they had made or were working on. Then the head pottery lady, the oldest and the fattest, grabbed a big glob of clay and smashed it on her knee, slowly patting it into a vase. Rolling out thin coils of clay, she proceeded to decorate it. "The opening is the sun," she said then pointed to the raised ridges on the side. "These are rays of the sun." Then she pressed on round dots. "These are the men's heads." The crimping around the center belly of the pot represented waves. On a large pot with similar motifs—waves, men's heads, etc.—fishermen and pointy spikes represented the "War Gate." Everyone creates their own design using combinations of these motifs.

Another large lady told me with a big crooked smile: "We dig the clay from the riverbank. Then we put the pots in an open fire and glaze them by rubbing a kauri-like resin over the pot while it is still hot." They were not the most graceful or sophisticated pots, but it was fascinating to watch the women work and to learn about the process. I tried to explain how I make pots on a wheel and could never make anything as big as their huge urns. At this the head "potter" giggled, her six chins quivering like chocolate pudding.

Meantime, an assortment of babies and toddlers crawled around us playing with clay and wooden paddles used for smoothing the clay, while the men sat outside. One young mother discreetly breast-feeding her baby said: "When a girl child is born, we put a lump of clay on her forehead to make sure she will grow up to be a potter. It is a special tradition of our village."

When my friend finished making her pot, she carefully wrapped it in newspaper and handed it to me with a big smile. "You take home. " I said, "*Vinaka*" (thank you very much), and gently put it in my backpack, having no idea how I would let it dry before it came to harm in a rolling sea. Now, after fourteen years, I still have that pot on a bookshelf in my library. We also bought a little glazed pot shaped like a spearhead, which the ladies decided was more like a boat. We called it "Ithaca." As we pulled away from the bank, all the ladies waved and said, *Vinaka* and *Moce* ("good-bye").

*   *   *   *   *

We left Fiji from Vuda Point on August 16th and headed toward New Caledonia. After a challenging eight-day passage, we very gratefully entered the harbor of Port Moselle, Nouméa, on August 24th. Plagued by rough weather the whole trip, the last day almost did us in.

It was on my early morning watch that dawn brought the vision of a big black thunderstorm off the port bow and another one on the starboard. A vibrant rainbow towered out of each one as if making a giant arch. Its beauty was spellbinding but deadly. Suddenly the sky above darkened, the water whipped up a maelstrom of white caps, and the wind increased from 15 to 25 knots in five seconds. I sheeted out the main and grabbed the wheel, yelling for Michael who was asleep below. The wind continued to rise and the boat heeled over violently. Michael came up dazed and grumpy because I had awakened him but immediately grasped the situation. Yelling, "Oh my God, hold on," he sheeted out the genoa and the main as far as we could while I held the helm over and we ran down the wind, at one point doing 13 knots.

"Didn't you see that coming?"

"Yes, but I thought it was further away. I thought I had more time." Suddenly THWAK! The boom detached from the mast and swung wildly to starboard. "What do we do now?" I cried in a panic. The halyard parted and the sail came down on its own. We both breathed, "Thank you, God."

Fifteen minutes later the worst of the storm had past and the boat leveled out enough so I could go forward and tie down the mainsail. Then I noticed the yankee sail bag dragging in the water. As I went forward to drag it aboard, the bow bucked like a rodeo horse. A huge wave buried my feet, and the varnished bowsprit became as slippery as an ice rink. I grabbed the bow pulpit rail with all my strength, leaned over the side, and pulled up the bag as another wave slapped me in the face. I tied the bag to the shroud and carefully inched my way back to the cockpit, gripping whatever handhold I could find until I was safely standing under the dodger where Michael handed me a soggy towel to wipe my face. "Good work, Mertis. I was worried there for a few minutes." I sat down trying not to show my shaking hands.

After the storm passed we assessed the damage. The giant bolt holding the boom to the mast had slipped out. Now the boom had to be lifted up and pulled into alignment with the mast so that the bolt could be replaced. Somehow we had to line up the holes so we could reposition the bolt and slip in the cotter pin at the bottom.

"Okay. Here's what we're going to do," Michael said in his calming take-charge voice. "We've lost the main halyard but I can lift the boom with the yankee halyard. Then we'll pull the boom back with a line leading to the starboard winch. That should get it into the approximate position." Then it was gravity, luck, perseverance, and prayer that did the rest as we clung to the mast and tilting port deck trying to line up the holes and insert the bolt. It took all morning.

That accomplished, we used the yankee halyard as the new main halyard and raised the sail again as if it had all just been a bad dream. It was one of the few times we have wished that we had a third crew member—for the obvious reasons, but also because it would have made a great video.

The next day it was time to get out my French conversation book and remember how to order café au lait and a croissant!

Rituals of the Western Pacific

B AD WEATHER HAD KEPT US IN FIJI LONGER than we had planned. Now we had to hustle through the Western Pacific islands of New Caledonia and Vanuatu to get to Australia by December. In many ways this was the most remote and interesting part of our journey across the Pacific. From Fiji we sailed southwest to the southern tip of Grand Terre Island in New Caledonia then zigzagged south to Ile des Pins, where we gorged on everything French for a hedonistic couple of weeks before continuing on to the Vanuatu island chain feeling civilization dim with each new landfall.

On Tanna, at the tip end of the Y-shaped archipelago of small islands named the New Hebrides by Captain Cook in 1774 but now known as Vanuatu, or "Our Land," we went back in time. For many years the government had wisely restricted tourism to a limited number of locations in order to protect the indigenous culture. Transportation was sketchy, roads few. Even though the island was beginning to open up to "ecotourists," tourism in general in 2003 was still limited and homegrown. Since that time, the movie *Tanna* has been filmed there, giving the tiny remote island worldwide exposure.

The Lonely Planet calls Vanuatu a Tower of Babel with the highest concentration of different languages per head of population than any country in the world. Bislama, a type of pidgin English, is spoken by more than 70 percent of the people, while English and French are the secondary official languages. At least 105 other distinct traditional languages are used, however.

A hairy trip by Land Rover to the still active volcano Mount Yasur on Tanna set the stage for what was to come. Sitting on a rim of jagged lava rocks, staring down at fiery embers percolating below as sooty flakes flew around our heads, we felt as if we were being assaulted by an angry god.

That we were in a different world was confirmed during the following weeks as we sailed up through the island chain to visit local "Kastom villages," so-called because they follow the ancient ancestral religious and social customs. It felt a bit like going into "The Heart of Darkness," where teachings of the Jon Frum Cargo cult are still believed, ancestral rites are practiced, ceremonial dances hold hypnotic powers, and witch doctors are real. Tall, carved spiky totems with Martian-like faces with furrowed brows frown down from the chiefs' houses or from the sacred spaces they encircle. Wooden masks decorated with feathers, flying fox fur, and human hair, axes of jade with intricately woven twine over their wooden handles, and curious tassel-like objects worn by the women—objects of great artistry and imagination—are still made by these people we call "primitive."

While many things were similar, each island nevertheless had its own particular customs, traditions, and beliefs. Like Fiji, land rights went back to the first ancestors. According to Kastom, land could only be transferred to those who are related to the clan, although it could be leased. Here, too, the women did most of the work while the men sat around the *nakamal* (village clubhouse) drinking kava. In some areas, however, a woman could not stand higher than a man nor could a man deliberately place himself below a woman. Just walking under a woman's clothesline or swimming under her canoe was forbidden.

All kinds of taboos governed life, particularly for women. Many traditional villages had a special area set aside where women were to give birth or to stay during menstruation. Pregnant women were forbidden to garden, cook, and fish. Ignoring this taboo meant you may be fined or banished from the village. It is almost inconceivable that such restrictions could govern women's lives when, as I write this, we in the United States could be about to elect a woman president.

In this part of the world, of course, it was assumed that only men could become chiefs, although the process of choosing them differed from island to island. In the southern islands, the position was either elected or inherited. In the northern islands, it involved a process of giving away everything you had to move up through the "Nimangki" system, where "prestige flows to those who have publicly given away their wealth by holding a series of spectacular ceremonies which are always accompanied by traditional dancing and feasting . . . Each step up the village social ladder is accompanied by the ritual killing of a pig." Thus, the Lonely Planet suggests, owning many pigs ensures your political possibilities as well as provides status in the afterlife. "By means of this conspicuous destruction of his assets the villager moves up the Nimangki grade, earning new respect from his fellows for his wealth and generosity." All the traditional dances that we saw involved some aspect of this process.

*   *   *   *   *

On the island of Malekula, while walking along Banan Bay beach, we were suddenly barraged by a group of children who burst out of the jungle—naked little brown bodies clinging and clutching, pulling our fingers, and chattering away. Their huge brown eyes and wide white smiles were enchanting, although being surrounded and pawed was a bit unnerving.

Taking our hands they led us through the bush to a cluster of huts where ladies were sitting under a thatched pavilion talking and preparing bundles of pandanus for weaving. Then we heard tom-toms and were led to a clearing in the woods marked off with fern-tree sculptures. Women were forbidden to enter, except female tourists, of course. Dixon, the headman's son, introduced each dance with a very brief explanation. While a handful of men, naked except for conical hats, wide belts, and green pandanus leaves wrapped around their penises, stomped and chanted. Some dancers had bunches of seed pods tied around their ankles which rattled as they pounded the dusty ground accompanied by Dixon and "Little Eddy" who beat small hollow wooden drums.

Next we were guided to a different location where women and children danced but the men were taboo. Two long lines of women—maybe twenty per side—wearing grass skirts, their breasts bare, faced each other while three ladies sat on the ground beating out the rhythm and chanting as the women swung their arms and jogged in place. When asked the significance of the dance, Dixon just said, "The ladies like to dance." The second dance was a little like a reel dance where the two lines crossed each other in the middle and then returned to their own side, leaving little children swallowed up in the dust.

Some clearly performed more wholeheartedly than others. After they finished, we went along the line and shook everyone's hand. Some were shy, some defiant, some very warm and friendly, and others utterly bored. I got the feeling that some of the younger women were unhappier than others that they never went anywhere outside of their village—except maybe the next nearest village—and that they admittedly had "too many babies." As a woman I identified with them and felt more uncomfortable for them than I did for the men—putting themselves on display clearly not by choice. They have so little to cover themselves with anyway—literally rags of T-shirts and bits of material—that to put themselves further on display for the pleasure of tourists and for money seemed less than an "authentic National Geographic moment" as cruisers like to call these type of events.

After the ladies' dance, we were led back to the men's dancing area where we were presented with coconut milk to drink. Dixon gave another speech and each of us was required to say something. Then a mat was laid on the ground where a green bundle was unwrapped revealing chicken pieces in a broth of butter and coconut milk surrounded by a flattened orangish mashed starch called lap lap, which you dipped in the broth. It looked hideous but was actually pretty good, except for the rubber chicken. After we finished, the dancers all swarmed around and devoured the rest.

* * * * *

October 17th rolled around again, as it does with monotonous regularity every year. This time my birthday happened to coincide with the rare performance of the Rom Dance on Pentecost Island. The day before there had been some kind of local village rally culminating with a young Indian from Canada giving what was reported to be a fiery speech about how the white man had taken their land, brought diseases, etc. Later that afternoon, when walking through the village, I felt a certain edginess, something less than the overt friendliness and "Halo" that we usually received from the local people.

Thus, on the day of the big event, it was with a bit of trepidation that we met up with Douglas, our "go-to guy," who was sitting with a group of men under a banyan tree—his little daughter clinging to him like a baby chimp, all arms and black eyes—their animated conversation replaced by sullen stares as we approached. Starting down the path into the jungle, we noticed that both Douglas and his companion, Ruben, were armed with very sharp machetes. Douglas peeled off at his workshop, and Ruben, who was to be our guide, sternly pointed down the jungle path with the tip of his machete.

The narrow, steep path followed a river gorge, under palm trees and tangles of tropical bush. At the crest of the hill we looked down to Waterfall Bay and saw *Ithaca*, serenely moored in a scalloped fringe of beach. It briefly occurred to me that this might be the last time we saw our beloved boat and shivered when a random breeze rattled the palm trees. I looked at Michael with raised eyebrows. He squeezed my hand. It slowly became apparent, however, that what we had mistaken for gruffness was simply shyness, and gradually Ruben began to tell us about his life. By the end of the pleasant one-hour walk to the village, we had become friends.

Eventually we arrived at a ramshackle village. We could hear chanting in the background and were led to a big dirt clearing fenced off with little stakes: the *nasara*, or dancing ground. Tall, carved totem–type drums were stuck in the ground next to the *nakamal*, a large bamboo hut, which was the men's house. Behind the nakamal, the male dancers formed a circle. Wearing elaborate bird masks and covered from head to toe in banana leaves, they stomped and chanted around a group of men inside the circle, some of whom were dressed in the traditional *namba* (penis covers) with bunches of leaves gathered above their buttocks. One chief had a bright red hibiscus in his ear; a few of the other men were in regular clothes.

Slowly the entire group of men progressed to the center of the nasara as dogs scattered and villagers clustered around the outside of the circle. Periodically one of the dancers would fly off and harass the audience and run around the nakamal to keep away the evil spirits.

To be a Rom dancer is a great achievement of status. Young men go through a period of fasting and preparation, and the price of a pig must be paid, to become initiates. We were watching the late stage of this process when they had completed the initiation. After the dancing, green bananas were brought to the center of the dancing ground and tins of food were piled on top of them. Then a pig was brought out and unceremoniously clubbed on the head with a crowbar, not one of those elaborately carved pig-killing sticks we had seen in the museums. No one seemed to pay much attention to the poor pig, which was left unconscious but still breathing as everyone drifted away; even the dogs lost interest. The chief was paid his money and that was it.

We shook hands with the now clothed chiefs and some of the dancers, who then flew into the jungle like startled birds. Later, as we were picking our way down a slippery path, there was a sudden rustling and stamping of feet as a pack of Rom dancers streaked down the hill toward us. We stepped aside and they ran on down through the greenery. It was a bit scary even though, Ruben explained, they were new initiates who could only scare people. Just the old guys could kill people. This fact did not calm my overactive heartbeat. Happy Birthday, Marguerite!

Magic in Eden

O CTOBER 22, 2003, ASINVARI, MAEWO, VANUATU

Bright sun, clear blue sky, gin clear water, turquoise/aquamarine spotted with dark purple, embraced by a perfect crescent of beach. I can see clumps of coral 35 feet below us and hear the sound of the waterfall's ceaseless rushing, hidden behind a cluster of three trees on the shore. Yesterday I took the dinghy to the waterfall and tied it to a tree while I tried to do some drawings. I seem to have lost the knack entirely but it was still fun rocking back and forth in the shade, scribbling on my little pad. Then I walked up to the falls and sat on a rock under the falling water as it gushed over my body. Through the palm branches I could see Ithaca rocking on her anchor.

* * * * *

Maewo is the wettest island in Vanuatu's mountainous north, with fast-running rivers, permanent springs, and abundant waterfalls. The people are light skinned and more influenced by their Polynesian heritage. The charming, tidy village of Asinvari is my picture of Eden.

When we took the dinghy to the beach to pay a visit to Chief Nelson at the newly rebuilt "yacht club" hangout—quite grand by ordinary island standards—he introduced us to a small teenage girl who was hiding behind him. "My granddaughter, Nani. We lost her father last year." A mop of rust-colored hair partly hide her face as she held his hand and stared at the ground

. "She'll be your guide." Then she looked up, smiled, and the sun came out. Limping slightly, Nani showed us around the well-organized village, pointing out the houses of all her relatives. Colorful plants lined neat paths through rock-lined flower beds and attentively weeded vegetable gardens. Then the path circled around the school, across the football field to the ocean side of the island, and back again to the yacht club.

Along the way we passed the grave of the chief's oldest son who died the year before. A faded photo of a middle-aged man stared out at the hillside of coconut trees and jungle bush under a crudely lettered memorial. "Beloved Son, husband and Daddy." Nani stood silently next to us. We didn't ask.

A gentle waterfall spilled down a broad expanse of rock face in several different sections, falling into a green pool created by a ledge of rocks piled between it and its route to the bay. We stood on the ledge absorbing the cool mist on our hot sticky faces, soothed by the endless cascade, then returned to the yacht club for ice-cold beers and conversation with our new friends. Here we met Chief Nelson's youngest son, Nixon, who was practicing with his string band group, a charmer with a ready smile, bright eyes, and two dreadlocks coming out of the top of his head like little horns.

The next day Michael, in a playful mood, performed his "eat your thumb" magic trick for a little boy who came by the boat in his canoe. Word spread that the man with the white beard did "magic," which is taken very seriously in this part of the world. Later on the beach he did a few more little tricks and had a whole gallery of kids begging for more as we rowed back to the boat. That night we went to the yacht club to hear Nixon's string band and partake of a special coconut crab dinner. After dinner the children begged for more magic, so Michael pulled a coin out of a little girl's ear as they clustered around him whispering in wonderment. Then a young man from the string band asked him if he would come to the school so all the kids could see his magic.

When we got back to the boat that night, Michael searched for whatever props he could use to "make magic," not having access to his basement trunk full of secret boxes, top hats, and hidden rabbits. "I think a handkerchief, a shoelace, a bit of string, a table knife, and a teaspoon might do it," he muttered to himself as he pulled out the galley drawer. "I need to practice. It's been such a long time since I've done some of these tricks." Bending my mother's silver spoons used to be our boys' favorite, mainly to watch the agony on her face. Michael practiced grimacing and pretending to put all his strength into bending a galley spoon then whipped it out straight. I giggled until I was blue.

On "Performance Day," Nixon escorted us to the school, playing his small, long-neck banjo-like instrument that he was never without. He introduced us to his brother, who taught at the school and was in charge of organizing the children from little first graders to eighth graders. Michael stood in a doorway under the eaves of the porch in front of a low table as the kids crowded around him. It was hard to know how they responded because they didn't make a sound, just looked wide-eyed at each other after each trick. The jewel rope trick was first and may have been a little wordy for them, but the knife-swallowing and coin tricks were clearly the favorite, as was the thumb-eating trick everyone loves because Michael is so funny when he does it, bug-eyed like a Maori warrior. In the middle of the "disappearing knot in your shoelace" trick, he looked around and suddenly realized the premise of the trick was lost on them since no one wore shoes. But he told it in such a funny way that they couldn't help but grin.

Later that day he was summoned by Chief Nelson to do the whole routine over again. The wily chief was perplexed by the knife-swallowing trick but even more mystified by the magic spots trick. So Michael said he would show it to him and leave him the card if he promised never to tell anyone. Several hours later the chief paddled out to the boat with some papayas and Michael showed him how to do the trick but, having started early on the kava that afternoon, he never quite mastered it—much to his embarrassment. Michael graciously assured him that it took years of practice.

On our last day in Asinvari we walked through the little village and followed a new track, which led up a hill to another very pretty village with a tiny church next to an immense banyan tree called "the Chief." Suddenly a large group of kids popped out from behind the tree yelling "Magic. Magic." It seems Michael had become the rock star of the island.

Back on the beach, we found Nani in a small grass hut selling baskets, fruits, and vegetables. We bought a kumara and some eggs then traded a pen, notebook, and T-shirt for a small woven basket and a bag of delicious cherry tomatoes. Still shy but sweetly vivacious, she shook our hands, as is the custom here, and, when we confessed we were leaving that day, she pouted slightly and said, "Oh, but I'll never see you again" as if we were her best friends. She stood on the beach waving as we pulled away over the black sand and turquoise water. I waved back and smiled, deeply regretting that we would, indeed, never see each other again or be under the spell of Asenvari's own particular magic.

* * * * *

By the end of October we were anchored in Luganville on the island of Espiritu Santo, where 100 warships had been moored during World War II and a huge strategic base, a virtual city, had accommodated more than 100,000 servicemen. Now, all had been swallowed up by the jungle. Only a strip of overgrown tarmac marked the once crucial runway. The shell of a beached plane lay rusting under a tree. A buried ammunitions bunker was hidden in vines, and Million Dollar Point—where the departing US Army had driven truckloads of spare parts, military equipment, and jeeps into the water—was a wreck-strewn beach. Snorkeling over the site one could still see engine parts, tire rims, and green coke bottles embedded in the coral.

Offshore we dove to 100 feet to see the SS *President Coolidge*, a 1930 luxury liner that had been converted into a troop ship and sunk by our own mines when it strayed out of the secure channel while entering port. Incredibly, all but two hands were able to abandon ship before it went to the bottom. Now huge fish lazily paraded the decks, snooped around discarded canons, and inspected '30s decorative bric-a-brac sequestered in an underwater garden.

All this abandoned abundance had sparked "cargo cults" across the island chain. Villagers believed that the "cargo god," Jon Frum—the name supposedly came from "John From America"—would come again and bring them the kind of wealth they had seen discarded. The cult had various permutations, but basically the believers thought that if they waited, as if for a prophet, Jon Frum would come and bring riches, so they waited. In Tanna the cult evolved into a controversial political movement of the late '70s. Versions of the cult still exist in some islands where men wear tattered camouflage shirts and treat bits of old engines and rusty machinery as holy relics.

As fascinating as these islands were, I was getting anxious to move on when we learned via email that Caroline, our fourth grandchild, had been born. Two days later we were on passage to Australia. It was seven wet and wild days, but fast. During one twenty-four-hour period we covered 165 miles, our fastest record ever. We made landfall in Bundaberg, Australia, on November 17th and immediately called home. All those excited voices so far away galvanized us like a magnet. Michael, the tenacious ship's travel agent, discovered we could get a space A flight from a US Air Force base outside of Sydney. A week later we took an overnight bus to the state capital of New South Wales.

Home for Christmas

BY DECEMBER 5TH WE WERE ON A C-17 Globemaster to Hawaii where we waited three more days for a flight to Charleston. By December 10th, after an agonizingly long drive from Charleston to Annapolis, we were home. Alexis was waiting in the driveway. I scooped her up in my arms trying not to cry. Then there was Calvin, Dallas, baby Caroline, and the whole family. Alexis took us on a tour of their new house—so cozy and settled in, so rich with the details of a lively happy family, photographs on every surface, every room bustling with life and love.

The days passed in a fever of family and Christmas activities—shopping, cooking, doctor and dentist appointments, school plays, sporting events, and neighborhood parties: Christmas Eve Mass at the Naval Academy with all of us squeezed together in one pew, our handsome sons belting out the hymns next to wives straightening neckties and calming babies; Danny shucking oysters for Christmas dinner; Pete pouring champagne, dapper in his bow tie; infant Caroline as baby Jesus in the church pageant swaddled in the arms of a recalcitrant Mary, watched over by off-kilter angels in tutus and toddling camels; Michael showing Calvin how to land an airplane on his new toy aircraft carrier; Calvin and Dallas in matching navy coats and caps; and Alexis in her velvet and plaid dress in charge of the movie camera at Caroline's baptism and her round face, furrowed forehead, and intense blue-green eyes looking up at me as we made a book about CC the Cat.

The weeks after the holidays flew by. In an instant it was February 22, 2004, and we were back on the boat in Bundaberg.

February 22, 2004, Bundaberg, Australia

The trip home was, as usual, by turns wonderful and difficult. We ended up staying two months because of M's dental work, which allowed us a little more relaxing time but still most of our days were absorbed by babysitting, laundry, shopping, being involved in other people's lives. Which is fine since we are gone so much of the time. It's strange, though, we are and we aren't involved. Often we felt a little left out of what was going on. Pete, having started his own company, worked late nights and weekends so we barely saw him. Danny, making his own way in the new company with a wife and baby, was under his own set of challenges.

Every year it gets harder and harder to resolve these disparate aspects of our life. I miss everyone so much and feel sad that we are not really a part of their lives, except when we are there. Then there is no time for anything else. We are almost too close. We want to absorb it all, get involved but we've missed all the middle part.

I certainly would never willingly give up our adventure, but it has its own set of sacrifices and losses that we can never retrieve. I can accept it somewhat with the grandchildren knowing that they grow and change so fast, but I feel like we are losing that sense of deep communication with our sons. I guess that happens naturally as the result of them having their own families and lives so separate from ours, even if we were living at home, but I felt it so acutely this time. I suppose it is all part of learning to "let go and let be"—that eternal lesson that I have to relearn every day of my life.

The things that cause me the harshest stab of pain all have to do with not letting go—of Jack, of Alexis, of old issues, of my sister, of my mother, etc., etc. Maybe why I love our gypsy life so much is that it really calls me to be in the moment, experiencing new places, new things, new people, new languages, new challenges, constantly confronting the unknown. It is the ultimate escapist life. No time for looking back to old worries, losses, angers, and disappointments.

Down Under Redux

T HE LANDSCAPE AROUND BUNDABERG WAS flat, dry eucalyptus bush interrupted by rolling sugarcane fields, which undulated across the plains like sea swells rolling out to the horizon. A few old terrace houses with rambling covered porches and roofs like coolie hats were scattered in the green or parched brown landscape. Waterspouts from the irrigation sprinklers made lazy little rainbows in the afternoon sun. The town of Bundaberg was famous for its rum but not much else. Shortly after we returned, it rapidly lost its charm.

March 15, 2004, Bundaberg, Australia

Can't believe it is the 15th of March and we are STILL here, weather bound and buried in boat fix-its. I spent all last week varnishing in spite of the constant humidity and heat, while M tried to figure out the water leaks over our bunk and replace the pressure switch in the hot water tank. I did finally have my tooth pulled after three more days of dreadful pain and a consult with the dental surgeon whose comment was "Pull it. You don't really need that tooth anyway." Great. Happy to know that.

I just finished reading a sublime little book, The Art of Travel by Alain de Bottom. Why do we lust for new places and what do we discover when we get there? How to appreciate it, see it in more depth is why artists paint pictures, writers describe, photographers photograph—the desire to possess what we love. The last chapter, about Xavier de Maistre's A Journey Around My Room, was particularly thought provoking. I need to make more of an effort to rekindle my own natural inclination toward more concentrated looking, exercise my eyes and mind, make more specific descriptions, more accurate word choices, not be so lazy, be more engaged with my surrounding no matter how pedestrian. The "art" of varnishing, etc. What do I think about, see, smell, feel? I need to make time to photograph around here, really look at the flat green horizontal ribbons of sugarcane against the patches of rich red-brown dirt under a cloudless dome of robin's egg blue—like the Midwest wheat fields with a "down under" accent.

I loved drawing Alexis because it gave me the opportunity to embrace every little detail of her face, memorize it, hold it, possess it. The particular translucent blue green of her eyes, electrified flyaway wisps of hair across her forehead. The creamy smooth ivory/pink skin and pale rose bow-like lips curved like a shallow dish below two dark nostrils of her upturned "little piggy" mound of a nose. The only image strong enough to focus my attention while I was having my tooth pulled yesterday.

Tomorrow we sea-trial the new autopilot, (christened "Dave" for the Aussi installer) then pull the boat out of the water for hull repairs and a little boatyard work while we are on a road trip—finally. Can't even remember where it was I wanted to go.

* * * * *

Once we got the boat work under control, we bought an old rattletrap station wagon, filled it with camping gear, and blithely headed out on a land trip south to Tasmania, an island off the southeast tip of Victoria separated from Melbourne by the treacherous Bass Strait. We forgot that Australia was so *big*—7,682,300 square kilometers big! About the same size as the forty-eight mainland states of the USA, and half as large again as Europe, it constitutes 5 percent of the world's landmass. This clearly wasn't country you could see in a couple of weeks, as we had in New Zealand.

Undaunted by distances, on March 19th—Michael's birthday—we started from Bundaberg, Queensland, in the middle of the east coast of Australia and headed south. Our goal was to get to Hobart, Tasmania, the storied finish of the famous Sydney-Hobart sailing race, since we weren't crazy enough to sail there like some Aussie sailors we knew. While much of the interior of Australia is a barren land of salt flats and semi desert, a fertile strip runs down the east coast of the continent, separated from the dry interior by the Great Dividing Range. We drove down the interior side of the Dividing Mountains and returned along the coast—days and days and days in the car—forty-one to be precise.

As we drove south toward the Bunya Mountains, miles and miles of flat grassland stretched to the horizon punctuated with hoop and bunya pine trees. At Munroe Cottages, wallabies watched us from the front lawn all night like we were going to steal the silver (if there had been any). Rosella, vibrant-colored parrots of red, blue, and green, chattered overhead. The next day more grasslands and small towns, each with a balconied Grand Hotel and bar on the corner. Old "western" style storefronts lined the streets. In the cattle and sheep country of New South Wales, more grasslands, gum trees, AND a biblical locust plague so thick you could barely see through their smashed bodies on the windshield. We had to stop at sporadic gas stations to wash them off the front grille so the car wouldn't overheat. Thankfully, the locusts departed as we crossed the Murray River into Victoria's pretty little towns and gardens.

By the twenty-third of March we were on the ferry heading for Tasmania, an island of blustery mountaintops, rocky coastlines, serene and sparsely populated highlands, small villages, abandoned mining towns, vineyards, art colonies, old prisons, towers of hops vines, and farmland ablaze with fall colors. We saw a Tasmanian devil—as you would suspect, mean, ugly, and intimidating—corner a quoll, an equally ferocious catlike nocturnal creature, over some choice bloody bit of dinner. In Hobart we had a beer at the Hope and Anchor Inn, billed as the oldest hotel in Australia, and visited the "Female Factory," a prison where brass plaques described the fate of the incarcerated women. One Irish woman intentionally stole a cow so she would be transported to Australia, not realizing that starving in the potato famine of 1845 would have been preferable to life in this prison where women were treated like slaves.

Back on the mainland, we headed north along the Great Ocean Road through a string of small villages clustered among craggy-fingered cliffs, which clawed at the foaming water. The "Twelve Apostles," huge sandstone sculpture-like formations, stood enchained and raging at the sea like Michelangelo's "Prisoners." Lighthouses warned mariners to stay well clear of "Shipwreck Coast," where the Cape Otway Lighthouse and Signal Station were the first light and sign of land seen by many people on their four-month sea voyage from England to Melbourne.

Then on to the gold field county of Bendigo and miles of dry, drought-affected brown paddocks cracked with dry streambeds. We sat at a picnic table under a clump of gum trees by a pitiful "lake" where a flock of noisy white cockatiels ranted above our heads and a kookaburra stared at us from a nearby branch. Then three very curious and vibrant red-and-blue rosellas flew at us like kamikazes, practically taking the sandwiches out of our mouths. This was supposed to be the mellow wine trail but we didn't see a single vine.

More driving up the Great Alpine Road into the Snowy Mountains, through Mallacoota, and across miles and miles of burnt forest to the state capital, Canberra. Then on to Sydney—a cornucopia of cosmopolitan treats: museums, elegant shops, great restaurants, the famous bridge and opera house, where we saw Aida and sipped champagne looking out over the sparkling waters of Sydney Harbor. Every day involved a ferry ride to a different area of the city. For yachties it was perfect. We were constantly on the water (and out of the car).

By the time we got to Brisbane, Brizzy to the natives, I felt like I was glued to my seat, permanently bent in a sitting position. Finally, after forty-one days, I was thrilled to be back in boring old Bundaberg readying *Ithaca* to tackle the "Insane Labyrinth."

The Insane Labyrinth

THE GREAT BARRIER REEF, KNOWN TO mariners as the Insane Labyrinth, stretches like a beautiful but deadly necklace of coral reefs and islands off the coast of Queensland in northeastern Australia. From Fraser Island, southeast of Bundaberg, to the Torres Strait, north of Cape York Peninsula a –distance a little more than that between Boston and Miami– it covers 133,000 square miles. According to Wikipedia, it is the largest living structure on Earth. Made up of coral polyps, which along with algae make limestone to build the reef structures, it has been "in process" for millions of years. Only now is it bleaching and dying, suddenly succumbing to the warmer water temperature caused by the plague of global warming.

It includes 3,000 coral reefs, 600 continental islands, 300 coral cays, and about 150 inshore mangrove islands. There are crescent reefs, flat reefs, fringing reefs, and lagoon reefs where more than 1,500 fish species live, including clownfish, red bass, red-throat emperors, several species of snapper, and coral trout, plus 5,000 species of mollusks, 17 species of sea snakes, 6 species of turtles, and 30 species of whales, dolphins, and porpoises. More than 215 species of birds dive, wade, and fly above this pulsing life, among them 22 species of seabirds and 32 species of shorebirds, including white-bellied sea eagles and roseate terns. All the while, saltwater crocodiles patrol the mangroves and salt marshes.

Sad to say we experienced little of this underwater majesty, one of the great disappointments of our journey. As it turns out, sailboats and reefs are mutually abhorrent. Adverse winds and tides made it impossible to find safe harbor and secure anchorage in all but the most developed offshore islands. Thus, we zigzagged our way up the coast stopping only at the more populated islands and marinas. It was a long journey, fraught with frustrations and challenges: jelly fish and crocodiles kept us boat bound; the engine-overheating problem persisted; the fridge went on the "fritz"; and the head stopped working on a port tack. But, as always, the joys of "new territory," unusual sights, natural beauty, and interesting encounters kept us constantly surprised and delighted.

At Nara Inlet on Hook Island, we anchored within a fjord-like bay surrounded by steep rocky hills of hoop pines. Ashore we discovered a cave with Aboriginal paintings that looked like lacrosse stick nets and jellyfish tentacles. We also saw zamia palm trees, with cones of poison seeds, and very large ugly spiders. Australia is indeed a hostile land. At every bend there are things that can kill you. Along with crocodiles and box jellyfish, poisonous snakes patrol the bush; even whales were on the warpath, streaming down toward us in their annual migration south. I longed for lovely green New Zealand where there is only one shy and seldom seen poisonous spider in the bush, all else in nature sublimely benign.

Shallow water caught up with us in the Hinchinbrook Channel, where once again we realized we weren't in New Zealand anymore, Toto. After safely transiting the shallow bar at the mouth of the channel, which had been our big worry, we got confused by markers for a creek off to port and were hard aground before we realized our mistake. "Damn. I thought we were home free," yelled Michael as the wind and current pushed us back against the sandbar with each inch we powered off. Even though the tide was coming in, the wind and current kept us pinned in the shallow water.

Lots of boats went by. We hailed them on the radio. We waved T-shirts. No one even looked in our direction. I shook my head. "This never would have happened in Kiwi land." We flagged down a fishing boat that reluctantly gave us a perfunctory tow, but it did not help. Then a little fat man in a "tinny" tried to help us, but his engine was too weak. "Sorry, mates" and he putt-putted away. We called the Coast Guard, but they only work on the weekends.

Such a horrible feeling: the boat banging on the bottom, rigging clanging; the whole boat shivering. I felt like the hull must be cracking and splitting open beneath us and there was nothing we could do.

About two hours later we finally worked ourselves off as the tide rose and the current went slack. Fortunately, our valiant new transducer, which was taking all the beating, continued to work and we eventually found 25 feet of peaceful water in which to lay our anchor.

"That wasn't any fun."

"Sure wasn't. Let's drink!"

Shallow water, unmarked reefs, adverse wind and tide, plus a dinghy gone walkabout kept the fun going until Cooktown, so-named for Captain Cook who brought his ship up the fjord-like entrance for repairs after HIS grounding. Here he climbed what is now called "Cook's Look" to find his way out of the Insane Labyrinth. It was then that he claimed all the surrounding land for England.

During the age of exploration, the Portuguese, Spanish, Dutch, and English had all stopped at various locations on the continent, been unimpressed, and moved on. Cook was the first person to see any value in the place, probably because he had the insightful botanist Joseph Banks with him. Their first landfall is now called Botany Bay, which almost became the first penal colony until Sydney Harbor was deemed more attractive. Meeting a tribe of Aboriginal people for the first time, Cook wrote, "All they seemed to want was for us to be gone." Primitive by some standards but dumb they weren't.

We also climbed Cook's Look, signed the logbook at the top, put stones on the cairn, and took photos of each other to prove that we had gotten this far, hoping the pilgrimage would ensure that we, too, would escape the Insane Labyrinth.

Luckily we got to the Escape River on the Fourth of July where we celebrated with hamburgers, corn, and cabbage and apple salad while fellow cruiser Neal, on his boat *Active Light*, played "Yankee Doodle" and "Our Country Tis of Thee" on his trombone.

July 4, 2004, Escape River

Can't believe it is the Fourth of July. I miss my family. We got a cute email from Lexi a couple of days ago in response to my complaint that I had to stay on the boat and couldn't go swimming because of the crocodiles. She wrote, "Sorry you have to stay on the boat. I'll swim extra for you."

* * * * *

We escaped the Escape River about 8:30 on the morning of July 6th. A favorable current and strong stern wind powered us over the flat water of Albany Pass at 10 knots, while we sat in the cockpit and had lunch in awe as Dave (our new electronic autopilot that replaced Henri) steered us past Possession Island and the monument to Cook's land grab. Never had we experienced that sustained speed. But the mellow moment turned to an "all hands" emergency when the engine-overheating needle inched up suspiciously as we approached the anchorage in Seisia. I turned on the hot water to see if that would help, but in the nervousness of making landfall, we forgot that the hot water tap was still on.

Once anchored, Michael went down below to fetch a beer. "Oh no. We forgot to turn off the water. I'm drowning down here." The water was up to his ankles. Being mutually humiliated by our forgetfulness was one thing, but now we had absolutely no idea how much fresh water we had left and would have to keep the engine going to run the water maker until we were sure we had enough to get through the evening. So much for celebrating being out of the Insane Labyrinth and "Over the Top"—now it was mop time.

On July 6th—roughly seven weeks since we left Bundaberg—we had finally dropped the hook in Seisia Harbor, a tiny village on the other side of Cape York, the tip of the top, which points like a fat finger into the Torres Strait. From Seisia we made the rough, two-day passage across the Bay of Carpentaria to Darwin and the lock-bound Cullen Bay Marina where we spent several weeks getting ourselves and the boat prepared for the passage to Indonesia. Each day I walked to the post office in hopes of mail from home and each day returned empty-handed and brokenhearted. I varnished, mended canvas, cleaned, and polished until we shone. One day a mail package arrived from the kids with T-shirts, a picture album, and a video that we watched until we had it memorized, then called home to hear their sweet voices.

Dreamtime in the Northern Territories

T HE NORTHERN TERRITORY, WHOSE CAPITAL city is Darwin, is the most barren and least populated area of Australia and the ancestral home of its Aboriginal people, whose ancestors came across the sea from Southeast Asia approximately 45,000 years ago. When the British landed in Sydney Harbor 200 years ago, there were between 500,000 and 1 million Aborigines in Australia who spoke 250 distinctly different languages. They were a nomadic tribal people who clung together in clans descending from a common ancestor, whose history was written in the land through totems, or "Dreamings."

"Dreamtime" was a little like our Christian creation story. It was the time when the totemic ancestors created the world and all living things, the laws, and the landscape. These ancestors, like Greek gods, could appear in human form but could also manifest themselves in natural formations or animals. The stories of Rainbow Serpent, Lightning Men, and Wandjina could be traced by paths marked both by a tree, a hill, a river or by animals such as frogs, snakes, and fish. In this way the totem ancestor communicated moral lessons, instructions about life that were passed on to later generations through songs and pictures. Thus, it was the responsibility of the clan to respect and protect those special places and animals that held such significance.

To the British colonizers these people were less than human and their land was considered "terra nullius"—a land belonging to no one. It didn't take long for this fragile but intricate Aboriginal culture to be bulldozed by land appropriation, enslavement, and disease. As sacred sites were destroyed, social fabric shredded. By the 1880s only small groups of Aboriginal tribes existed in the very remote regions of the outback, and a long history of abuse and disregard ensued. Only occasionally did the government implement policies to help the tribes, but these did little to reinstate the dignity and rights of these "original" people. In spite of modern humane efforts at reform, too many Aboriginal people still live in abhorrent poverty, suffering from the modern plagues of alcoholism, substance abuse, and domestic violence.

Interestingly, while the Aborigines themselves have been segregated and marginalized as a cultural group, their art forms and indigenous signs and symbols have been appropriated as something uniquely "Australian" and are seen on everything from coffee mugs to upscale textiles. Some authentic Aboriginal paintings sell for thousands of dollars in galleries in Sydney. This art is strongly graphic, simple or complex; it is often colorful and abstract, its stylization naturally appealing to the modern aesthetic. All these dots and wavy lines and stick figures are freighted with meaning and densely literary, however. Dot painting, for example, evolved from ground painting in which dots were drawn on the ground to reflect a dreaming journey; cross-hatching represented different clans; animal tracks corresponded to different ancestors. A digging stick drawn as a straight line represents a woman. A boomerang or spear shape represents a man. Concentric circles represent dreaming sites. All tell stories that can be traced to centuries-old cave paintings, and Arnhem Land in the Northern Territory contains the world's most important collection of what is called "Rock Art." Obviously, we had to go there. So, leaving *Ithaca* safely ensconced in the marina in Darwin, we rented a car, packed our camping gear, and once again headed out into the bush.

* * * * *

Arnhem Land is closed to independent travelers and can be entered only with a special permit. Making a low river crossing into the East Alligator River floodplain, we stopped at the Red Lily billabong, a beautiful little oasis of green reeds, lily pads, egrets, various waterbirds, and one lazy crocodile floating along the water's surface, before picking up our guide, Thompson, in the small village of Oenpelli.

Our next stop was the sacred Aboriginal site on Injalak Mountain. Here thousand-year-old paintings sequestered in crevices, caves, and rocky outcrops were painted in red ochre and black, mixed with blood or spit, which penetrated the sandstone rock. The paintings of fish, birds, and animals indicated what kind of food could be gathered in the area. The tall skinny stick figures, *mimi* (spirits of the dead), told cautionary tales. The abstract "dream paintings" told creation stories of the Rainbow Serpent.

One at a time we squeezed through a narrow chasm and stepped onto a ledge overlooking a valley divided by a meandering river that seemed itself to be painted in patches of green and blue. Wild brumbies sheltered under shade trees, and the village of Oenpelli floated on the horizon. Michael and I uttered a collective gasp when Thompson said, "In the peak of 'The Wet' this whole area is flooded, but in 'The Dry' the earth is brown and cracked, just a landscape of mud puddles." Luckily, we were in the in-between time.

We sat in silence. A canopy of red fish, crocodiles, kangaroos, and mythical figures swam over our heads. Thompson served us tea and biscuits and wandered off by himself to smoke yet another cigarette. He was a shy little fellow, bare black feet sticking out of tattered long pants, grizzly gray beard crusting his black face, and a fizz of hair flying out from an old ball cap. He spoke softly and only when asked a question. Apparently, Aboriginals as a whole are very shy and hesitant to talk about their people and culture, which makes them charming companions but not inspired tour guides. On the way down the mountain, however, Thompson did point out a very curious line drawing of a woman with swollen joints who "had been punished with an evil spell from her husband for her philandering . . ."

Back at our campsite we had a drink, made a fire, and cooked chili under a big moon casting filigree patterns in the shadows. "A nice place to visit but . . . ," Michael joked as he sipped his G and T.

The next day we drove to Katherine, where we set up our tent in a green carpeted camp, and then headed to the Nimiluk National Park for a trip through three of the thirteen gorges carved out by the Katherine River, which begins in Arnhem Land and becomes the

Daly River before flowing into the Timor Sea roughly 50 miles (80 km) southwest of Darwin. Steep cathedral-like cliffs towered above us, some painted with Aboriginal icons thousands of years old. We moved slowly along the river listening to the rather annoying patter of a young Maori guide who filled us in on the nature of the floods during The Wet, when surging water turns this river into a frightening maelstrom of destructive power. Tea under an overarching paperbark tree was pleasant, but forgoing the opportunity for a swim seemed wise when we saw a freshwater crocodile, his nose peeking out of the water on the edge of the swimming hole, eyeing a clump of tourists on the beach. Although assured by our guide that they are completely harmless, what does a Kiwi Maori really know about crocodiles?

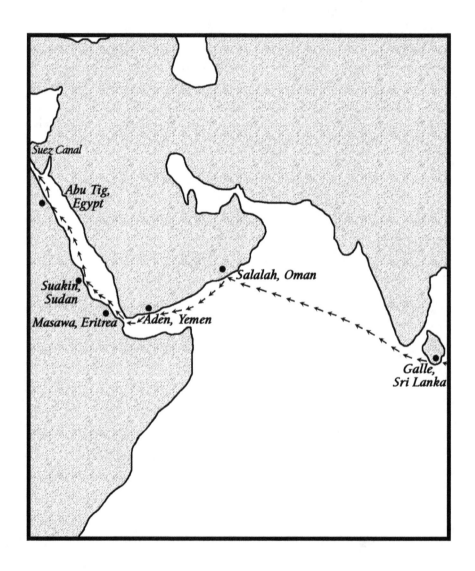

Suez Canal

Abu Tig,
Egypt

Suakin,
Sudan

Masawa, Eritrea

Aden, Yemen

Salalah, Oman

Galle,
Sri Lanka

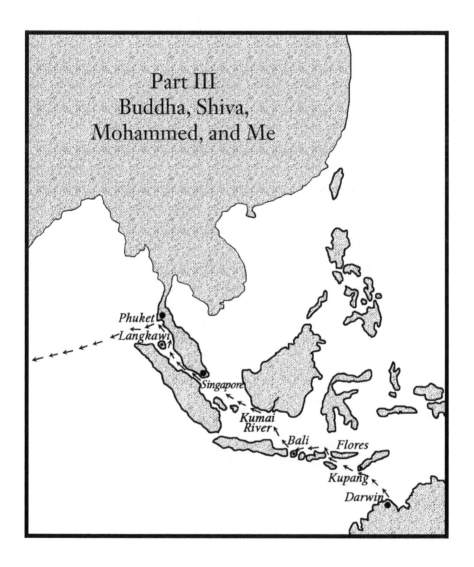

Part III
Buddha, Shiva,
Mohammed, and Me

Phuket
Langkawi
Singapore
Kumai
River
Bali
Flores
Kupang
Darwin

Indonesia Intro

AUGUST 7, 2004, 28 MILES FROM TIMOR WAYPOINT

7:30 a.m. Still motoring. A pale bluish-gray dawn blushes to pink haze on the horizon, which slowly reveals a light purple undulating line of peaks and valleys, too distinct to be clouds. Indonesia introduces itself as subtly as the journey—slow, gradual, no fanfare, drama, wind, or seas. In fact, we have motored almost the entire way with respites of mellow sailing in the afternoon and evening.

Yesterday morning glassy, flat water rippled silver at the bow by arching dolphins, racing and twisting, surfacing and blowing, water puddling blood-red pools in the sunlight which raked across the eastern sea under a bank of trade wind "puffies" that brought no wind. Hanging over the bow sprit, I tried to film them diving through the dark shadow of my reflection, but in a heartbeat the shattered mirror stilled and they were gone.

I've been reading, trying to get a handle on the history, geography, cruising, and anchoring possibilities of the country, as well as trying to learn a few words of the language. Naturally, there is too much to see and do and not enough time. This always provokes difficult discussions with the Captain, trying to match up the Lonely Planet romance with the Cruising Guide reality. In this case, the Cruising Guide info is rather sparse and hard to sort through. But what is clear is that, once again, a lot will fall through the cracks. I just have to focus on what we CAN do and how extraordinary it is to be here at all, instead of what fascinating, off the beaten track, undiscovered paradises we are missing.

* * * * *

Indonesia lies on its side like a quarter moon across the equator for nearly 3,100 miles (5,000 km) between the Pacific and Indian Oceans, total land- and sea mass two and a half times greater than the land area of Australia. Indonesians call their country *Tanah Air Kita*, "Our Earth and Water." Of its 18,000 islands, 6,000 are inhabited, and 231,330,000 people make up the country's diverse population, the world's fourth largest after China, India, and the United States. Three hundred ethic groups speak 365 languages, have different cultures, and practice different faiths. They live in rural and urban, dry and jungle-like, primitive and sophisticated environments. Previously known as the Dutch East Indies, it only became Indonesia in 1945. Its history is multi-layered, its politics are complex.

For instance, in the ninth century, Buddhism and Hinduism produced sophisticated cultures in Central Java, as evidenced in such monumental temples as Borobudur and Prambanan. Islam arrived with traders in the twelfth century and became blended with Hinduism and animist beliefs to produce a hybrid religion that predominates in much of Indonesia today. The Portuguese, Dutch, and British brought Western ideas of freedom, democracy, independence, and the complications of forging a new nation out of this vast and varied country. (East Timor's bloody battle for independence being a recent example.)

Ithaca arrived in August 2004. For two months we cruised the southern archipelago from Timor to Bali, then up to Kalimantan (Borneo of old) and on to Singapore. Skirting unmarked nets, reefs and rocks by day, at night the challenge was unlit and shifting fishing boats. Anchoring off remote villages and tourist dive resorts, we dove along hanging gardens of coral-encrusted walls and snorkeled shallows where fish poisoning and underwater bombs had turned the reefs to bleached bones. We trailed Komodo dragons on Rinja Island and tracked the wild orangutans of Kalimantan. We learned about *Ikat* (local textiles) and devoured mounds of *kepak* (the local noodle dish). We struggled with the language, and thanks to the patient ministrations of the Captain, managed to keep *Ithaca*'s engine moving us forward when wind failed and sails hung slack.

Most rewarding of all, we made new friends and established bonds that continue to this day, years after home ports were reached and anchors "swallowed": Sam and Bill on *Blue Banana*; Captain Ron on *Gemini*; Christian and Cybil on *Subeki*; Phil and Janie on *T/Solo*;

and many others too numerous to name whose companionship and support lightened the difficult times and helped create the best ones.

* * * * *

Many times, though, we were completely by ourselves. On Solor Island (in the Lesser Sunda Islands), we anchored in 30 feet of water close to the shore off the village of Lawgong. Women pounded their clothes in the "washing hole" on the beach amid splashing children. Two men sat on their haunches in the shade of a beached fishing boat, the low rattle of their conversation floating through the steamy air. Fishermen called to each other across the water. A motorbike roared by. A ferryboat got under way. The sinking sun poured stage lighting over the bright slashes of pink-and-green boats on the dark muddy beach, palm trees, and hazy mountains as *Ithaca* slowly swung on her anchor just off the bow of a fishing boat—a delicate birdcage construction of bamboo poles and outriggers.

A few days later saw us moored on the north coast of Flores, floating between two reefs off the small village of Wailamon, thanks to navigational charts on C-Map, our computer-based chart system. We were the only boat there. Kids in a canoe paddled around *Ithaca* and stared at us from a distance. When we took the dinghy in to the beach, hordes of them came out and stood around looking at us as if the Martians had just landed. The older boys led us into the village where we discovered that what we had seen from the boat was, in fact, a Catholic church. A young man named Bius, who spoke some English, walked up, introduced himself, and invited us to his house, where he climbed up a tree and cut two coconuts for us to drink. While we sat and talked, more kids encircled us; they stared and giggled when we said, *Selamat sore* (Good afternoon). A few young men stood around, with one or two women holding babies and the usual assortment of pigs and dogs.

Other than Bius, no one spoke English, but everyone was very friendly and smiling. His little daughter, Tian, bent over the back of my chair and stared at my Indonesian phrase book. She pointed to the English translation, which I then read to her, and she pronounced the word in Indonesian. Strands of dark hair fell across her face as she looked up at me with a shy, earnest smile. I wanted to hug her.

When we came back the next morning for Mass, Bius's wife brought out black sweet tea and buns, and the whole village gathered around again. It turned out that the church service just started when everyone got there, and there was no priest, which we suspected. So, the service was just a few communal prayers led by the village headman. Things happened here when they happened, not necessarily as advertised. We, however, were on a schedule dictated by the weather. Anxious about opposing wind and tide on the way to our next anchorage, we reluctantly took leave of our new friends. I took one last photograph of Bius sitting in a white plastic chair under a palm tree with his arm around Tian in her frilly pink church dress. Then the village boys shoved us out into the lagoon, waving and shouting *Selamat jalan* (Have a good journey).

"What an amazing experience. After twenty minutes I felt like they were family, and I barely knew two words of the language."

"Yes," I agreed. "We were total strangers from a different world who washed up in their backyard one day and in a few hours formed a memorable bond."

We still talk about that encounter and wonder what happened to all those kids.

Roads Less Traveled

A BOATBUILDING VILLAGE ON SUMBAWA (another Lesser Sunda island). How could we resist? According to our Lonely Planet travel guide, large wooden Bugis schooners were still being built in the village of Sageang, in the Wera region northeast of Bima. How could we get there? Our "Boat Boy" Budi had said he could arrange transportation, but, when we got to the pier, the original driver had mysteriously disappeared. Budi said he could make a cheaper arrangement with another Bemo driver, but there seemed to be a lot of confusion about who that was. A large crowd gathered. The new designated driver gave us a long and animated song and dance that he couldn't take us because he had a stomachache. Budi drove us all around town to locate someone who was "healthy," finally piling our gear into a fourth Bemo, whose very surly driver reluctantly started driving out of town toward the coast in the direction of what we hoped was indeed the boatbuilding village.

It was much farther than we thought, on a very rough, potholed road up over dry, windy mountains and into valleys of rice paddies lined with tidy, tile-roofed houses. After three hours we came to the end of the road—*literally*. We looked at each other. The driver got out of the car and pointed to a ridge. We walked over it and behold, the boatbuilding village. A small cluster of wooden houses along sand streets lined the beach. In front of them rose at least twenty huge wooden schooners, some with bare ribs of hulls looking like giant beached whales. All were in various stages of completion. Other smaller boats, strewn along the littered beach, were being painted, repaired, and re-caulked.

An old man beckoned to us from a bow 15 feet above our heads. We climbed up the rickety bamboo ladder and were swarmed by kids while he continued to pound his wooden spikes into the deck planking and attempted conversation with very halting English. The village was a boatbuilding co-op, but, because of the language barrier, we really could not find out much more than that. The old man pointed toward the end of the beach where a partially completed boat was ready to be launched, her blue hull gleaming with fresh bottom paint. We watched a crew dig away the sand under the boat. Mounds of sandbags propped up her sides, as several men dug a hole by hand under the keel and positioned logs for rolling her down the beach into the water. Sadly, our driver was getting impatient, so we couldn't stay to see the mission accomplished. It must have been a monumental task, with all the villagers lending a hand.

When we got back to town, another large group of yelling men had gathered. After we paid our driver, the money was snatched from him by an angry man with a large potbelly. The crowd got bigger and uglier. Deciding it was some kind of Bemo Mafia altercation that didn't concern us, we left as soon as we could get our dinghy untied and the engine going.

It had been an interesting day but a bit uncomfortable, each of us secretly wondering if we were being kidnapped by some irate Muslim fanatic to be held hostage in a hovel somewhere in the dry brown mountains of Sumbawa. Our sullen driver had never smiled except when I commented on the music he was playing as *"Musik bauo,"* meaning, I hoped, "Nice music." Only then did he manage a meager indication of pleasure with a subtle nod of his head.

At the time I wrote this in my journal.

August 2004, Bima, Sumbawa

Language is such a barrier. There is so much we miss because we can't communicate, so much we misconstrue out of ignorance. Even just a few words make a big difference. It would be wonderful to be able to travel with an electronic translator. There's a useful technological tool now to break down the barrier of cultural separatism and promote peace. [Guess what?

Twelve years later we have it, but the world is even less peaceful. What do I know?]

In the meantime, we muddle through with a well-thumbed phrase book and a handful of key words. This is the adventure of travel that I love, to go beyond the boundaries and barriers of the known. To have one's comfort level constantly challenged and learn more about this amazing world, which in some ways gets smaller every year yet remains a universe of mystery and wonders. This adventure is the only thing that could keep me from you, Alexis, and move me to give up so many other things in my life. This challenge, this constant questing and learning, seeing and doing.

Bali Pictures

FROM SUMBAWA WE CROSSED THE channel to Lombok, made lush by streams of water pouring down the volcanic slope of Mt. Rinjani and ringed with popular dive sites. While the indigenous Sasak people, whose religion is a unique mix of animism and Islam, make up 90 percent of the population, a large minority observe the customs, language, and religion expressed by Balinese Hinduism—an exotic world of gamelan (Java and Bali's traditional ensemble music featuring mainly percussive instruments), stone temples, and dollhouse-like shrines where candles flickered, flowers bloomed, and petite, dark, big-eyed women in vibrant sarongs and gold jewelry smiled shyly at strangers. Lombok was simply an hors d'oeuvre before the main course, Bali.

By early September we were tied up in the Bali Marina in Denpasar on the southern tip of the island. It was the beginning of the full moon season of annual temple festivals where every town, small or large, comes alive with dance performances and processions in which hundreds of men, women, and children—draped in exquisite fabric, donning elaborate headdresses, and laden with gold jewelry—carry ornately designed flower and food offerings to one of at least three temples in every town. A continual score of gamelan rhythms floated on the sultry air 24/7. This richness of culture made up for much of the tawdry tourist development of some areas around Kuta, where the "Bali Bombing" in a local bar was now touted as a tourist sight. Having access to "real" grocery stores and an opportunity to renew our stash of pirated DVDs—fifty for $1.00—was an extra bonus. Shopping opportunities were legion, both tacky and elegant.

When not working on the boat, we traveled around the island, going to dance performances, watching processions, visiting temples, and traveling to out-of-the-way villages in the highlands. I photographed ravenously. Our driver, Waylan, navigated the traffic, lack of street signs, narrow and sometimes washed out mountain roads, and awkward language barriers. But he always seemed unusually nervous when he saw anyone in uniform.

"What's the problem, Waylan?" I finally enquired.

"The police are bad men. They can stop you anytime and extort money for any small, unreasonable infraction. The whole country is corrupt. The government runs on bribes, even the schools. You can pay your teacher to get a good grade."

So much for the picture postcard idyll. But we were lucky. We were tourists. We could indulge in storybook romance, which we did unabashedly.

In Ubud, the mountainous "cultural center" of Bali, we enjoyed the elegant surroundings of the garden-like Hotel Tjampuhan, looking out from our balcony over a tangled, terraced hillside of tropical plants, pools, and curving stone steps. Since Colin McPhee's *A House in Bali* had given me a rudimentary understanding of gamelan music and dance, I became almost as fanatical about seeing every performance as I was about finding every remote Mayan ruin. I was in love again, mesmerized by the music and the movements.

Balinese music and dance/drama are a blend of religious and aesthetic expression, largely based on stories from the *Mahabharata*, a Sanskrit epic from ancient India which is as important to Hindu culture as the *Quran* is to Muslims and the *Bible*, Shakespeare, Homer, and Greek drama are to Western culture. In many of these stories, mythical characters representing good and evil are forever locked in a battle for balance in the world. In the Barong Dance the beast, Barong, in the form of an impressive lion, represents good locked in perpetual battle with Ranga, the evil witch. The dance reminded me of a Shakespearean play, with high drama, low comedy, and dramatic crisis; unlike in the Bard's plays, however, there was no final catharsis. Evil is never totally vanquished. Kris dancers fight their exhausting battle with the self-destructing sword into eternity—a uniquely Eastern philosophical position, but deeply personal and universal.

Gamelan predominantly consists of percussive instruments (gongs, xylophones), as well as strings and woodwinds. It is a complex sound of overlapping and crisscrossing notes, vibrant and hypnotic, blending seamlessly with the angular expressiveness of the dance/drama and underscoring the absence of "resolution."

Sometimes dancers are possessed by demons. In the Sangyang Dance, for instance, the dancers go into a trance and walk on hot coals or stab themselves with daggers. In Ubud we watched the Legong Dance under a canopy of stars where tiny, doll-like girls performed intricately choreographed movements—fingers, hands, arms, hips, feet, and facial expressions all coordinated to reflect the layers of percussive sound. Children are actually taught to dance with their hands before they can walk.

Michael was ever indulgent and patient, but when he threatened to burn my Lonely Planet, I knew it was time for a break. And, thanks to that travel guide, I found the perfect place: the Villa Cepik, in the mountainous village of Sideman, where we spent a weekend sitting on the tile terrace of our very own *balé* (Balinese pavilion house) overlooking a small swimming pool surrounded by dripping bougainvillea, bamboo, palm trees, and hibiscus. The hillside and valley beyond were completely sculpted with rice terraces and thatched huts. Gamelan music from the temple across the valley tinkled and crashed with agitated syncopation and then faded to a solitary drumbeat, slowly gaining momentum again. A soft mist hovered over the scene as the early morning sun gradually burned through. In the valley, a solitary man in a coolie hat bent over his hoe.

We sipped our coffee in silence. Nibbled on papaya

"How much longer do you think we can do this?"

Jolted out of my dream I said, "Do what?"

"Keep traveling. How many more years? Eventually we have to go home."

"What do you mean 'go home'? We're not even halfway around the world."

"But at the rate we're going, it will be years."

"So?"

"I just think we should think about it."

It was a conversation we were to have many, many more times.

The kaleidoscopic drive back to the Bali Marina was a welcome diversion. The cascade of images kept my mind off our conversation: rice paddies, clear rushing streams, a rice *sawah* being plowed by a water buffalo, people harvesting peanuts, quaint tile-roofed houses, walled compounds of mushroom-shaped shrines and pavilions, ornate split gates, and temples decorated with long, arching poles made of bamboo and palm leaves which symbolized the Snake, the god of water. Made by individual families during temple ceremonies, these pennants were ubiquitous, lining the roadsides and announcing village entrances. Each was a unique work of art.

At an Aga village we met the descendants of the original Balinese who had inhabited the island before the Majapahit. One soft-spoken young man explained that in his community everyone had to marry within the village. He chose his wife by throwing a camellia over a wall that enclosed all the eligible girls. Whoever caught the flower became his wife. As good a method as any, I guess. According to Waylan, modern Balinese custom still requires that a couple not only gain the approval of both families but also the whole village before they can marry. Maybe not a bad idea either.

* * * * *

Back in the marina bar, we met up with Sam and Bill on *Blue Banana*. (Later, we often lovingly called them the BB's, as it was cruiser protocol to refer to boat crews by the name of their craft rather than their given names.) We had met them briefly in Flores when they dinghied over to our boat and invited us to a "trash party." Despite our double takes at the implication, a trash party turned out to be when cruisers, buried by their garbage on the boat, took it to the beach and created a giant bonfire, accompanied by liberal amounts of party liquids, munchies, and a modicum of "trash talk." How could we resist? Everyone turned out to be very simpatico. So much so that we ultimately formed a little ad hoc tribe, staying in contact and meeting up in various ports throughout Southeast Asia and the Mediterranean for many years to come.

"Where are you two from?" I asked Sam.

"California, the Monterey Bay area."

"No kidding. So am I!" And it went on from there.

Although Sam was ten years younger than me, we shared a network of common friends. She had the same riding instructor, haunted the same bars in her youth, and loved the rugged, wild Pacific coast as much as I did. Upon further discussion, I discovered that Bill had grown up in Pasadena, California, where I had lived as a child, and that his twin sisters and I had all attended fifth grade at the Westridge School for Girls the same year. I recalled them vividly. We all wore the blue-checked uniforms and saddle shoes, but I particularly remembered their matching ponytails. It was astonishing to make such connections halfway around the world on our way to Singapore.

At the trash party Sam suggested that we make a detour to see the orangutans in Kalimantan. Absolutely. Why not?

Up the Kumai River on the "African Queen"

O CTOBER 10, 2004, MOTORING UP THE KUMAI RIVER, KALIMANTAN (BORNEO)

It is 5:30 a.m. I have just awakened to find myself sleeping on the deck of a wooden riverboat, under a canopy of netting, floating on still, coffee-colored water, tethered to a black tire on the reedy shore. M is sleeping next to me. Bill and Sam are on the bow and Rod and his Indonesian girlfriend are on top of the cabin, the crew on the stern. A cacophony of animal noises is emanating from the hazy forest. A bug crawls lazily up the netting through which a misty jungle looks like a painted stage backdrop. We are floating on the Kumai River in the southern central part of what used to be called Borneo and is now Kalimantan, going deep into the jungle on a riverboat to see orangutans ("forest men") in the wild at the Leaky Wildlife Preserve.

* * * * *

Having left our boats anchored and watched over by the ramshackle Harry's Yacht Services at the mouth of the Kumai River, we started our journey on what I dubbed the "African Queen." Up a narrow tributary, deeper and deeper into the jungle, the huge pandanus rushes were so close we could lean out and touch them. Slowly the water turned from café au lait to blackish brown, which was caused by the tannins but in fact was cleaner than the muddy Kumai River polluted by runoff from mountain gold mining. By two o'clock that afternoon we had tied up to the pier at the Camp Leakey Recovery and Research station, which recovers orangutans from the wild because their habitat has been destroyed by mining, logging, or fires. The research center feeds the animals twice a day and monitors them in the hope of releasing them into the wild again.

Our guide led us through the jungle on a system of muddy paths and boardwalks to a feeding station where we waited to see if anyone arrived to eat the large pile of bananas stacked on the platform 15 feet above the ground. The Kalimantan orangutans are big orange-brown herbivores with long arms and legs. The mature males have cheek fat that protrudes on either side of their face like little face wings. Females don't. Apparently cheek fat is caused by stress. Interesting.

As we proceeded through the jungle, a huge male swung down on a vine in front of us and hung by one hand, blocking the way. Our guide warned, "Never get between the male and his mate," which we had inadvertently done. "Look up there." He pointed behind us where the female and her baby were lazily ensconced in a tree branch over our heads. "We just have to wait until one of them decides to move." The four of us tried to remain motionless and uninterested while the guide enticed the male with bananas and called to him repeatedly. But it was clear that the big orange guy knew who had the power and that he was definitely in control of the situation. After a nervous fifteen minutes, hunger overcame protective instincts and he lumbered down the path to the feeding station, where he sat in a huge furry lump concentrating on piles of bananas. Shortly thereafter, his mate and baby came crashing through the forest and swung down a vine to sit next to him, munching and staring out at us nonchalantly.

We sat quietly on wooden benches, closer than might have seemed safe, but the orangutans were much more interested in their family picnic than our intrusion. Mom alternately picked lice out of the baby's head while Dad gave it a random swat just to show who was boss. About forty-five minutes later they wandered off into the jungle and we walked back to our floating home.

That night the cook, who remained sequestered in the galley next to the engine and head (which was literally a poop deck on the stern of the boat, where you sat on a Western toilet but flushed it into the river with a bucket of water), prepared a feast of vegetables, rice, and fish. While we were having dinner, mattresses were laid out on deck and mosquito netting was arranged.

After dinner we all sat around with the crew, some of whom played American songs on guitar, cooking pots, and water bottles and sang in Indonesian. We laughed 'til tears rolled down our faces when the boat captain sang "No Water, No Rice" to the tune of Bob Marley's "No Woman, No Cry." In the middle of Borneo, in the middle of the night, Sam and I drank cold beer, sang old '70s favorites, and formed a lifelong friendship.

* * * * *

Two days later, sitting on *Ithaca*'s starboard deck in the shade of the dinghy, I turned my face toward the brief zephyrs of air stirred by our own forward motion. The flag hung motionless. I could barely breath in the stultifying air and dense, polluted haze. Long boats putt-putted by us. A quintessential "tramp steamer" passed to port followed by a large Indonesian fishing/ferry-type boat with scooped-up bow and jaunty doghouse sitting on the stern like a rakishly tilted hat. Other exotic watercraft, logs, and clumps of unidentifiable debris floated by, the biggest hazard being floating islands of river weeds that would break loose, drift down the river, looming out of grayness unexpectedly in the unpredictably shifting water depth. Following *Blue Banana* and the waypoints we used to transit up the river, we managed to survive another "Insane Labyrinth," but the challenge took a mental toll on us, as did the local poverty.

At the end of our river trip on board the *African Queen*, Danon, one of the knowledgeable guides with whom we had had such laughs the night before, led us down a dusty river levy, shored up with broken sandbags and sunken boats. We passed by a handful of decrepit-looking huts where people peered out at us from the dark interiors to arrive at a small Dayak village for some local culture and a hope that we would buy *something* from the pathetic little tourist handicraft hut leaning into the river. He explained that they were mostly rice farmers, but I didn't see any tidy, colorful rice paddies, just a lot of garbage in a muddy stream where a little boy was wistfully pulling a chip of wood along like a boat.

The handicraft shop was stifling. A pile of crudely woven hats, bags, and assorted baskets sat on dusty shelves—a project started by some Dutch social workers in hopes of providing the villagers with some income, although a rough sign implied that purchase of these items also supported the National Park and orangutan rescue program.

Regrettably, no one bought anything in spite of the hangdog looks from the few villagers sitting around. Later I was left with a haunting sense of guilt for not purchasing some crude, unwanted something just to help the people. It still bothers me, as does the fact that Michael left a meager $2.50 tip for all three boat crew who worked so hard to make our adventure so comfortable. It may seem like a lot of money to them, but they know it is nothing to us.

These thoughts nagged me there as they certainly had not in Bali, where I was swept away with the beauty, sophistication, and sense of spiritual coexistence with the environment in spite of the repulsive tourist hype and endless grot shops. At least Bali offered the hopefulness of enterprise. I confess I am an unabashed romantic who can't help but prefer aestheticized experience to cold, capricious reality. Singapore, on the other hand, was almost too sanitized, orderly, and safe, with the world's most efficient transportation system, a complete lack of slums, and not a gum wrapper or (God forbid) discarded piece of chewing gum nor drop of spittle on the street. Its modern museums, good restaurants, and world-class shopping were glitzy but dull. Where was the ethnic authenticity?

Singapore to Malaysia—After the Deluge

T HE SINGAPORE STRAIT IS ONE OF THE busiest waterways in the world. Freighters, tankers, ferries, fishing boats, huge logs, islands of debris, rough water from wakes, and eddies of swirling, bubbling current threaten the small-boat sailor. Strolling around the Republic of Singapore Marina grounds, however, one could easily believe they were in a very expensive resort with swimming pools, bars, and an ornate dining room. Most welcome of all: a world-class locker room of gray-and-white marble, fluffy white towels, shower shoes, combs, hair dryers, shampoo and body wash in the glass shower stalls, and a background score of soothing music. I stood in a steady stream of unending hot water, barnacles dropping from my hair and months of tropical mold sluicing off my body. Divine.

More than anything, Singapore is a shopping city. Never have I seen so many shopping malls, centers, courts, strips, giant stores, and high-rise apartment buildings. On Orchard Road, the Alpha and Omega of shopping, Sam and I stalked the shoe stores with glassy eyes, practically comatose with choices. "Oh my God, look at this store. Have you ever seen so many fabulous shoes?" We sounded like a couple of kids from Appalachia visiting the big city. Finally we took refuge in a quiet restaurant called My Humble House, which was anything but humble. Here, in a crisp, black-and-white Asian ambiance, the fusion food was so artfully presented it almost overwhelmed the dish.

"I can't eat this. It's too beautiful."

"Look at the white salad bowl. It's as big as a bathroom sink!" I joked back.

The horn-shaped beer glasses were more like an instrument than a drinking glass.

Later, at the Fullerton Hotel, we sat on big comfy couches with brocade pillows and had a "pick me up" cappuccino, surrounded by the low hum of elegance and money. Here, too, the extraordinary restroom made going to the loo an aesthetic and spiritual experience: the mirrors made you look twenty pounds thinner and the lighting twenty years younger. On the bus "home" we giggled like schoolgirls over our adventures all the way back to our "humble" boats.

* * * * *

Our first Christmas away from home, ever, was in 2004, moored in the posh Admiral Marina in Port Dickson, Malaysia. A 12-inch-high plastic Christmas tree decorated with tiny balls and mini lights strung around the cabin created a festive ambiance. We hung out at the pool to escape the heat, while a "turkey roll" we had bought in Singapore for the occasion roasted in our small oven. We had cranberry sauce, stuffing, gravy, just like home—but it wasn't. No matter how much red wine we drank, or how much we joked about how simple everything was, we missed our family and the usual chaos of the holidays.

It wasn't until December 28th that news began to trickle down to us about the Boxing Day tsunami that devastated coastal villages from Sumatra to Sri Lanka. We called home.

"Where are you guys?" Frantic voices yelled over the speakerphone. "Are you okay?"

"Yes. We're fine. We were motoring up the Malacca Strait toward Penang Island, so we were completely protected from the waves by Sumatra. We didn't feel a thing."

"Where's the boat now? I can't believe the destruction."

"We're in Penang. It's not too bad here. Just a couple of roads washed away, but we're just starting to hear stories about how bad it is in Phuket. One person told us a lot of people drowned when they walked out on the beach to pick up the fish that had washed ashore and were then washed away themselves by the second wave. I don't think any cruisers died, but several boats were lost or seriously damaged."

As details trickled down to us from other yachting friends in Langkawi—an island off the northern coast of Malaysia near the Thai border—we began to sense the scope of the tragedy. It was hard to imagine such devastation only a few miles northward while we were peacefully sailing along in calm waters on a beautiful day. Gradually, however, we began to see dead fish and debris floating in the water.

When we arrived in Langkawi in the first week of January, we met Hugo at the marina bar, a short, ruddy, delivery boat captain. In collaboration with the nonprofit United Sikhs, he had helped to organize a volunteer group of cruisers called Waves of Mercy (WOM). They were collecting food, medicine, and clothes to send to Aceh, the major town at the northern tip of Sumatra that took the brunt of the waves. Because cruisers owned small boats that could get to remote, out-of-the-way villages along the western coast of Sumatra, they could operate immediately and under the radar of government regulations.

In his strong Scottish brogue Hugo filled us in. "The *Sean Paquita* was one of the first boats to reach some of the inaccessible villages down the coast which haven't received any help since the tsunami two weeks ago. Whole villages are completely washed away with nothing but rubble and decomposing bodies on the beach. Every day the captain radios us with details of what the survivors need. We collect it the best we can and send it on local ferries. We'll be loading one tomorrow. Do you want to help?"

"Sign us up."

Volunteer yachties formed long chains to move hundreds of twenty- to forty-pound sacks of rice from a large shipping container to waiting pallets, which then would be forklifted to the edge of the pier, where another chain of people would load them onto different parts of the ferry. It sounds much simpler and more organized than it was, but everyone was very willing. It was hot, hard work in ninety degrees and 80 percent humidity. Although there were some young crews from mega yachts, for the most part the volunteers were moms and pops on small sailboats and crusty single-handers—all solidly middle-aged or older. It was an impressive effort that continued steadily for two months. In spite of our many different languages and frustrating delays with clearances, paperwork, or getting supplies out of customs, everyone felt a tremendous sense of dedication, accomplishment, and camaraderie.

Nevertheless, as in all ad hoc organizations, it was a bit chaotic. A big problem was that the ferries were very long and exceedingly narrow. Many worried that we were loading them too heavily to be safe in a seaway, but communication between the Malaysian captain, the crew, and the WOM staff was confusing. Even people who spoke the same language sometimes didn't understand each other. There was endless discussion and indecision about what was to be loaded first and where it was to be stowed. Eventually, Michael became the "load master" and the loading process was improved significantly.

Over time I took on a more organizational role: I planned meetings, helped smooth out communications, and kept the blog current with information and photos. It was a full-time job for which I discovered I had some skill. As the needs grew, I found myself involved to the exclusion of every other aspect of my life, which began to cause stress on *Ithaca*.

"You know, the world won't end if you don't get the WOM Web site up tonight."

"I know, but I really want to get my article and photos out. Maybe you could just go on to the Chinese restaurant with Bill and Sam and I'll meet you later."

"Don't you think you are getting a little nuts over this?"

"NO! It's important." I slammed my hand down on the nav desk.

"To who?" Michael yelled over his shoulder as he stomped down the pier.

In time, my dedication became a bit like a disappointing love affair. At first one is full of love, hope, commitment, and willingness to put your whole heart and soul into the project, make it better to the exclusion of everything else. Then a gradual realization of some fundamental problems ends in a separation over irreconcilable differences.

An argument broke out in the bar. Phil, one of our cruising friends who had spent weeks in Aceh building latrines for the villagers, argued that the mission needed to change because donated clothing was lying in abandoned heaps in every village and by continuing to supply free rice, we were hurting the little markets that needed to be patronized to survive. What people needed were jobs, money, self-respect—not welfare.

I agreed with Phil, but Hugo didn't seem to see it that way. Conflicts among some of the volunteers also made it clear that not everyone was ready to listen to constructive suggestions about how to improve operations and update our mission. Thankfully, roads were cleared, shops had reopened, and large NGOs had taken our place with more money and government connections. Michael was right. We were redundant. It was time to move on. We did a good job, helped a lot of people, made a lot of good friends, and I learned some important lessons. Thank heavens. I was redundant. It was time to move on.

December 31, 2005, Kota Beach, Phuket, Thailand

Looking back what did we do, what did we accomplish, what did I learn? Did I really help? Did I grow, become a better person? The Tsunami aid experience was an eye opener for me on a global as well as a personal level, where I learned a lot of surprising things about myself---certainly not all positive. My ability to organize and take charge surprised me but my frantic need to control things that were out of my control, my emotional involvement, my own need to "look good" were a disappointment but a good lesson. My arrogant streak dangled like a ripped slip beneath the frilly party dress of Christian love.

How often that slip gets in the way of daily relationships. I always think I'm right about nutrition, childrearing, lifestyle, about how to run a relief organization. I get tangled up in these emotions born from an equal measure of concern and arrogance to the point that, even if I am right, I am definitely wrong if I allow my thoughts and opinions to damage family or working relationships. In some ways I am not any different than my sister even though I think I am the loving kind one.

Thailand—"Marooned" and Meandering

S OUTHERN THAILAND HANGS DOWN FROM Bangkok between the Gulf of Thailand and the Indian Ocean like a long tail touching the northern tip of Malaysia. As we cruised up the Thai coast between the offshore islands and the mainland, the damage from the tsunami became increasingly evident.

On the petite island of Phi Phi Don, for example, the destruction was visible from the boat. Much of the bustling tourist town was completely gone. Down one rubble-strewn sand street our friend Marco, from *Shazam*, was helping some backpackers and cruisers form a work party. Further inland a few ramshackle wooden buildings were still standing, remnants of a main street where small businesses were rebuilding and hanging out signs.

Two small, delicate, dark-haired girls standing under a balcony beckoned to us. One said, "Want massage sir? Lady?" "Cheap," said the other. Michael and I looked at each other a little skeptical and then said, "Why not?" We climbed the rickety wooden stairs to a large room lit only by sunlight from the adjacent balcony. A screen partitioned two massage beds. Silently the young girl began to massage my shoulders as I stared out the balcony at the skeleton of one very large tree still standing near the town center, draped with orange and yellow fabric. "The colored flags are in honor of the spirits of the people who died here. I lost my mother and brother."

For the next two years, everywhere along the coast we met people with tragic stories related to the tsunami and saw towns hewn in two. Often a distinct line delineated where the waves stopped, leaving part of the town unscathed but the shore side obliterated. Every beach was littered with sandals: small ones, medium-sized ones, black ones, pink ones, fancy ones, and simple rubber flip-flops scattered among the tattered bits of fishing nets and particles of Styrofoam. Each one representing a person presumably lost to the waves. Slowly most of the area got cleaned up, particularly along the tourist beaches and resort sites, but it took a long time. Tent cities attempted to provide a sense of safety and community, and gradually clusters of cement houses were built to house the homeless. But land disputes slowed recovery and aid money often went into the pockets of politicians and construction company cronies who built roads that went nowhere.

With the exception of our yearly trips home, we spent March 2005 to January 2007 cruising Thailand's picturesque islands off the Andaman Sea coast. We battled tour boats for anchorage in crowded coves, explored caves in the jagged Karst cliffs, strolled the beaches of elegant tourist resorts and hung out around their pools and bars pretending to be guests. It was a great life, much of which was shared with our dear friends on *Blue Banana*. The food was so good and so cheap that cooking on the boat was silly. The beer was abundant, the Thai people charming, the landscape exquisite, and the culture fascinating—aside from an element of disturbing sleaziness born of easy sex and cheap alcohol prevalent in some areas of Phuket and Bangkok.

All was not play, of course. Months at a time were spent in Boat Lagoon Marina, in Phuket, dubbed "Boat Maroon" by Sam. It was here that we finally resolved our long-nagging engine problems by simply and expensively replacing it with a new Yanmar. I varnished, sewed canvas, polished, and primped *Ithaca* until she shone. Michael worked on the head, the fridge, and every other moving or mechanical part that kept us afloat and under way. In the hot afternoons we swam in the marina pool. At night we rode our bikes out to the food stalls and hung out at Mama's Pad Thai shack with our many cruising friends, consuming mountains of pad thai and mussaman curry and quaffing gallons of cold Thai beer—for literally pennies. It was a very social time. But my mood was as changeable as the monsoon weather.

April 1, 2006, Phuket, Thailand

*Varnishing and cleaning all week, sorting books to sell or send home
to make room for new ones—always an agonizing chore. While I was
varnishing yesterday I was thinking about what I would write were I
to actually try to write about our journey, beyond the boring "and then
we went . . ." The image of a river is so appropriate for this ongoing
journeying. We are swept along by the geography of the world's weather
patterns and seasons. A broad route determined by these issues already
predetermines a certain direction, a path, a flowing pattern within which
eddies and swirls sweep us into unexpected, strange little corners of the
world like the San Blas Islands or Asanvari, Vanuatu.*

*But what about the inner journey? How do I discover the route there, the
pattern, the sense of it, if there is one? Is there any relationship between the
inner journey and the outer journey? Have I learned anything, changed,
grown? Sometimes I think that as the years have gone by I have just
atrophied. Certainly in creative energy and ability. I have a locker full of
art supplies that I never use. I have all this sophisticated digital computer
stuff capable of doing wonderful things if I could figure out how to use it.
Or had any interesting ideas of what to do with it.*

*It is as if all I have left is an empty shell of a mind that I have to keep
feeding with foreign sights and sounds to just keep it stimulated enough to
stay alive. Curiosity is my only life's blood now, the engine that pushes me.*

* * * * *

And thus we traveled: bus trips to Bangkok, train trips to Chiang Mai,
road trips to towns and villages off the beaten path to track down
historical sites and ancient temples. From northern Thailand we
took an overgrown sampan down the muddy Mekong River to see
the iridescent temples of Luang Prabang, Laos, then bused through
a narrow tortuous mountain pass to Vientiane and crossed the border
into Cambodia which, after forty years, was still desperately poor but
fueled by a new sense of industriousness. Angkor Wat, one of the
largest religious monuments in the world, had become a major tourist
attraction. The mix of Hindu and Buddhist iconography, the friezes
of dancing gods and goddesses, the monumental Buddhist heads, the
serpentine roots of jungle trees strangling temple terraces still create
a powerful atmosphere of mystery in spite of all the tourists. More

temples had been cleared and war damage had been repaired, but you could still find a random bullet hole in Shiva's belly or a gouge in Buddha's enigmatic smile.

Further afield, in Beijing, we took the newly opened speed train over the tundra of the northern plains to Tibet, the highest train track ever laid and for years thought to be impossible to build because of the freezing and thawing of the ground. But, like the building of the Panama Canal, where there is an economic will there is a way. In spite of the unsurpassed engineering challenges and vehement Tibetan fear that remote areas of Tibetan culture would be swallowed by the rapacious wave of Han Chinese development, the Chinese government persisted, spurred by the economic imperative to relieve their crowded cities.

For three days and two nights the train roared across vast fields of brown stubble, frozen pools, and melting glaciers which feed the Yellow and Yangtze Rivers, while a recorded voice pointed out landmarks and reminded us that the landscape reflects Chinese nature which "withstands everything and walks straight ahead." At night a full moon tinted the barren hills, snow-covered peaks, and glowing ridges shades of silver and brown velvet. By day we passed small walled enclosures, herds of Yak, and lone pilgrims walking to Lhasa, periodically prostrating themselves on the frozen ground. At 17,000 feet we breathed pure oxygen through nose respirators provided in our very comfortable compartment. Those in second class weren't so lucky.

A government-sanctioned guide was required to travel in Tibet at that time. Luckily our man, Ngodup, was Tibetan. A small, serious young fellow with round wire-rimmed glasses, he met us at the newly constructed cavernous Lhasa train station and practically slept with us for a week. In the privacy of our car, however, he was surprisingly frank. "Tibetan children have to pay to go to school, but Chinese kids go to school for free. So, Tibetan children end up begging in the street and ultimately turn to crime to survive. Even the money made from tourism goes to the Chinese government, not the Tibetan people." Often we witnessed colorful Tibetan shops and houses crumbling in bulldozed, dust-filled streets to make way for blocks of dreary cement apartment houses sprawling across the city like a disease. All the plagues of a modern city—the effects of traffic, pollution, overcrowding, and unemployment—were unmistakable.

The Tibetan spirit, however, seemed indomitable. It was the beginning of the pilgrimage season when chores were done for the year and ruddy-cheeked pilgrims walked miles from their villages to parade through the temples burning yak butter, muttering prayers, and leaving offerings. Beribboned, draped with jewelry and bundled in fur-lined, brocaded coats, each a slightly different style representing their home village, they flooded the city. Shy children and old folks with wrinkled toothless smiles stared at us in bewilderment, while Ngodup, a devout Buddhist, ushered us through the temple rituals. At the Drepung Monastery, one of the world's largest, we followed the pilgrims' path through the glowing yak butter light, rubbing our bodies against the thrones of the various Dali Lamas and walking under the long cabinets that hold books of wisdom and bring the pilgrims longevity. I now hope to live a very long and holy life.

Joining the steady stream of pilgrims flowing clockwise through and around the Potala Palace and the most holy Jokhang Temple, we spilled out into the Barkhor market maze of stalls and alleyways where monks and beggars swung prayer wheels, chatted with stall vendors—all crowding, shuffling, and pushing, playful and serious. A great flow of humanity united by the ancient rituals of their faith. One particularly jolly pilgrim grabbed Michael around the neck with a huge grin and gestured for a photograph. No charge.

On our last day I photographed Ngodup standing under a string of flapping prayer flags against a background of snowcapped peaks. He pressed his name and email address into my hand and whispered, "Don't forget us."

* * * * *

Traveling in Myanmar, formerly known as Burma, was in some ways even more restrictive. It wasn't required that we be accompanied by a guide at all times, but we always felt we were being watched. Just getting a visa to enter the country required a week of bureaucratic haggling in Bangkok. In addition, there were no ATMs in the country, no one accepted credit cards, and there was no way to get local cash. Everything had to be paid in dollars, crisp new ones. Dirty, torn, or bent bills were not accepted. You had to bring in all the cash you expected to need. We traveled through the country for three weeks always anxious that we would run out of money and on edge carrying so much cash.

In some ways Myanmar reminded us of Cuba minus the fifties cars: the streets were crowded with bikes, the cities full of crumbling, colonial buildings, sporadic electricity, disintegrating roads, and a population that seemingly lived on the street and struggled to stay alive. But there was no music and no joy. The government was repressive, and "Saint" Aung San Suu Kyi was locked in her house overlooking Inya Lake in Yagoon while her people sat glumly on broken buses and stranded trains or in darkened houses wrapped in their longis, their bleak faces painted with a granular yellow paste that looked like cornmeal meant to ward off evil spirits, hoping the golden Buddhas of the 2,600-year-old Shwedagon Pagoda would welcome them to another world.

We cruised up the Irrawaddy River to Mandalay; visited the extraordinary 100-temple-site at Bagan, and poled through the watery, floating islands of Inle Lake. All scenically captivating, but the most memorable image I will always carry with me was the sight of women and children bent over along the road, picking up a landslide of rocks by hand in the heat and depositing them in large wicker baskets which they then carried on their heads to a waiting truck bed. A sight I was clearly not supposed to witness, much less photograph, so I shouldn't have been surprised when my camera bag with all the film from the trip mysteriously disappeared on the flight back to Bangkok.

* * * * *

When another Christmas rolled around, we once again decided not to fly home. It didn't seem like too much of a hardship at first. We were anchored off the pristine white sand beach of Nai Harn with a large group of other yachties. A big beach party was planned, and

Michael—the only one with a red jacket AND a Santa Claus hat—played the jolly Big Guy, one of his best roles. Everybody loved him.

As the evening wore on, I walked down the beach and sat down in the sand with my glass of wine. I needed some quiet.

Sam came up and sat down beside me. "You okay?"

"I was just thinking about my mother. She died two days before Christmas the year before we left. This time of year always makes me a little sad."

"I was thinking about beaches. All the beaches we've been on. This is beautiful, but my favorite is still Carmel Beach."

"Right. 'The dog beach.' I loved it. I loved to take Mom's dog there and ride horses with my sister along the surf in Pebble Beach through that beautiful misty morning fog."

"Don't tell Bill, but my dream is to finally sail *Blue Banana* into Stillwater Cove, anchor right in the middle of all the kelp and sea otters, row to the beach club, and celebrate our circumnavigation with all our friends around the pool." She paused, looking out at all the anchor lights twinkling in the harbor. "Yeah. I miss it. But it's fun here. Come on. Let's go track down Santa Claus."

* * * * *

Weeks went by. The alternator still wasn't working, installation of the new engine had stalled, and numerous other fix-its were not fixed. It was a stressful time. Michael was anxious about making our window to cross the Indian Ocean and continue up the Red Sea. I was miffed because I had wanted to travel to Vietnam but did not really have the courage to suggest it. Finally, over a beer at Mama's just outside the marina, I tentatively introduced the topic.

Vietnam Revisited

E VERY MARRIAGE HAS MINEFIELDS THAT, WHEN recognized, are best artfully avoided. Michael and I never talked about Vietnam. As a US Navy fighter pilot who served in the Vietnam War, he has memories that are raw and ambiguous; mine are angry and political. "The War" is a topic we had long ago declared taboo. We acknowledged a mutually respectful but passionate disagreement. Further discussion was not productive. When our odyssey on *Ithaca* took us to Southeast Asia, however, a flood of disparate thoughts and feelings poured out of Pandora's box.

The Vietnam War was a budding sore when we were married on September 11, 1965. Two weeks after our wedding Michael left on an aircraft carrier headed for the Western Pacific. Not long afterward I realized that the life of a stay-at-home Navy wife was not for me. I booked passage on a freighter bound for the Philippines, where the carrier would be based. I waved good-bye to friends and family in San Francisco having no idea where I was going or what was looming over the ensuing longitudes. It was the beginning of a lifelong romance with Asia, one that Michael did not share.

When I met the ship in Yokosuka, Japan, with a book on Zen Buddhism under one arm and reservations to stay in a Japanese inn in the other, it was almost the end of our young marriage. Michael had anticipated a steak dinner and a Western bed and time with his new wife who had, after all, recently converted to Catholicism. "What is all this Buddhism stuff about?"

That aside, those eight months traveling by myself throughout Southeast Asia were among the most formative of my life. Tourism had yet to swamp Thailand, and the magic of its glistening temples and peaceful rural villages is still vivid in my heart. Angkor Wat, largely entangled in jungle, had yet to become a battlefield. Saigon was full of soldiers and sandbags, but elegant women speaking French still graced the cafés and proudly strolled the boulevards in silk pajamas and straw hats.

Now it was 2007, and we were back in a part of the world that held vastly different memories and significance for each of us. Michael finally agreed to go, but the night before we were to leave we both had a little too much beer at Mama's and conversation slipped into argument and then shouting. He said, "I'm not going." I said, "Fine. I'll go by myself." He said, "Fine" and stomped off into the night. But the next morning he was silently waiting at the taxi stand.

* * * * *

Our 6:30 a.m. "Welcome to Hanoi" was a little problematic when a very loud loudspeaker started playing martial music and broadcasting a voice spouting angry-sounding Vietnamese: Rallying the workers? Reading the morning news? Exclaiming anti-Western sentiment? Michael was not amused.

The extreme traffic was another shock. Motor scooters and bikes flowed along the narrow, curving roads like a river. Crossing the road one had to have the mind-set of a floating log or a rock and just let the constant stream flow around you. Walking on the sidewalk was equally challenging since it was both a motorcycle parking lot and a restaurant, where clusters of miniature stools and tables were crowded with people who slurped pho (Vietnamese noodle soup), drank tea, and socialized among the cauldrons of bubbling noodles, makeshift vegetable stalls, and insistent fruit vendors whose shoulder baskets banged you in the shins while a woman stood nearby washing sheets in a big tub of hot water.

"Everyone looks too young to remember the Vietnam War," I observed.

"Yes. I was worried about that, but it's ancient history to them."

At dinner time, traffic subsided and the remnants of a graceful old city materialized: the multi-balconied, French Colonial buildings with their mansard roofs, shuttered windows, and patina of peeling pastel paint; a tombstone cutter next to a little boulangerie; a man selling hand-cut stamps on the busy corner next to a cozy coffee shop. Hoan Kiem Lake shimmered in the city center; there was not a single glass-and-chrome skyscraper in all of Hanoi. I thought, "I could love this place." Michael thought, "Where's the exit?"

Temple of Literature was, naturally, at the top of my must-see list. This ancient Confucian University with its typically simple, elegant symmetrical layout, calming pools of water lilies, and beautifully balanced architecture was an oasis in the noisy chaos of the surrounding city, as was, surprisingly, the Ho Chi Minh Mausoleum, Presidential Palace, and Ho Chi Minh's stilt house that had been his home from 1958 to 1969. The mausoleum, looking appropriately grim and gray, was closed. Ho had been sent back to Russia for his regularly scheduled "maintenance" because, according to Michael, he continually banged his nose spinning in his grave over the extreme entrepreneurship and capitalism happening in his "Communist" country.

The Old Quarter was the real treasure trove. Dating from the thirteenth-century period of guilds, each street was named for specific merchandise. Although now many of them could have been called "Tourist Trinket Street," there was still the street of furniture, the street of birdcages, and the street of Christmas and New Year's decorations where everything was red and tinselly. Men squatted on the sidewalk making cookware and light fixtures on Tin Street. Bolts of exotic fabric, intricate embroidery, lacquerware, and water puppets crammed mind-boggling blocks of long narrow shops along Silk Street. I stopped to photograph a shop window. Not one to linger, unless it was at a hardware store, Michael disappeared into the crowd of motorbikes, bicycles, fruit vendors, and cycles. I ran after him, not wanting to get separated.

"Could you just slow down a little?"

"I was looking for a restaurant. Aren't you hungry?"

"The Lonely Planet suggests the Green Tangerine. It's only a couple of blocks away."

I suspected it would be a glitzy tourist place with mediocre food. It was not. We ordered scallops, Michael's favorite. They arrived arranged on a checkerboard of pumpkin squares and aubergine, dabbed with clumps of caviar, floating in balsamic vinegar. Ribbons of tomato-flavored potato puree accented the corners of the square glass serving plate. It was a work of art. The subtle combinations of tastes and textures were heavenly, scallops still whispering "the sea." A nice glass of white wine, when chilled with a lump of ice, was the perfect accompaniment.

Dessert (how could I resist?) was a small scoop of delicate coconut ice cream set on a bed of warm pineapple and minced date pressed into a round patty type form over which arched two curling sail-like wafers of almond biscuit—a far cry from the hardships of war when many people only had grass to eat.

*　*　*　*　*

Our sleeper compartment on the train to Hue turned out to be two "soft sleepers," that is, the upper bunks in a small compartment that we shared with a very old Vietnamese woman and her extended family. Nose pressed to the ceiling, I finally fell asleep and woke to a gauzy Chinese landscape of small villages and rice paddies unscrolling outside the compartment window. Each house faced east and featured a little porch and a koi pond. Burial sites, randomly perched on hillocks in the rice fields, increased as we approached Hue.

North of Hue we passed through what had been the DMZ. It was starkly barren except for a few young trees and low scrub. No towns, no rice paddies, just forgotten clusters of grave sites—mounded, circular enclosures, some strangely dusted with what looked like powdered sugar sprinkled over the red dirt.

The Perfume River flows through the city of Hue, once the seat of the Nguyen Dynasty and national capital from 1802 to 1945. The nineteenth-century Citadel, encompassing the old Imperial City on the north side, is linked to the modern city by the graceful Truong Tien Bridge. The Citadel, originally built in 1687, had for centuries been the cultural and political heart of South Vietnam. Its elegant palaces, pagodas, and lily ponds had, through the vicissitudes of history, been the site of grand celebrations and cruel suffering, none more lacerating than the Tet Offensive in which more than 10,000 soldiers and civilians on both sides died in a two-week period; 150 of them were US Marines.

We stood in the middle of the bridge and watched sampans drift by beneath our feet. I wondered what Michael was thinking but I didn't ask. We walked through the multi-tiered Ngo Mon Gate where the last reigning emperor of Vietnam, Bao Dai, ended the Nguyen dynasty when he abdicated to a delegation sent by Ho Chi Minh's provisional Revolutionary Government. It was eerily quiet as we wandered through the moss-covered ruins, palaces, and fortified towers. A low mist hung over a lotus pond like a congregation of spirits, while voices of boys playing soccer on a grassy field outside the enclosure drifted on the damp air.

Later we floated down the Perfume River on a dragon boat, traveling back in time to Vietnam's romantic past with a stop at the Thien Mu Pagoda, where young monks were doing their homework under the trees, their heads shaved except for a long forelock flipped over one ear. Even in this romantic and isolated setting, however, the pulse of commerce beat as we fended off a barrage of vendors selling paintings, embroidery, silk shirts, baby pajamas, etc., and met with very sad faces when we made it clear we were not interested in buying anything. It was always so awkward, embarrassing, and, finally, annoying when a friendly smile and cordial "No thank you" were met with hostile resentment. The couple who ran our boat seemed like very hardworking people, but they still displayed an attitude that we owed them something more, even though we gave them a reasonable and completely unnecessary tip. Maybe we did.

* * * * *

At the summit of the Hai Van Pass between Hue and Hoi An we looked down at a large bay ruffled with rolling surf. Clusters of fishing boats bobbed in the swell, and Danang sprawled out on the southern curve—a rather dismal and busy city, we were to discover. It was warm, humid, and tropical. The road along the coast was littered with graves, ramshackle houses, and old hangars. It was hard to believe that this was all that remained of the sprawling major US base of the Vietnam War.

Michael reminisced. "I remember flying in here a couple of times, when the carrier couldn't take us aboard due to a crash on the flight deck, and going to the Officers' Club. I remember it was called The Doom Club, open 24 hours a day. Then I spent the night in a tent and flew back to the carrier the next morning." The Doom Club had disappeared into the mists of history.

* * * * *

In Saigon, Michael had booked a "junior suite" with a big bed and a nice view from the fourth-floor balcony, but the hotel had given our room to someone else on the pretext that it would be too hard for us to walk up the stairs. (I guess we looked pretty tired after sailing halfway around the world to get there.) Michael was aggravated because the room they gave us in the sister hotel was very small, dreary, and a bit tacky—not a good way to begin our sojourn in Saigon.

Over breakfast the next morning I pulled out my list of "see and dos." Buried in the *International Herald Tribune*, Michael folded the paper and said: "Look. Let's just have a leisurely breakfast for once and then I need to find an Internet café so I can check on the mechanic."

I sipped my coffee and stared out the window, dabbing my eyes with the corner of my napkin.

"What's the matter?"

"I don't know. It's just all so sad and pointless."

"What's sad and pointless?"

I had promised myself that I would never address the topic of The War. Even though it was physically invisible—with the exception of an odd bunker, a gun turret, old photographs and news clippings in a dusty museum, or overgrown and neglected cemeteries—to me it subtly resonated everywhere. So many people died here for, from my point of view, no reason except political pride, fear, and ignorance of history and culture.

It was hard for me to imagine how anyone could spend even a day in this country and not be moved to consider the past, but all Michael seemed to want to talk about was the broken water maker, an email to the mechanic, and the new engine installation. What did I expect? Why did it matter? Slowly I calmed down and realized, once more, that discussion was counterproductive. Here was a man who spent thirty years as a dedicated naval officer who loyally served his country's call, regardless of politics, cultural pressure, or fear for his life. This moral steadfastness and faith were what I loved about him.

He generously changed the subject to what was next on my list and we took a taxi to the History Museum, which dealt with different periods of Vietnam's history from the Stone Age to 1945. Here it was suggested that Vietnam's continual battles with the Chinese and Mongols throughout their history strengthened them in the belief that they could eventually defeat any foe, French and American included. The sad truth is that the apparent inevitability of violent conflict throughout the history of the world is the ultimate and inescapable tragedy of the human condition.

* * * * *

After dinner we walked around the corner to the Majestic Hotel where we had both stayed at different times in 1965. It was all very modern and "done up now," but the shell seemed familiar. Dodging a steady stream of trucks, we walked across the street to watch the tourist dinner boats disgorge their hordes of Japanese tourists.

We stood together watching the dark water. A dim shadow of a fishing boat, barely visible under all the illuminated billboards, sparked an elusive memory like a familiar scent, tantalizing but unidentifiable. I had been, perhaps, at that very spot on a freighter forty years ago. I was twenty-five then and rumbled along this dark river in the back of a truck with the ship's captain and some friends to some place, maybe it was the Majestic, for dinner. I remember seeing a lot of soldiers and sandbags . . . and feeling like I was the heroine of a grand adventure, having no idea of the tragedy that would soon befall this part of the world that I loved.

Indian Ocean Incident

NOW, FORTY YEARS LATER, I STILL SAW MYSELF as the heroine of a grand adventure—most of the time. Adventure, however, implies peril, scary moments when you wish you were reading about it instead of living it. By that definition, our trip across the Indian Ocean, through Pirate Alley and the Bab el Mandeb, was "it."

Early morning, January 22nd, we left the anchorage in Phi Phi Lai, Thailand, for the last time and closed the chapter of our Southeast Asia cruising. Genoa unfurled, main reefed, we headed into 25 knots of wind on the beam. Next stop, Sri Lanka.

The wind switched. It was a rocky night. Big rollers slammed the stern and white caps crested into the cockpit. A small freighter snuck up our six o'clock position. I pressed the ignition button. Silence. My body prickled with panic. I held my breath and tried again. The engine spurted to life and we powered out of harm's way. The likely diagnosis was water up the exhaust pipe as a result of high following seas. It was very troubling, but our friends on board *Blue Banana* had lost a shroud, so, as always, we thought, "Things could be worse." Nevertheless, strange meteorological events seemed to bode ill: round lightning on the southern horizon and a meteor or large orange ball falling into the sea with a green streak. Michael saw it too. I wasn't hallucinating.

A week later 10-foot seas were chasing us through the Great Channel between the Nicobar Islands and Sumatra. A parade of huge freighters, car carriers, container ships, and natural gas tankers kept us vigilant. Upon seeing our large American flag off *Ithaca*'s stern, an American car carrier captain called us on the VHF and chatted in his thick Southern accent, asking Michael who we were and where we were headed. A delightful surprise, as usually ship captains simply ignored us while we prayed that they at least saw us and didn't run us down.

We were still having problems starting the engine, however, despite Michael's very clever rig using my walking stick to hold down the flapper valve on the exhaust, which we hoped would prevent seawater from entering the system. With 900 miles to go to Galle, Sri Lanka, this was developing into a serious a problem.

Michael checked all the wiring and connections. Everything looked fine. This is the kind of uncertainty we had hoped to avoid by spending more than $10,000 on a new engine. Now we were worried about charging the batteries. The good news was we were moving along at 6 to 7 knots, which would get us to Galle a day early. A full moon made night watches more pleasant, and the water maker was chug-chugging along so there was plenty of water for showers and hair washing, a great mood booster.

February 1, 2007, at sea, 359 nm to Galle, Sri Lanka

I am writing by the light of the radar to save power. We have not been able to start the engine for two days. The wind vane and solar panels have kept basic functioning going but beer in the fridge feels warm. At least I have clean hair for now. GRRRR.

* * * * *

The final diagnosis was water in the oil. It took two hours to pump out all the old oil, kneeling in the cramped galley space, taking turns on the pump. Then Michael took out the injectors and seawater gushed out of the engine, covering the cabin with salty spray.

"Oh no," I groaned in desperation.

"Leon [the engine mechanic in Thailand who installed our new Yanmar] must not have positioned the exhaust hose high enough to prevent water creeping up the exhaust pipe into the engine. As a powerboat mechanic, I guess he forgot he was working on a sailboat that leans her rails in the water with predictable regularity."

"How can that be? He was such a nice guy. We trusted him."

Michael looked at me in disbelief that I would say something so stupid.

The next day we removed and secured everything in the port cockpit locker. Michael then squeezed himself into the small space to reach the exhaust hose and force it up to a higher position where I could lean down and tie it off on a cross beam while the boat rolled rail to rail and the bulkhead bit into my stomach. That mission completed, we re-stowed all the gear, put the engine back together, and spent another three hours sitting on the floor, laboriously hand pumping more thick, cold watery oil out into empty plastic oil cans, arthritic joints burning. Taking turns pumping and checking for ships every twenty minutes while Hans steered the boat, we felt like he was a real person taking care of everything while we did what had to be done. Fortunately, there was plenty of wind. Averaging 6 or 7 and sometimes even 8 knots, we were almost sailing too fast. By 6:30 p.m. all bits and pieces were put back on the engine and the critical moment arrived. When the engine jumped to life as Michael turned the key, we cheered, hugged each other, and shook our heads with disbelief. We had dodged another bullet.

It had been an arduous and worrisome three days; at any point we could have "lost it" completely. Joyfully we cleaned up the boat, put away tools, started the fridge and water maker, and turned on lights and radio. After a hot shower and hair wash, we gratefully celebrated with a beer in the cockpit and mellow dinner under the full moon.

* * * * *

Two days later we were in Galle, Sri Lanka (aka Ceylon), tied against three ugly black tires along a rough cement pier, negotiating with the Sri Lankan Navy personnel who had boarded the boat with obvious "attitude," demanding "presents" of gin and cigarettes for the privilege of checking us into their country. Good humor was sparse when more boats arrived and were directed to raft up bow to stern and port to starboard so that everyone had to walk over everyone else's boat to get to theirs, gunnels rubbing, spreaders banging in the strong fore and aft swell, enforced togetherness a shock after solitary days and nights at sea.

More enforced togetherness ensued when we took a tour with three other cruising couples, old friends including "The "Bananas" with whom we had agreed to make the Pirate Alley/Red Sea passage. Loner that I am, traveling in a group is not something I normally do, but Michael needed some new company and the BBs were always a lark. Loaded into a mini bus with "go-to-guy" Leel, now wearing a tour guide hat, we headed out on a five-day excursion up into the central highlands.

Sri Lanka, shaped like a teardrop at the tip of India, has, like so many places in Asia, seen a long tumultuous history of invasions, colonization, and cultural clashes. The first Singhalese arrived from northern India in the fifth or sixth century B.C.; then traders and fishermen from southern India made it home, followed by Portuguese, Dutch, and British colonizers. Over the centuries Hindus, Buddhists, Muslims, and Christians have staked claim to this island all the way back to Adam, who is said to have left his footprint on "Adam's Peak" (Sri Pada) as he turned for a last look at Eden; not to be outdone, Buddha left his mark in the same place on his way to Paradise.

While religious and cultural strife are an undeniable strain of Sir Lanka's history, at Kataragama, a holy place along a river, Hindus, Muslims, and Buddhists gather periodically for a month-long feast and celebration where multicultural rituals are celebrated. Here we were led through a ceremony offering fruit to the peacock-riding god of Kataragama, blessed with a peacock feather, offered more fruit to a local elephant, and then prayed over with a flaming coconut bashed against a stone, hoping to a man/woman that this prayer would keep us safe from pirates on our journey to the Red Sea.

In spite of this token ecumenicalism, however, violence still rocked the country in 2004. The Tamil Liberation Tigers, Hindus originally brought to Sri Lanka by the British to work in the tea plantations, feeling discriminated against by the Buddhist government, had settled in the north and had long been demanding an independent country. Hostilities on both sides had the whole country on edge with military checkpoints everywhere. At night a naval barricade regularly deployed depth charges in the harbor to preclude a stealth invasion—a bit disconcerting when we felt the repercussions on the boat at 2:00 a.m. Our tour was confined to the southern part of the island largely because of the Tamil Tiger threat in the north.

We left Galle Harbor on Valentine's Day after the usual checkout rigmarole with the Sri Lankan Navy personnel coming aboard, fingering everything, and asking for cigarettes. A Navy runabout with a machine gun mounted on the bow pursued us as we were motoring out of the harbor entrance, inducing a panicky moment until we realized they just wanted "smokes." Good pirate practice.

After an exhaustingly rough night, we arrived on February 20th at an Uligamu anchorage in the Maldives in company with *Blue Banana* and *Gemini*. Walled compounds made out of coral and a mud-cement-limestone mixture lined the empty sandy roads. A handful of men prayed in one mosque and four or five women prayed in a separate mosque. The shops were scantily supplied with dusty packages of cookies and boxes of ancient onions. "What do these people eat?" Sam and I wondered. Finally, we discovered "Moag's" company store where we found a little bread, wilted lettuce, and a few oranges, tomatoes, and cucumbers.

"Damn the Torpedoes . . ."

M ARCH 2, 2007, AT SEA, 418 NM TO
SALALAH, OMAN

I've been reading the Red Sea Pilot and whatever other info we have about where we are going. Sounds challenging with adverse winds, currents, shipping, but at least we are finally on our way. Shipping is starting to pick up now—not my favorite thing at night. Everyone is getting a little more edgy about "Pirate Alley." Fortunately we have a way to go before we are in the designated danger zone.

This morning two dark men in a small open boat approached us at high speed, powering along our port side. Even though I know we are not in Pirate Alley yet, my heart pounded so hard I could practically hear it over the engine. Fortunately they just wanted charts, which we thought odd, but were grateful that our friendly manner and several packs of Marlboros mollified them. Later two fishing boats came up alongside wanting liquor or cigarettes. More cigarettes. No problem. We were just happy that was all they wanted.

Every day I try to do some kind of little project. Today I finally got around to waxing the cockpit. It looks so much better. It was a joy to sit out there this evening in clean clothes, after my shower, sipping a cold beer and nibbling popcorn as a setting sun spread a deep rose stripe halfway around the horizon. A concerto grosso by Handel provided the movie score as Ithaca skimmed over the purple water, sails billowed out in a perfect 8-knot breeze. It was so peaceful and relaxing I didn't want to move or talk, just sit there and soak up the perfectness of the moment, forgetting all frightening stories about pirates in this part of the world.

* * * * *

On March 7, 2007, we anchored in the busy commercial port of Salalah, Oman, with about twenty other boats. Mohammed—an ebony Eddie Murphy look-alike dressed in white robes and a jaunty little fez-like skullcap—was our self-appointed "go-to" guy, who arranged everything from fuel to rental cars but, unfortunately, failed at finding any kind of guidebook. Undaunted, Michael and I and Bill and Sam set off in a rental car armed with a faded Xeroxed copy of a map from 1962 and drove into town across a barren, brown, dusty landscape, impressive only for the shock of being in such an alien place.

Camels munched stubby bushes by the side of the road and had right of way over the few cars. Fort-like structures with crenelated towers and Moorish windows dotted the desert. After the human crush and sensory assault of Asia, this seemed like an empty page, a world devoid of color and life. Stark white buildings were the only contrast against a beige background of haze and sand. Empty streets, slight traffic, men in long white robes the only pedestrians. Occasionally, a woman in black, like a cypher, fleeted around a corner, trailing a black train like a comma, a black-gloved hand silhouetted against a white wall.

We stopped for lunch. A sign made it clear that women had to go through the "family entrance" and sit in a screened-off area. Sam and I, wearing long skirts and suitably draped with head scarves, could eat in the men's section because we were tourists, but we felt very odd and out of place. Arabia, what are you? As mysterious and hidden as your black-enfolded women.

After lunch we persevered into the desert to find the remnants of Sumharam, the fourth-century B.C. trading center that exported frankincense around the world. The rumor was that the Queen of Sheba had a palace here and had brought frankincense to King Solomon. But the "palace" turned out to be an indistinct mound of sand.

We spent the rest of the day tracking down the "footprints of the sacred camel" and Job's tomb. The camel is considered one of the ten animals allowed to enter heaven, along with Jonah's whale, Noah's dove, and the ram that Abraham sacrificed instead of his son. That quest took us up into dry mountains and across a completely barren plateau where the road ended in a dusty village. We backtracked and finally found the tomb just outside of town in a hut—perched on a hill overlooking the surrounding parched countryside—next to a small mosque, which of course we could not enter. A green silk blanket with gold fringe covered the low mound of his supposed grave. A stick of frankincense burned slowly in a small terra cotta dish. No guard. No ticket. No postcards. No Orangina stand. If you want to get off the tourist route, look for Job's tomb.

* * * * *

While we were in Oman, we held a strategy meeting with the crews of the other three boats with whom we had agreed to transit Pirate Alley, the area between Oman and Somalia that, based on recent statistics, had been designated the most likely place to encounter pirates. We were all good friends who had known each other since the WOM (Waves of Mercy) days in Langkawi. That we were all friends complicated the issue.

Someone asked, "Who has a gun?"

"Not on *Ithaca*," Michael replied. "If we had a gun on board, one of us would have shot the other years ago."

"Well, what are we going to do if a hostile actor approaches us?"

"My theory is never assume they are the enemy until they do something aggressive," I ventured.

"No. You have to be proactive. We have to have a plan."

The most paranoid and an old-school skipper insisted on applying completely inappropriate World War II flotilla tactics to the situation. Another swore by his firepower, while others agreed that weapons only helped aggravate volatile situations. After much delicate and not-so-delicate discussion, we worked out a set of fairly reasonable procedures regarding radio contact, running lights, and steaming positions. Although, as it turned out, we were more in danger of running into each other than running into any pirates.

Michael was designated the flotilla leader, partly because *Ithaca* was the slowest boat but, in reality, because he was the most levelheaded and patient skipper of the group, a master at gently herding these very disparate "cats" and mitigating some increasingly difficulty personality conflicts. I just tried to stay focused on what I had to do and not add to the tension.

In the end, we left Salalah against Michael's advice and promptly headed into 20-knot headwinds, which necessitated falling way off course and motor sailing into a very confused sea to make any headway against adverse wind and current. Luckily, we had three extra jerry cans of fuel, but fuel conservation was still a worrisome issue. The plan was to motor in a "box formation," with *Gemini* off our starboard quarter and *Michalo II* and *Blue Banana* about a mile behind us.

Before we even drew close to the designated pirate area, we were approached on three different occasions by boats matching the pirate profile: open boats, going very fast, with three to five persons on board. The first boat sped toward us from the Yemen coast, as if to check us out, and then veered off. The second boat approached out of the west and sped through our flotilla to the east. Then, later, two boats approached from the north. One powered alongside *Michalo II*, who threw them some cigarettes, while *Gemini* broke ranks and moved up alongside *Ithaca*. That confused *Blue Banana* as the second fishing boat approached them, and our carefully planned strategy melted like ice cream on a hot sidewalk.

Minutes later another boat came alongside us, hovered, and finally waved. I waved back. Then they slowed up. My heart skipped several beats. They pulled away just as Michael issued a pan-pan on the radio. On calmer reflection, we surmised they were all just fishermen heading to the islands off the coast of Somalia that belong to Yemen. A bigger worry was fuel. That afternoon we would enter the "scary area," which extended for about 60 miles. To maintain the box formation at 6.5 knots would just kill our fuel.

Everyone was nervous and still a little shaken by the confusing maneuvers earlier in the day. I was worried about fuel. But as luck would have it, the wind came up to 14–20 knots off our starboard stern. We rolled out the genoa and cruised. It was a very rough, dark night, but at least we knew that the chances of any small boat approaching us in such weather were very remote. We got through the night and morning, but then *Blue Banana* and *Michalo II* wanted to change course because they could not sail very comfortably. So, we had to roll in our collapsing genoa, which couldn't hold the wind on the new course, and motor the rest of the way. We put in our last three jerry cans of fuel and prayed.

March 17, 2007, Aden, Yemen

Hallelujah. Anchored in Aden harbor yesterday afternoon. By 7:00 were having a stiff sundowner. The last couple of days have been very stressful. We are all still physically and emotionally recovering from an exhausting passage with four different boats, different sailing strengths and weaknesses, different fuel capacities, different sailing styles and, most of all, different personalities. True to his Navy roots, M was a masterful flotilla Captain, patient yet firm when it came to dealing with "pirate paranoia" and, most of all, reasonable and respectful of everyone's opinions and wishes. But it was a strain, one with which I did not distinguish myself when it came to dealing with difficult personalities. I wasn't in charge for good reason.

Now we are bobbing up and down in a very crowded anchorage with 31 other boats, surrounded by all the hubbub of a commercial port and the exotic allure of an ancient Arabian City sprawled up the hillside behind us. I have been reading Arabian Sands by Wilfred Thesiger about his life wandering with the Bedouin through the "Empty Quarter" from 1945 to 1950. Much of his journeying was through Oman & Yemen, so it is particularly interesting since I know nothing about this part of the world. I must read T. E. Lawrence's The Seven Pillars of Wisdom. I feel a new romance coming on.

Daggers and Suit Coats

T RAVELING ACROSS ROCKY, DUSTY FLAT LAND through mud towns and villages that stair stepped up the mountainsides to 10,000 feet above sea level, we were in biblical times, except for the motorized bus conveying us, which, truth be told, was pretty ancient itself. It was Friday, market day in Yemen, and the streets of each town were crowded with men buying and selling *quat*—a mildly narcotic leaf that the men stuff into their cheeks and chew or suck like tobacco. There were no women anywhere. All marketing appeared to be done by men, gossiping and milling about the busy market stalls in congenial groups.

The national costume seemed to be a long white shirt or robe gathered at the waist by an elaborate embroidered belt with a curved dagger stuck in the front. A suit coat was worn over this and a scarf over the shoulders or wrapped around the head in an artful turban, which could be arranged in different ways depending on the wearer's sense of style or mood. Some men forsook this costume for a simpler sarong-type wrap in a zigzag American Indian–looking motif, folded around the waist, and a long-sleeve shirt and scarf or turban. Even the most impoverished had a rakish sense of style that was quite appealing. As Michael ruefully pointed out, however, never have we been in a country where the men dressed in skirts, wore weapons, and quite unselfconsciously walked down the street holding hands with their male companions.

The women—what ones you see—were completely anonymous in black swirls of fabric with perhaps a bit of embroidery, eyes peeking out behind black veils and hands enclosed in black gloves or occasionally tattooed with red and black henna that looks like lace gloves with black fingernails. Sam and I always wore long skirts, our arms covered and scarves hiding our hair.

As we bumped along the barren, brown land stretching between mud brick towns on the way to Sanaa, the capital, we could see small villages in the distance, which rose from the hilltops as if they had grown from the rocks. Sometimes it was impossible to determine what was man-made and what was God's work, except for the litter of plastic bags along the sides of the streets and blown up into the trees like bleached, deflated papayas.

Halfway we stopped for lunch in the world's noisiest restaurant—filled as it was with yelling men. A huge piece of flat bread that covered the whole table was unfolded. Then a small bowl of squash and lime soup, a whole fish in peppery cumin barbecue sauce, an interesting hummus, and a potato-vegetable dish were set before us. All of which we tucked into with our hands, pulling chunks of the "bread tablecloth" off to scoop up the food, as is the custom in this part of the world.

Later on, after five hours of bouncing over dirt roads in the bus, we arrived at our hotel—a tower house in the old section of town—molded out of stone with thick walls, small low doors, and narrow stone steps and passageways. The walls of the rooms were all whitewashed and the latticed or stonework grilled windows were inset with stained glass, which cast iridescent patterns across the gray bricked floor. "This is so cool," Sam and I exclaimed in unison. (Not so the 5:00 a.m. call to prayer the next morning.)

In spite of the approaching "cocktail hour," we dragged Bill and Michael out to explore the crowded market and got completely lost amid the narrow streets of little shops and stalls. It felt like we were the only tourists in the whole town. The fabric souk was packed mostly with men. As the darkness fell, the lights in the shops illuminated the most fantastic array of colorful patterned, sparkly, and sequined fabric, a fairyland of shimmering color.

"Where are the women who buy all this?" Sam wondered.

"And where do they wear clothes made from it?" I added.

Suddenly a sense of panicked disorientation gripped us as we realized we had no idea where we were. Catching up with Bill and Michael I asked, "Where the heck are we?"

Even the world's two best navigators themselves were confused.

"This way."

"No. I think we came that way. I remember that kiosk."

Then from around a corner three black figures flew at us like marauding blackbirds, stopping directly in front of us as if to block our path. "Good evening" the tallest of the three exclaimed in aristocratically inflected British English. Stunned, we replied in unison, "Good evening."

"My sisters and I want to tell you about Islam." I thought, *Could you please just tell us how to get back to our hotel instead?* "We have reading material for you and a CD in English that will explain our faith" she continued, holding out a small plastic bag of pamphlets. Her black veil puffed out with each word. Her dark eyes sparkled with the humorous recognition of our stunned fearfulness. The other two young girls giggled nervously. Michael took the packet.

Sam asked, "Where did you learn English?"

"In London."

"Really?"

"Yes, really."

I said, "Do you mind?" as I lifted my camera.

And suddenly they were gone, as rapidly as they had appeared, back around the corner. The four of us looked at each other in astonishment and silently picked our way back to the street of window makers and a familiar alleyway near our hotel where we headed up to the observation tower, unwound on giant Turkish pillows, and secretly sipped G & Ts from travel mugs. Below our birdlike perch, a sea of fanciful towers, houses, and minarets, their windows topped with arched filigrees of tan-and-whitewashed zigzagged patterns, turned sepia and beige pink in the dying light.

Now as I write this in 2016, we watch on the evening news as Sanaa is being pounded into dust, its unique birthday cake buildings destroyed, its proud, dapper men and invisible women having become a motley crowd of dislocated, angry, and confused people. History is not kind.

Bad Bab

SOON YEMEN WAS OFF OUR STERN. NEXT EVENT: the Bab el Mandeb, at the entrance to the Red Sea, appropriately named the "Gates of Hell." It was rough and windy with big seas "up the bum" most of the way. An accidental jibe yanked the mainsheet block off the traveler and the boom went flying wildly out over the starboard rail about 2:00 a.m. on our second night—a very dark night, naturally. Michael finally found a fitting to replace the pulley, but pulling in the boom to reattach it took all our strength. Unpredictable ship traffic added to the stress. Neither of us got much sleep the remainder of the night.

The next morning we found two small tears in the mainsail and we reduced sail to the second reef, which was fine because the wind increased and seas built to 15 feet, which made our passage through the needle-like entrance about 8:30 that morning even more challenging—cliffs on one side, rocks on the other, and oncoming ships in the middle—white-knuckle all the way. Dave couldn't handle it so I took the helm and immediately got drenched by a huge wave that broke over my back into the cockpit. Michael and I alternated on the helm the rest of a very tense, tiring day, each of us just getting snippets of sleep. The constant parade of container ships, freighters, and stern waves kept us nervous and wet.

"*Ithaca. Ithaca. Blue Banana.*" Sam's voice crackled on the radio as another wave doused my head.

"*Blue Banana. Ithaca.*"

"How are you guys doing?"

"It's a little hairy out here." Crash. The bowsprit plunged into a trough.

"Take heart. We're a couple miles ahead of you and it's beautiful here."

"If I live that long."

"You will."

And I did. Slowly the wind and seas abetted, making it possible to adjust course and cross the shipping channel to the African coast. Before we knew it, we were sailing up the coast of Eritrea toward Massawa in calm waters, ready for new adventure.

The Dreaded "Red"

A TRIP UP THE RED SEA CONJURES DIFFERENT images for different people. Divers tout its world-class dive sites. Geographers, historians, and politicians cite the significance of the Suez Canal and the Sinai Peninsula. Archaeologists wax ecstatic over the treasures of Luxor and the Valley of the Kings. Tourists pant and salivate over a camel ride around the pyramids and the Great Sphinx. But for sailors, the Red Sea is the "Dreaded Sea" of constant headwinds, adverse currents, sandstorms, and isolated, untenable anchorages—that is, if you make it that far having had to negotiate the triple threat of Pirate Alley, Sudanese warlords, and the "Gates of Hell."

Years before it was physically on our horizon, the thought of the Red Sea crouched in the back of our minds like a bleak prophecy. If you wanted to do a circumnavigation, it was either the relentless wind of the Red Sea, political instability, and pirates, or the notoriously rough passage around the Cape of Good Hope. Big guns or big waves. We chose the Red Sea because it was the best route to the Mediterranean, but we still worried about the intractability of wind and politics. It turned out we got through just under the wire. In our wake the Arab Spring disintegrated into a long, destructive winter of discontent, where today clashing ideologies and bitter wars threaten every country we traveled through in 2007. A tragic irony, but nothing new.

* * * * *

Massawa, Eritrea, was our first landfall in the Red Sea. An ancient port city and trading hub once known as the "Pearl of the Red Sea," it now lies derelict and battered, remnants of whitewashed buildings, porticos, arcades, and trellised balconies clinging to old Turkish houses, 90 percent of which were destroyed by Ethiopia during Eritrea's struggle for independence in 1990. After another convoluted port entry, we hooked up with Bill and Sam for a four-hour bus ride to the mountain capital of Asmara, where the air was cool and a vibrant blue sky domed over shimmering pastel Art Deco buildings.

Once a convenient staging post in the caravan trade, the entire town is a cultural anomaly: old chrome espresso machines crank out strong coffee in little cups, European pastry shops and Italian restaurants abound, and snatches of Italian can be heard on street corners. In the evenings the sidewalks throng with the traditional *passeggiata*. Designed by Italian architects under the orders of Mussolini, Asmara was intended to become the future capital of the Italian East African empire. Every corner presents a unified impression through design, paint, and planting. Even though its makeup is beginning to fade and its skin is cracked, this aging Italian beauty's bones still delight. In all our travels only Havana and Sanaa had this same wonderful sense of a city as a complete work of art, arrested at a particular moment in time. Everywhere I pointed my camera the scene fell into a coherent composition of light, color, and shape.

Buon giorno said the waiter with a little bow when we sat down at the small round table. *Grazie* said we when he brought the steaming cups of cappuccino. "Are we in a Fellini movie?" Sam said with a grin. "I think so," I said looking around for Marcello Mastroianni.

* * * * *

By April 11th we were anchored off Sheikh El Abu Island, happy to be there after strong winds forced us to return to Massawa twice. It was hot and humid. Blowing sand turned every inch, seam, and crevice of the boat red. Which is not the reason they call it the Red Sea but might as well be. (In actual fact, the water does turn vermillion due to periodic algae spores—which we never saw.) For the next ten days we clawed our way north against constant 20-knot headwinds, which set up closely spaced rolling waves known as the Red Sea chop. Power sailing into this was slow and exhausting, tacking unproductive.

When forward progress slowed impractically, we retreated to a *mersa* (a small bay carved out of the sand dunes), where we could hunker down in flat water, if not calm winds, to rest, do boat repairs, and wait for the wind to diminish or change direction. Usually in the company of two or three other boats, we entertained ourselves socializing on each other's boats, troubleshooting fix-it projects, hiking the dunes, and organizing potlucks on the beach. Sometimes there would be interesting snorkeling, but the water was murky most of the time. It was tedious. Except when we stopped in unusual ports and explored "new territory."

Picking our way up the Shabuk Channel along the Sudanese coast, for instance, we threaded through reefs and little islands up to Suakin using the series of waypoints in the *Red Sea Pilot*, our bible for the duration of the journey. The flat, arid land along the coast was dotted with gray-green scrub bushes that extended out into a mirage-like haze from which steep mountains carved a pale purple line against the smoky blue sky. Along the beach an occasional boat with a lateen sail shaped like a shark's fin beat against the 15-knot winds and camels waded in the rippling shore waves. Motoring past the crumbling slave trade center of Suakin, we anchored in the boat basin at the end of the channel. Later that afternoon, yet another "Mohammed" came aboard to check us in and arrange for fuel, propane, and laundry.

The rubble-strewn town was crowded with donkey carts pulling metal drums of water or sacks of produce. Camels munched on sparse weeds at the side of the road, and men stood around leaning on their donkeys, gossiping and sharing sips of liquid from large burlap containers slung across the donkeys' backs. Tea shops lined the dirt streets of the market area, where men in long white robes and turbans lounged, drinking tea from little glasses or thimble-size cups full of coffee, which they poured out of small teardrop-shaped metal flasks. The low afternoon light tinged everything with a painterly glow, but whenever I showed my camera, everyone turned away.

* * * * *

Continuing on our slog up the Red Sea, periodic stops in isolated mesas provided lots of reading time. A book titled *The Photograph* by Penelope Lively that had caught my eye in an English language bookstore in Bangkok led me to this mental meandering in my journal:

April 20, 2007, someplace off the coast of Sudan

I'm reading The Photograph, a beach read but saved by an interesting cubist structure where events are described from the points of view of different characters. Kath, the main character who is deceased, makes an appearance in everyone's life, allowing the author demonstrate how we are all total mysteries to one another. Even though we may be sisters or an old married couple, we usually only communicate on the most superficial level. We are too busy with our own personal survival tactics to worry about anyone else's, too self- absorbed to discover who this person really is that I've grown up with or been married to for forty years.

It reminded me of my sister who, on one occasion long ago, said exactly the same thing as Kath says to her sister: "I always wanted to be like you." Now she hasn't spoken to me since mother died. Why, I'm not really sure . . . and M. We are so different it is really hard to find anything serious to talk about other than the house, the boat, the kids. We both have faults that annoy and frustrate each other but we can never talk about them. He has no idea who I am as a whole person and maybe I don't really know him, though I think I do.

He is reading Soul Mountain, however, a book he is, to my surprise, enjoying and even has shared a chapter or two with me which he never does—and always apparently hates it when I read something to him. It was wonderful, poignant, poetic writing about love, lust and ageing; quite unlike M to be interested in reading anything so introspective. Usually, in his own words, he "just likes a good story." But, there ya' go . . . What do I know about him really?

* * * * *

By May 1ˢᵗ we were in Egypt, tied up to a long cement bulkhead in Port Ghalib in front of six other cruising yachts. After the lengthy and expensive check-in procedure, we pooled our hoses and washed down our boats. It took several hours and 1,000 liters of water to wash off two months' worth of sand and salt from *Ithaca*'s topsides. For a brief interlude she was clean and gleaming, but by the next day, a fine layer of reddish-brown sand coated her decks.

After a week of waiting for weather in Port Ghalib, we continued north to Abu Tig, a huge resort area with a marina, condos, vacation villas, a market, restaurants, and shops. It's a fake, instant town built along the shores of the Red Sea but largely empty, unfinished, and abandoned to blowing sands. It was clean, safe, and secure, however, with plenty of water to wash the boat. Best of all it was a perfect place to leave *Ithaca* unattended while we traveled. A few days later we were on the bus to Cairo, a rather boring six-hour ride up the Red Sea coast along the Gulf of Suez, interrupted by brief stops when someone would get off the bus and walk toward a huddle of tents in the barren desert, reminding me of what bleak places many people in the world call home.

Cairo was a jolt, a bit Alice in Wonderlandish. Like Cuba, things were never what they seemed, and people were not always saying what you thought they were saying. For example, "in one hour" meant at "one o'clock" not sixty minutes later, and taxi drivers often didn't know how to find your destination or would take you to some other place for a shopping opportunity first. Merchants jumped out at you from their shops, grabbed your arm, or blocked your way to engage you in conversation: "Hello," "Where you from?" "What's your name?" "Come have a cup of tea," "Buy my rugs." Shopping was a contact sport and baksheesh the weapon of choice. Everything required a "tip" or a "gift" or a "contribution." It was difficult to navigate such extreme aggressiveness.

We persevered as politely as we could and spent the first day in the Egyptian Museum, across from Tahir Square, now more famous for political demonstrations than icons of a glorious past. But in 2007, all was peaceful. Only tourist groups crowded the square. After several more days exploring, we boarded a sleeper train at Giza station and headed to Abu Simbel in Aswan.

Here one of the greatest stories of archaeological salvation resulted in the re-creation of the temple of Ramses II and Queen Nefertari's temple of Hathor. Originally hewn out of a solid rock mountain on the west bank of the Nile between 1274 and 1244 B.C., the temples were built both to proclaim Ramses II's magnificence in perpetuity and to honor his beloved wife. Over the centuries, the shifting of the Nile and desert sands buried them, seemingly forever, until they were rediscovered in 1813 by a Swiss explorer. It took five years to dig away the sand to reveal the monumental exterior statues and ornately carved interiors.

Four colossal statues of Ramses II guard the entrance to his temple, each more than 65 feet (20 meters) high, although one toppled over centuries ago. The falcon-headed figure of the Sun God Ra-Horakhty stands over the entrance. Inside, reliefs on the walls depict Ramses as ever glorious and victorious, particularly at the famous Battle of Kadesh, where he inspires his demoralized army to triumphant success and stands boldly in his chariot shooting arrows at his fleeing enemies.

Nefertari's Temple of Hathor is slightly smaller and fronted by six statues, each nearly 33 feet (10 meters) high. Four represent Ramses and two represent Nefertari, who, typically, is not portrayed as large as he is. Even though he built this temple to honor her, he can't resist filling it with images of his own prowess as a warrior. Boldly he smites his enemies while she watches with a raised hand, probably meant to signify her blessing, but to me she looks more like she is saying, "Oh dear, must you?" or "Enough already." Her manifestation as Hathor, the cow, riding on a barque serenely through the lotus and papyrus reeds, is one of the few feminine images in the temple.

In the 1960s, when the rising waters of the Aswan Dam posed a new threat to the temples, a UNESCO-sponsored rescue team cut the temples into more than 2,000 huge blocks weighing from 10 to 40 tons and reconstructed them inside an artificially built mountain 210 miles away and 65 meters higher than the original site—re-creating their original environment and orienting them in the same direction so that the exact path of the sun's rays, so important in Egyptian worship, would be maintained. It cost $40 million and took more than four years, but Ramses II, like his avatar the Sun God, rose again.

* * * * *

Not surprisingly, Michael and I always fantasized about sailing down the Nile. On our last night in Luxor, we did. Floating among the water hyacinths as the sun sank over the western hills, Michael persuaded our fifteen-year-old captain to let him take the tiller. We sat together in the stern skimming silently over the dark water while the boy leaned over the gunwales and picked a water hyacinth for me, and the illuminated pylons of Luxor, rising majestically above the string of lights along the eastern shore, drifted off our port rail.

Then a policeman came alongside and demanded a bribe because it was illegal (he said) for foreigners to sail the boats. At the end of the hour, the young captain skillfully beached the boat on the western shore and Michael gave him a big tip.

* * * * *

Port Suez, at the southern end of the Suez Canal, marked the completion of our Red Sea transit, where, luckily, we tied up to a mooring just before the beginning of the afternoon big ship convoy south. It had been an anxious passage, partly because Pete and Alexis were coming to Cairo. We were so excited to see them we could talk of nothing else, but suddenly it looked like we would be a day late.

The Red Sea gods got in their last licks about 9:00 the night before, when the wind suddenly swung from southwest to north and the seas, whipped up by 18 to 20 knots, had us inching along at 2 knots. All night long *Ithaca* plunged into surfing waves that crashed up against the bowsprit, catapulted into the troughs, shaking and shuddering. The sea state, as well as our disappointment, made sleep impossible. Just as we were thinking we would have to spend another night at sea, the wind slowly dropped and the seas calmed a bit so we could actually make 3.5, then 4, then 5 knots over the ground. We were elated when we realized that, yes, we would actually be able to make Port Suez before dark. Never had we been in such a body of water where weather predictions seemed to mean nothing but a cruel joke making planning almost impossible.

June 13, 2007, Cairo, Egypt

We are finally finished with the Red Sea. Hooray. The constant blowing sand, baksheesh, touts, and general impossibility of doing business here have made even me ready to leave. Everything is a money hassle, from buying a melon to paying port fees. Everything has to be negotiated. It is draining. The laundry was $20.00, which was way too much for soggy, wrinkled *clothes. After much haggling we paid half, thinking it was settled but still the laundry man returned wanting us to "be happy" and, after a long spiel, still wanted a T-shirt or a present. It wears you down.*

Sitting on the balcony of our hotel room on the 6th floor of the Flamenco Hotel in Cairo, overlooking the Nile, watching the early morning sun tinge the mosque and houseboats across the river a soft orange, I finally feel calm. At last we are here and all the hassle of the past months is a distant memory. When we walked into the hotel lobby yesterday afternoon and Lexi turned around, saw us, and yelled so everyone in the whole hotel could hear her, "MERTIS," I couldn't help but cry. Then Pete said, "Hi Mom," and they both gave me a big hug. I still can't quite believe we have the next ten days to see a tiny, exotic slice of the world together and share something of our amazing life with two of our favorite people.

* * * * *

Lexi was ten years old, and this was her first experience in a foreign country. Nothing could have been more foreign, but she navigated it like a trouper and was enthralled most of the time. After our trip to Cairo several weeks earlier, we knew how to get around and had planned a few special excursions that we knew she would like. Having inherited "Olympic" shopping genes from her mother, the Khan el-Khalili Market was a must.

The labyrinthine bazaar, where better men have been known to get lost for days in the honeycomb of narrow winding streets and alleyways, was crammed with brass shops, jewelry shops, rug shops, perfume shops, fabric shops, spice shops, little shop after little shop overflowing with copper teapots, Bedouin dresses and belly dancing costumes, glittering glass lanterns, snake-like hookahs, shiny brass trays, ornate inlaid furniture, stacks of backgammon boards, candlesticks and jewelry boxes, gold bracelets, seas of beaded necklaces, dangles and spangles of semiprecious stones, and earrings and bangles by the basketfuls. She was speechless, head on a swivel, little straw hat spinning like a top from shop to shop as she and Pete, hand in hand, slowly made their way through the crowds ahead of us looking for a present for Mom.

Eventually we found our way to Fishawi's, Cairo's oldest coffeehouse, open day and night for the past 200 years. Here men in turbans and robes sat sucking on *sheeshas* (water pipes) around copper-topped tables, and drinking mint tea in a long corridor hung with ornate mirrors off a cramped alley. Lexi sipped her iced tea with all the self-possession of the Arabian princess she must have been in a past life.

The real fun came when Michael, aka "Da," being fixated on buying a small square oriental rug for our galley, got trapped by a rug salesman who popped out of his shop to accost him with the usual spiel. We went in, against everyone's better judgment. Michael explained that he just wanted a 12-inch by 12-inch square rug but the rug salesman pretended not to understand and proceeded to pull down rectangular rugs, ovals, runners, large room rugs, prayer rugs, and little entryway rugs, extolling their beauty and cheap price, while high on a shelf in an obscure corner stood a stack of little sample rugs that might fit the requirement. Michael gestured toward them, but the rug salesman just pulled down another prayer rug.

Michael was getting more and more exasperated and finally yelled, "Don't you know what a *square* looks like?" Lexi stood by wide-eyed and then started to giggle. The rug salesman stopped for just a heartbeat and then pulled down another very expensive, lovely handwoven floral-patterned large rectangular wool rug and said, "Now look at this, sir. Very fine quality . . ." We all put down our thimble teacups, said, "Thank you very much," and left, trying not to laugh out loud until we got out in the alleyway.

Ever since, "Don't you know what a *square* looks like?" has been code in our family for, "Are you really dumb or what?" which predictably elicits peals of laughter from Lexi.

Two days later, with Lexi and Pete in tow, we headed back to the boat in Ismailia. The next day we were on our way to Israel, with one last leg of the Suez Canal still to complete. Of course, the pilot who was scheduled to come at 6:00 a.m. didn't come until 12 noon. Thankfully, though, he was practically invisible, and we just read, rested, and watched the big ships and sand dunes role by. At 6:00 p.m.

we were in Port Said and a pilot boat came alongside to take him ashore.

And then we were out . . . in the Mediterranean! We cracked a bottle of champagne and celebrated. Lexi even had a sip.

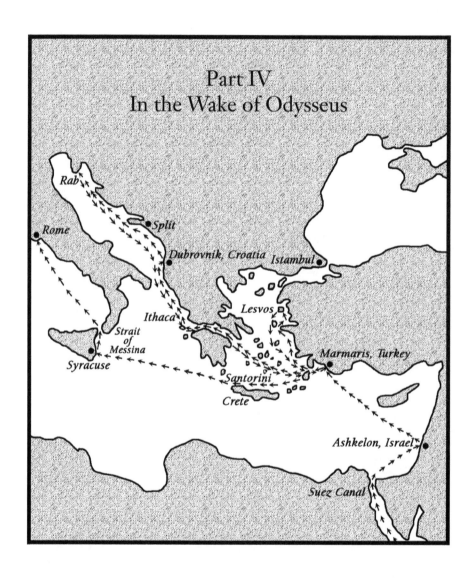

Part IV
In the Wake of Odysseus

Out of Arabia—From the "Red" to the "Med"

A SHKELON, ON THE SOUTHERN COAST OF Israel, was a twenty-four-hour passage from Port Said but worlds away by other measures. Women were visible everywhere and didn't mind displaying themselves in tight blue jeans and sexy tops. They had attitude. After so many months of not seeing women on the streets, or if you did they were covered up and anonymous, it was a shock to see these ladies. They had real presence. No one was going to make *them* stay home. You sensed it immediately. Way before the United States let women serve in the military, these ladies were on the front lines with guns.

Equally obvious was the sense of a country under siege. Although Israel had withdrawn from Gaza in 2005, now, two years later, relations were still tense. Ashkelon, only about 9 miles from the border, continued to experience random shelling, and the coast of Israel was heavily monitored. As we approached Israeli waters, observation helicopters tracked us, repeatedly hailing us on the radio. Ten miles out a navy gunboat, appropriately named *Bad Boy*, roared over the horizon, throwing up a rooster tail wake, and circled *Ithaca* several times. An angry voice yelled at us over the radio to stop dead in the water and identify ourselves. More angry questions erupted from a megaphone as *Bad Boy* drew closer. We put up our hands and pointed to our American flag. Finally, they were convinced we were not a security threat; they backed off but kept us in their sights until we entered the harbor. The marina was almost empty. Most people had moved their boats north away from the erratic gunfire. It was a bit unnerving. But we were on a pilgrimage, anxious to share the next few days with our son and granddaughter following in the steps of Jesus.

After getting our bearings in the marina, we rented a car and drove to Jerusalem. Entering the old walled city through the Damascus Gate, we followed the twisting alleys where Stations of the Cross are etched in Roman numerals along the Via Dolorosa, much of which is now lined with tourist grot shops. Lexi touched each number and looked up at her father who smiled down at her like she was a beneficent angel.

The "way" itself is one of the many supposed routes that have been conjured up over the years, the exact location being impossible to know. Emperor Constantine's mother, Helena, probably had a hand in it. She was a devout Christian, who, on a pilgrimage to the Holy City 300 years after the death of Christ, chose the site of the Church of the Holy Sepulchre in the belief that Hadrian's temple to Venus and Jupiter, previously on that site, had been built to dissuade the early Christians from worshipping at the true location of Jesus' crucifixion and burial.

The last five Stations of the Cross are, in fact, inside the Church of the Holy Sepulchre. The Franciscans run the chapel where Jesus is said to have been stripped of his clothes. The Greek Orthodox church runs the chapel where Jesus was nailed to the cross. Other chapels designate where Jesus was crucified and where Jesus' body was taken down and handed to Mary. The final, fourteenth station, the tomb of Jesus, is inside a very small chapel in the center of the church. Silently the four of us squeezed together and knelt before a candlelit altar over the spot where Jesus was buried. Lexi's face glowed in the candlelight. Pete squeezed her hand. A tiny tear glistened on her cheek as we knelt shoulder to shoulder in the cramped space contemplating the significance of the place and the moment. Geographic exactitude mattered not.

By the time we got to Jerusalem's Wailing Wall, Lexi was a little bored and detached. But we persevered, Michael and Pete going to the men's section, Lexi and I to the women's section, skirting the phalanx of old ladies sitting on plastic chairs begging. Then, looking for a taxi, we suddenly found ourselves embroiled in a heated argument between two drivers over the fare. Hot and tired, we looked at each other, got in the back of the nearest one, and tried to remain politically neutral while the Jewish taxi driver harangued us about the dishonest, mendacious, and cheating Arabs.

The next day, our excursion to Bethlehem was even more fraught. It was prohibited to take a rental car into the West Bank, so we had to park outside the border wall, scrawled with angry graffiti and covered with barbed wire, walk through the checkpoint, and get a taxi to Bethlehem on the other side. The intractable hostility between the two sides was palpable. Once across the border, we arrived at the Church of the Nativity in Bethlehem just in time to follow a small candlelight procession of chanting Franciscans down into the crypt, where they gathered around us like attending angels, their voices reverberating in the small space. Lexi bent down and kissed the silver star marking the spot where Jesus was born. We crossed ourselves and said a Hail Mary.

Then, coming back through the checkpoint into Israel, it suddenly felt like we were in prison. Loudspeakers barked orders and hostile gun-bearing guards forced a Muslim women in front of us to remove her veil and overcoat. I felt the Palestinians' indignation, personally—a deep spiritual experience bookended by hatred and suspicion.

The next day we were back on the boat for a farewell steak dinner, and an early trip to the airport the following morning. A quick photograph of Pete and Lexi in a smiling hug just before they boarded the plane, and then they were gone. I stood at the gate watching their backs disappear in the sea of other travelers, trying not to cry. "Come on," Michael said as he grabbed my hand. "We've got stuff to do, places to go, things to see . . ."

We did, and spent the rest of July doing it: touring the country by following biblical names we had known all our lives. First was Caesarea, the ancient city on the coast where Herod built two large breakwaters totally enclosing a port which, in its day, rivaled those of Alexandria and Antioch; the Basilica of the Annunciation, in

Nazareth, built in 1969 over four other previous churches, marking the spot where the Angel Gabriel appeared to Mary and announced she was to give birth to Jesus; and the Church of St. Joseph, which in theory was built over Joseph's carpentry shop. Who knows, really, but there was something powerful about just being in the general geographic location where the Bible tells us all these things occurred.

We drove around the Sea of Galilee and stopped at the stunning Church of the Beatitudes, high on a hill overlooking Galilee—Tiberias to the south and Capernaum to the north. This is where Jesus supposedly delivered the Sermon on the Mount containing the Lord's Prayer and the beatitudes—"Blessed are the peacemakers . . ."—inspired by the serenity of the landscape, no doubt.

But my favorite was the Church of the Primacy of St. Peter at Tabgha, a small chapel on the pebbly shores of the Sea of Galilee, set in a garden of babbling springs. After the noisy tour group from Naples left, we had it all to ourselves except for a bewhiskered Franciscan who was muttering prayers on a bench by the entrance. It was here that the resurrected Jesus said to Peter, "You are Peter and upon this rock I build my church." As a recent convert to Catholicism, I named our first son Peter, praying that he would always have that rock on which to build his life. Now, almost fifty years later, I continue to pray the same prayer.

*   *   *   *   *

It was a five-day motor sail from Herzliya, Israel, to Marmaris, Turkey. Once a sleepy fishing village with a natural harbor, commodious enough for Lord Nelson to assemble his fleet there before his attack on the French at Abukir in 1798, the landscape of mountainous islands and bays is still stunning. The town of Marmaris, however, has become a tacky pile of high-rise cement buildings catering to hordes of northern European tourists who flock here to don bikinis and escape the northern cold. It is also a mecca for cruisers. Boats from all over Europe fill the two large, secure, and well-equipped marinas, where you can haul your boat, have work done, or store it for the winter at very reasonable prices. Restaurants, markets, shopping, marine equipment, and fabrication facilities of every kind are plentiful. It was another one of those places where sailors come and stay for years, supported by the strong sense of community and ease of living. We walked into the marina restaurant and instantly found three couples sitting at the bar that we had known from Southeast Asia, including Bill and Sam.

Ultimately, Marmaris became our home port for the next three years, but not before we had another one of "those conversations," which started with Michael proclaiming: "Okay, now we're in the Med, what do you think? Another year and we'll head home?"

"What? We just got here. Don't you want to cruise the Greek islands like we always planned, go to Italy and Spain, maybe do the canals?"

"Don't you get it? I want to go home. I want to finish this circumnavigation before I die. I'm sixty-seven."

"That's not old."

"It feels like it sometimes."

"What if we kick out our renters and do those renovations we've always talked about? Then we can live part-time in Annapolis and part-time in the Med, since we can fly home space A from here so cheaply?"

"That's a thought."

It was a perfect compromise. Of course, it got complicated. Like our boat refit in New Zealand, a small house beautification project escalated into a major renovation. Starting with a new well and septic system, we soon had an architect and builder, and we were living in one room sealed off with plastic to keep out the drywall dust—a little like living on a boat. A brief respite stretched into six months.

Epping "Home Work"

S EPTEMBER 1, 2007, EPPING FOREST, ANNAPOLIS
We have been home more than a month. Soon the leaves will be off the trees and it will be winter. A solitary swan swims off the point at sunrise. There used to be a pair that lived up the creek but now this elegant bird is only kept company by her reflection.

Progress on the addition is slow. The foundation is finished and we are awaiting the inspector, next week the framing. Everywhere I look something needs to be done, decisions to be made, chaos to be cleaned up. This porch overlooking the river is my refuge.

How many years have I sat here at different points in my life, in sadness and joy, worry and peace, love, disappointment, laughter and tears. Like my own life, this half acre of ground has changed, shed pieces and grown in surprising new ways. Major trees have died, limbs fallen. New land taken shape, new vistas opened. Like all things, it is constantly evolving, sometimes painfully, sometimes gracefully, sometimes with the jolt of lightning or landslides, other times with the slow decline of an aging tree. It is a living, visible expression of all I have come to know about life and only truly understand in brief moments of introspection such as this.

* * * * *

For the next six months, every day was crammed with "must dos" and events surrounding house and family. Slowly I made peace with the changes and constantly shifting dynamics of life all around me. Now as I look back, it seems like a movie of someone else's life. An early snowstorm welcomed Danny and Lauren's second child, Laird Burnes Copeland Welch, into the world at eight pounds eight ounces, who over the ensuing six months grew into a chunky, cheerful little guy who patiently endured big sister Caroline's aggressive affection and being passed around like the family football. As I write this, he is a funny, hunky seven-year-old, inquisitive and athletic.

Our last family picnic plays through my mind: the boys and Caroline dumping each other out of the hammock; the gleeful giggles; Danny and Lauren sitting on the swing; Pete, Alexis, and baby Laird lolling on the grass with new puppy Sky; Tracy gossiping with her parents around mother's glass-top garden table; Michael barbecuing chicken. One of many family gatherings we had shared to mark birthdays, deaths, and special arrivals of boats and babies. Hiking, boat rides, lacrosse games, family projects, school plays—all part of the fabric that weaves our lives together, so much of which we had missed for many years. I took a family photo of everyone assembled haphazardly around the porch steps, subconsciously leaving a hole for my sister.

To see our house come together so beautifully as an expression of our joint dreams amazed me after the agonizing decisions, delays, and dilemmas. The dismay at suddenly having my house full of mother's furniture. Would it still be my house or hers? Miraculously, every piece found its own home and looks like it was always meant to be there. Even her portrait in my workroom settled in. Having her there while I was frantically trying to finish the cushions for the living room with my dying sewing machine was reassuring—a comfort, a calming presence—although I could feel her looking askance at my obvious lack of skill. Often I would find myself conversing with her, remembering the time she made me put in a zipper three times until I got it right.

Toward the end of our stay we made a pilgrimage to the Eastern Shore to visit Jack. We always went to visit him whenever were home and he would always pretend like he didn't know me at first and then slowly come over and put his head on my lap and wiggle his tail. It hurt my feelings but I understood it was his way of just letting me know I wasn't entirely off the hook for leaving him. We also had kept in touch with him over the years through update post cards from his new family and knew he was adored by all, especially the grandchildren. But now we knew he was coming to the end of his days as Major of Oxford and that it was probably the last time we would see him.

I was shocked to see that he couldn't get up. I sat down next to him. He put is grey muzzle in my hand and thump his tail on the floor. I rubbed his head and tried to suppress my tears. It was time, I knew, to put him out of his discomfort but I couldn't say anything. He was not my dog. When we got back to Marmaris there was a postcard saying that Jack was buried in the Pet Hospital in Oxford with a head stone that read, "Here lies our friend Jack, Acting Mayor of Oxford."

Back on the Jazz

FTER A FAMILY BREAKFAST AT THE CITY DOCK coffeehouse and hugs on the sidewalk, Pete drove us to the airport—a quick embrace and momentary eye contact communicated all the love and sadness of leaving. Twenty-four hours later Michael and I were checking into the Orient Express Hotel in Istanbul. Driving into the city I recognized the skyline from old photographs I had seen in Orhan Pamuk's *Istanbul*. As we bumped over the narrow cobblestone streets to our hotel, seagulls, white as milk, swirled around the minarets of the Blue Mosque, reminding one that this city, at the confluence of the Bosphorus and the Golden Horn, has been a seafaring port and meeting place of East and West for centuries.

The magnificent Hagia Sophia, first a Christian church, then a mosque, and now a museum, was a shock of gold, the massive dome and delicate mosaics of a surprising tonal range. The breadth of it, the vastness, the four large gilt discs of Arabic letters suspended at the corners of the immense dome blending with the Christian iconography, a metaphor for peace between the two faiths.

The glittering Topkapi Palace was a whole day's romantic getaway. According to our Lonely Planet guidebook, it had been home to "Selim the Sot," who drowned in the bath after drinking too much champagne; Ibrahim the Mad, who lost his reason after being locked up for four years in the infamous palace *kafe* (cage); and Roxelana, the beautiful, malevolent consort of Suleyman the Magnificent. Fact, myth, and magic swirled through its shimmering light like facets of a diamond, every room, court, chamber, and hall a kaleidoscope of colored tile, a garden of intrigue expressed in intricate floral motifs.

Exhausted after cramming in every sight we could, we boarded a bus back to Marmaris. After a grueling overnight trip, we were finally back aboard *Ithaca*, preparing to cruise north along the Turkish coast and then back south through the islands that cascade down the eastern Aegean along the border between Greece and Turkey.

May 26, 2008, Kuruca Buku, Turkey

My first swim in the Mediterranean this morning was symbolic but cold. Afterward I stretched out on the deck in the hot sun, luxuriating in the warmth on my skin, the slight breeze rippling the water and Salsa music coming from the small resort ashore. Another mellow Mediterranean dream. I feel guilty. I should be doing boat work, varnishing or something, but I am too lazy to move.

* * * * *

By June 1, 2008, we were anchored up a protected bay behind a small peaked island topped by a crumbling Byzantine fort in the fjord-type harbor of Keri Buku. Here we settled in next to Blue Banana for a week with Bill and Sam, floating quietly on the glassy water, which glowed like a black pearl. Every morning I would get up before the sun, put a coat of varnish on the toe rail, then reward myself with a swim. Later, Sam and I would go ashore in the dinghy for marketing, walking, or eating at the family-owned waterfront restaurant. Flat bread stuffed with greens and feta cheese served with tomatoes and cucumbers from a local garden was our favorite, or Gözleme, a thin crepe filled with cheese, spinach, and potato, another yummy local specialty.

Sam was the best walking companion. She knew instinctively when to absorb the ambiance, when to comment, and when to chat. She also loved to sprint out and get some exercise when we both were feeling a little boat bound and fat. There was a long valley behind the restaurant in Keri Buku that stretched uphill between mountains covered with pine trees. Rhododendrons, roses, grapevine-covered patios hugged stone cottages clustered amid gray-green olive trees, their gnarly trunks silhouetted against the surrounding golden wheat fields. Little vegetable patches were stuck in every nook and cranny. Quizzical, bearded goats peered at us through the tall grass, and wrinkled peasant ladies in long skirts and elaborate head wraps nodded responses to our cheerful but shy Turkish greeting *Merhaba*. In the luscious pinky gold afternoon light, it looked like an impressionist painting.

Days later we motored to Knidos on the Datça Peninsula, a fourth-century BC trading city—one of the six cities of the Dorian Confederacy—famous for Praxiteles' statue of Aphrodite, the first statue of a female nude. (The story of her romance with a shepherd who kissed her thigh is enticing but too long to record here. Worth a Google search, though.) Here we literally anchored among the ruins in a bowl of rocky foundations, marble steps, and tumbled columns that had collapsed into the water along the shore. As soon as we got the anchor down we went exploring.

The hillside was covered with purple and yellow wildflowers drying in the hot June sun but not much in the way of identifying signs or information about the site. The Greek theater was instantly recognizable, however, built as it was into the natural curve of the hillside overlooking the harbor. I remarked on the arched entryway as a later Roman addition, since it was the Romans who perfected the technology of the arch. We sat high up on the stone seats and looked down at *Ithaca* and *Blue Banana* floating like toys in the dark blue lagoon. What must it have been like to live here, walk the streets of this busy trading town, live in the villas above the *odeion* (a small building for music performances), shop in the market? According to Lonely Planet, the ship taking St. Paul on his way to Rome for trial stopped here to wait for better weather. Caught in this eddy of ancient history, we, too, had to wait for weather.

In Bodrum we anchored under the charmingly be-gardened Crusader Castle of St. Peter, which houses the Museum of Underwater Archaeology, where we saw relics of shipwrecks from the Bronze Age to the Ottoman era. Colorful, gleamingly varnished charter gullets, like pirate ships, jostled for space along the quay across from a long street of sidewalk cafés and restaurants crowded with camera-toting tourists, as boat captains paced the pier looking for possible passengers.

In centuries past, Bodrum was known as Halicarnassus, home to Herodotus, the "father of history," and one of the Seven Wonders of the Ancient World. Built as a tomb for the Persian King Mausolus (circa 376–353 B.C.) by his wife, it was an enormous white marble "mausoleum" topped by a stepped pyramid that stood almost intact for nineteen centuries until it was destroyed during the crusades in 1522. Supposedly, pieces of it can still be seen in some of the city's old buildings and walls but now nothing remains on the site except a commemorative garden, bits of columns, and parts of the original drainage system.

It was here, after a delightful lunch (probably with too much parsley), that I had a massive allergic reaction, the kind that spontaneously erupts seemingly without any reason. I had had them before over the years. I knew the symptoms, starting with itchy palms, itchy throat, itchy feet, my heart racing until my face swells up like a Shar pei's muzzle and I am in full anaphylactic panic and can't breathe. It is ironic that this should have happened in a place renowned for its giant mausoleum but I didn't see the humor in this at the time. As we were walking through town, slowly my hands began to itch but I ignored it, hoping it would go away as it sometimes does.

Unfortunately, my symptoms increased and my Benadryl and Epi Pen were on the boat, which was a long walk and dinghy ride away. I remembered seeing a pharmacy somewhere. Frantically we searched for it as the itching spread. No one on the street spoke English, but it had been our experience that pharmacists usually do, and we finally found one. There was no Benadryl, but he gave me something else. I took three tablespoons and we continued walking toward the dinghy landing. It had no effect. Now my tongue starting to swell up and my eyes were puffy. The only thing to do was get back to the dinghy and the boat as rapidly as possible.

It was raining, the streets were slippery, and we were a little lost. Miraculously, we passed a window where, written in English in big red letters, was the word MEDICARE. Inside I asked the doctor in very rough Turkish if he spoke English. He answered with a slight Boston accent that he had studied at Johns Hopkins. My guardian angel had intervened again. He gave me a course of pills and instructions for what to do. Then he gave me his mobile phone number and email address to contact him if it didn't get better or happened again. I rested there for half an hour and slowly the itching and swelling went down.

It is a fear I lived with the entire journey, particularly when we were at sea for long periods of time with no access to an emergency room. Against my allergist's advice, however, I refused to consider this condition as a serious enough reason to stop sailing. I always believed God would take care of me, and He did, especially as we sailed north and I developed an intestinal affliction that proved to be more difficult to resolve, ultimately requiring a trip home and consultation with doctors I knew, in a language I more or less understood. More on that later.

At this point in the story, we are back with the BBs, leisurely cruising up Turkey's southern Aegean coast, center of ancient civilization and the location of more well-preserved ancient sites "per square kilometer than any other region in the world," according to my faithful guidebook. Enthralled, we could often see them towering on hilltops or sprawled along the shore in stark contrast to the miles of ugly high-rises and tacky white boxes that also clump the "Cement Coast."

Ephesus (near Kusadası, Turkey) was the crown jewel as the Roman capital of Asia Minor. One of the most intact Roman cities extant, it was the best-preserved classical city in the Mediterranean. It was probably the most crowded with tourists as well. We just had to imagine that they were all wearing togas rather than cruise ship attire, and that they had come to the city for a pagan festival. It did kind of feel like a rock concert venue.

* * * * *

After five days of exploring together, we said good-bye to Sam and Bill, who were on their way to Greece while we continued north. By June 22nd we were in a marina in Ayvalik. My intestinal issues had become chronic. The good news was there was a hospital across the street from the marina. The bad news was no one, not even the doctors, spoke English. Enter Zorbert, the marina manager, who also doubled as guardian angel. Having lived in the United States, he not only spoke perfect English but also was a kind and patient man who led us through the ornate protocols of Turkish health care; arranged for me to see a doctor the next day; and waited in the crowded hallways with us and translated the doctor's diagnosis. Actually, he was more like a saint, never revealing the slightest embarrassment with having to listen to and translate the details of some crazy American woman's intestinal drama.

Fortunately, while we waited for the lab test results, there was a diversion nearby: Troy. Imagine it! The site of the Trojan War described by Homer in the *Iliad*—a real place. Turns out it was a "real place" for a very, very long time. Nine different ancient cities were built on top of one another, dating back to 3000 B.C.—Troy VI or Troy VII being King Priam's city of Trojan War fame. The history is dense but the site is sparse, nowhere near as dramatic as Ephesus. Even after seeing the on-site informative tourist film, it was difficult to sort out the layers.

Apparently, the nineteenth-century amateur archaeologist Heinrich Schliemann discovered the site by studying Homer's descriptions of Troy and matching them to the surrounding landscape. Ultimately, we got eight more ancient cities in the bargain. Once again—with the exception of two Japanese tour groups who always cluster together, fly through, and are gone like a quick squall—we were the only ones there. Standing on what was once the outer wall of the city, we looked across the *troad*, a low rolling area of wheat fields and olive groves that still resembles Homer's description. Nearby was the site of the Skaean Gate where Achilles and Hector fought a duel.

The next day we drove south to Pergamon/Bergama and the famous medical center of Asclepion, where Galen (131–210 A.D.), the greatest early physician, ran his medical school and clinic. His work was the basis of Western medicine into the sixteenth century. Treatments included massage, mud baths, drinking sacred waters (which looked pretty icky to me), use of herbs and ointments, and diagnosis by dream analysis. (He must really have been from California.) There was also a theater because the arts were thought to be therapeutic in getting one's mind off one's ills. I was glad I didn't have to drink the icky waters to cure my own sickness, but wandering around this lovely peaceful site did get my mind off my infirmities.

Back in Ayvalik the test did not show anything. Nevertheless, the doctor prescribed some antibiotics, which did not help. I was feeling weaker by the day. Michael said: "I think it's time to go home. It's been six weeks and you're not getting any better."

"I'm fine. It will go away. I don't want to go home."

Michael stared at me and said in his stern, military I'm-in-control-here voice, "We're going."

We went. Luckily, we got a quick flight to Frankfurt and flew home from Ramstein. Slowly the symptoms disappeared. After a CT scan and two colonoscopies, I declared it simply a bad dream, and by August 24th we were back on board *Ithaca*, the only boat anchored in a small bay just north of Mytilini on the island of Lesbos, the third largest island in Greece. There was a tiny seaside chapel off the bow and a charming taverna off the port. We could see the buried shank of our anchor in 15 feet of clear green water, the chain pulled out perfectly. What more could one want.

* * * * *

Directly across from Ayvalik on the Turkish coast, Lesbos was until recently famous for its world-class ouzo and the Greek poetess Sappho, who was born on the island. That made it the mecca of lesbians who swamp the place every September to worship their "goddess" at the Women Together Festival. Now, sadly, Lesbos is best known as the mecca of migrants fleeing chaos in the Middle East.

Further north the cliff-side village of Anavatos, on the island of Chios, seems to have prefigured this tragedy when, in 1822, during the Greek War for Independence, the villagers abandoned their gray stone houses and hurled themselves over the precipitous cliff rather than be taken alive by the invading Turks. The empty, crumbling village remains a monument to their loss, a scene we saw repeated in Greek and Turkish villages alike over the years.

Sailing the "Wine Dark Sea"

B Y THE END OF OCTOBER 2008, THE BOAT WAS back in Marmaris "on the hard" and we were on our way home to spend the winter in Annapolis, feeling quite worldly to be splitting our time between Maryland and the Mediterranean. After an eight-month Epping Forest hiatus full of festive holidays, school plays, birthday dinners, Sunday barbeques, boat rides, and the usual small scrapes and abrasions of family life, we were more than ready to return to *Ithaca* the following May. We had a long, ambitious voyage ahead of us. The previous season had been spent cruising up the coast of Turkey and down through the northern Aegean islands. Now we would stray further afield, across the southern Aegean to Athens, through the Corinth Canal into the Ionian Sea to Corfu and north into the Adriatic Sea to Croatia and the Dalmatian coast above it . . . and back! Along the way we would find Ithaca (Ithaki), Odysseus's island home, a long-dreamed-of goal.

The journey began in the Cyclades (pronounced "kick la dees," although we coined ruder names). Sprinkled like sugar cube stepping-stones across the southern Aegean, these islands on the major trade route from Anatolia to Greece were once the center of ancient Mediterranean civilization. Consummate whitewashed Greek islands of myth and tourist brochure, swirling in a hurricane (*kykos*, or circle) around the central "eye" of Delos, they have been bound together by commerce and culture since the early Cycladic period of 3000–2000 B.C., occupied by the Minoans, Mycenaeans, Dorians, Athenians, Ptolemaic dynasties, Macedonians, Romans, Byzantines, Venetians, Ottomans, and Italians during World War II, to be finally vanquished by twentieth-century package tourism. For a sailor, they are legendary and lethal when the midsummer meltemi wind sweeps down along the eastern coast of mainland Greece and rages through the islands, imprisoning sailors in port for weeks.

Our first Cyclades island was one of the most famous and symbolic of this turbulent territory: Santorini (Thira), blown apart by a volcanic eruption in 1650 B.C. that destroyed the great Minoan settlement of Akrotini. The previously round island became a huge C-shaped cliff, embracing a deep caldera formed when the center of the island collapsed and the sea occupied the vacuum. This cataclysmic event destroyed the sophisticated and powerful Minoan civilization that had dominated the Aegean in the third century B.C. The resulting tsunami flattened Crete and reached as far as Israel. It changed history for millennia to come, periodically re-erupting and spewing havoc as recently as 1956, when scores of people were killed and houses destroyed.

In recent years the primary danger has been the thousands of tourists who pack the tiny streets when daily cruise ships disgorge their guests. A well-placed elbow to the eye, swipe of a Gucci bag, or shove off the crowded cliff-side walk could do one in just as permanently as flying rocks and foaming lava. Luckily, we had discovered early on in our travels that a museum was the best place to escape the marauding hordes and the Archaeological Museum of Ancient Akiotini, in the main town of Fira, did not disappoint. Tucked among the sprawl of white blocks tumbled on the cliff top overlooking the caldera, its cache of Minoan and Akiotini pottery and frescos spun tales of ancient life and ritual with whimsical, seductive style. Pitchers with bird beak spouts and bulbous bodies sprouting tiny tits kept me clicking my Nikon for the good part of an hour.

But the red swirl of the meltemi on the weather map warned we had better "get outta Dodge." Bill and Sam had told us about Schoinoussa, a small island north of Santorini where they had sheltered the year before. It sounded like a good sanctuary. On the weather map the tiny Bay of Mersini looked like a blue donut hole of tranquility surrounded by raging yellow and orange indicating very strong winds and turbulent weather for the rest of the week.

Like many of the Greek islands, Schoinoussa had a smattering of buildings around the small fishing port where a local ferry periodically brought people and supplies, but the real action, such as it was, happened in the hora, the town on the hill where most of the shops, cafés, and restaurants were located. Unlike many other Greek islands, however, Schoinoussa is very low key and only appealed to the more adventuresome, independent tourist. There were no discos, jewelry shops, or extreme sports, no ATM (when we were there), and only one Internet café located in a small resort on the other side of the island. We had to make our own fun.

It turned out this was not hard. There was a pleasant taverna on the quay steps away from where we were lashed in a cat's cradle of lines between a 25-foot sloop *Many Moons* and a 31-foot ketch *Filalou*. The American couple on *Many Moons* and the German couple on *Filalou* became our best friends and playmates, sharing gallons of a lovely Greek white wine appropriately called "meltemi" while the real thing beat the sea into a froth all around us.

When the meltemi eventually broke, we all made a dash for Serifos whence, five days later *Ithaca*, said farewell to her four friends and moved on to Kythnos. Like so many of the Cyclades, it is parched, brown, and stitched together with an amazing network of stone walls, some of which run right over cliffs into the sea, and hillsides stepped with stone terraces where nothing sprouts but the odd vacation complex.

Thinking the winds would be manageable we left for Athens early one morning. Had we known that stronger winds than forecast and large rolling seas would make it so uncomfortable, we wouldn't have gone, but then we would still be in Kythnos. A day later we miraculously arrived in the flat calm safety of Zea Marina in Piraeus, with no broken gear or crushed bones. Worried about how smaller boats like *Many Moons* and *Filalou* fared in such heavy weather, we were happy to hear on the radio that night that both the boats and their crews survived with no damage. Sailing Homer's "Wine Dark Sea," we discovered, is not for wimps.

Finding Ithaca

ATHENS WAS A TOUCHSTONE OF YOUTHFUL days for both of us. Michael's mecca was Syntagma Square, a club sandwich, and a bottle of retsina to relive his experiences of thirty years ago, when as a young US Navy pilot stationed on the aircraft carrier *Independence*, he and his squadron mates would spend hours hanging out "watching the girls go by"—or so I'm told. Naturally, it wasn't the same. The resin-flavored white wine wasn't on the menu, the club sandwich was expensive, the flood of outdoor tables with attentive servers had significantly shrunk, and the distinguished, well-dressed Greek waiters morphed into indifferent, tattooed, twenty-somethings. We ordered a couple of lukewarm Heinekens.

After an exhilarating four hours at the Archaeology Museum, we had barely enough strength for the Acropolis. Walking up steep steps and through the Propylaia, we stood in front of the Parthenon, speechless, hand in hand, our heads tilted backward until our necks hurt. Both of us had been in that same spot separately many years before: Michael with his Navy buddies and me on a summer abroad when I was twenty-one. I had been squired around the city by a charming hustler named Tony. Then, the famed Parthenon was completely unhampered by cranes, scaffolding, construction huts, or security. One could wander at will, sit on the marble steps in the late cool evening, play at being in love, and enjoy the view of the city like it was one's own front stoop. Now everybody and everything was considerably older, more complicated, and more crowded, but not necessarily less romantic—beauty and romance largely being in the eyes of the beholder.

"Still majestic but not like I remember it."

"Nothing ever is."

* * * * *

From Athens we sailed south, traversing the Saronic Gulf, stopping at the islands of Poros, Hydra (Ydra), and Spetses. Sailing up the Argolic Gulf between the thumb and forefinger of the Peloponnese, we anchored in the harbor of Nafplion. A major port at the head of the bay since the Bronze Age, it was by turns held by the Venetians, then the Turks, then the Venetians again, and then the Turks again, finally becoming the first capital of Greece after its independence.

The town was charming, but it was nearby Mycenae, the iconic site of Greek myth and epic poetry, that we had come to see. Trudging up a steep ramp to the Lion Gate, famous as a pinnacle of ancient architectural problem solving, we stood beneath its massive lintel, above which huge blocks in successively projecting courses created a "relieving triangle" where two lions sat facing each other on either side of a column that rose from a central altar. We passed under wondering how many generations of humans had walked through before us.

Now we were standing on the site of Agamemnon's palace—he the commander and chief of the Greeks during the Trojan War who was murdered, on this very spot, by his wife and her lover when he returned with his new conquest, the Trojan princess Cassandra. Next we were inside the giant *tholos*, or "beehive tomb," that Agamemnon called the treasure of Atreus. I had seen nineteenth-century engravings of it, but to look up at that vast, conical space and contemplate how it could have been built was on a par with seeing the Egyptian pyramids for the first time.

* * * * *

A day later we were back on the fast track to Ithaca, the home of Odysseus and, for many years, a dream destination. It turned out to be not so fast, however, as we tacked and beat up to the entrance to the three-mile-long Corinth Canal, as dramatic as it is expensive, with a transit fee of nearly $75 a mile. Every Tuesday the canal is closed for repair because the sides are so steep that erosion is a continual problem. As we slowly traversed the narrow channel, we could see the earth being washed away under crumbling bits of bulkhead. We were happy to get through without being sunk by a rock-slide.

The town of Galaxidi, midway through the Bay of Corinth, was a convenient place to stop for the night. A rosy-pink harbor shimmered below a hill of stone houses, tile roofs, blue windows, and a domed, spired church, which crowned the hilltop like the cherry on a sundae of peach ice cream with blue sprinkles.

As usual, the first day was spent with chores, which required every locker to be opened and every surface to be covered with tools. The fridge had to be fixed—again—with a new filter dryer and topped up with Freon. Then, after an hour of troubleshooting, Michael determined that a blue pen stuck in the bilge pump float switch had been causing its malfunction. The mysterious small leak over our bunk, on the other hand, remained mysterious, and the recalcitrant wind/speed instrument had to wait for a flat sea before we could make a safe trip up the mast to repair it.

"Was living in our house this problematic?" I asked Michael as I handed him a beer after the long frustrating day.

"Maybe, but the house won't sink if the sump pump doesn't work."

Needing to get off the boat, we dinghied to town for a walk. The town square was paved with large marble slabs and fringed with outdoor tables where parents could hang out and have a drink while their little kids tooled around on training wheels, boys kicked soccer balls, and preteens huddled together with their cell phones. It made us long for our own family and a warm summer evening on the porch watching the kids chase fireflies. As we meandered back to the dinghy along the quay, crushed with yachts of all types and sizes, *Forty Love* loomed above us, four stories of blazing lights, bright chrome, and loud music. "A wealthy tennis player, perhaps?" I joked. A small boy next to us looked up at this monolith, amazed and a little frightened, as if it were an insurmountable mountain. Michael asked him, "What do you think?" The boy opened his eyes wide, raised his eyebrows, shrugged his shoulders, and walked away.

*Getting ready to leave Galaxidi tomorrow and move on to another
place. It always reminds me of the lyrics from a song in Kiss Me Kate:
"Another opening, another show, from Philly, Boston to Baltimore . . ."
We constantly move from place to place, glimpse lives being lived, observe
characters as if in a play, read in their faces, gestures, and environment
something about their lives, real or imagined, and then move on again.
Like sharing a few words with an interesting person in the intimate space
of an elevator, one can only guess who that person was or what his life was
like. Then the elevator door opens and you both go back out into the stream
of the world, never to see each other again but always wondering what
would have happened if . . .*

*So much of our traveling is like that, because often we can't communicate
beyond a few pleasantries and we are always just passing through. We see
the world through the enclosed bubble of our own experience; delightful as
it often is, it may have nothing to do with reality. It is whatever we choose
to make it mean.*

* * * * *

We arrived in Ithaca on the afternoon of July 17th and anchored in
the commodious harbor of Vathy, surrounded by a long circular quay
lined with neoclassical pale pink and salmon buildings. As the sun set,
the harbor filled with gold, and we were sitting in the pot at the end
of the rainbow, elated to have finally arrived at our long-dreamed-
of destination. Even though our arrival had not gone exactly as we
had always planned, with billowing sails and a brass band, it was
thrilling to have achieved such a significant milestone in our travels.
Disappointingly, the Port Captain was not particularly impressed
with the name of our boat and that we had sailed her three-quarters
of the way around the world to see him. We thought he would at least
buy us a bottle of ouzo. Never anticipate. We polished off a bottle of
champagne in the cockpit—and didn't invite him.

The actual location of Odysseus's palace is controversial, as is
everything having to do with the actual geography reported in the
Odyssey. It has been the game of scholars for centuries, like finding
your way in a hall of mirrors through "glittering seas and shadowy

islands." Some archaeologists speculate the palace was located on Pelikata Hill, near the ancient port of Stavros, because from that hill there is a view of the three bays described by Homer. That was good enough for us.

We tracked down the Fountain of Arethusa where Odysseus's swineherd brought his pigs to drink; visited the "Bay of Dexa," west of Vathy, thought to be ancient Phorkys where the Phaeacians safely delivered Odysseus home; and tramped around the rocks of Pelikata Hill reciting bits of C. F. Cavafy's poem *"Ithaca"* (which he wrote in 1911), imagining Penelope at her perennial loom and feeling like we were Schliemann discovering Troy. We were in Ithaca and we did not "find her poor." But we could not stay for long. Time, tide, and history wait for no man, or two kids in a small boat sailing around the world.

* * * * *

According to the story, Odysseus returned to Ithaca from the land of the Phaeacians, what is now Corfu but known as Scheria in ancient times. He had been instructed by Calypso to build a raft and navigate from Ogygia to Ithaca by the stars. Three days away from home, angry Poseidon sent a horrific storm that destroyed the raft and left Odysseus washed up on the foreign shores of Scheria, where he was found by Nausicaa, King Alcinous's daughter. She, rather smitten, took him to her father's opulent palace of gold doors, bronze walls topped with enamel tiles, and gold and silver dogs standing as sentries—a magnificent palace where the gods themselves would appear during sumptuous feasts. After Odysseus revealed his identity and told his harrowing tale, King Alcinous sent him home to Ithaca in a boat that, with no rudder or oars, steered itself by the thoughts of the crew. "Siri" on steroids? The precursor to the driverless car?

We never found the palace with the gold doors and great food but we did enjoy the scenic delights of Corfu in spite of the nasty smear of cruise ship tourism. The shimmering cliffs and coves, ebullient Venetian architecture, pastel arcades and balconies, picturesquely crumbling cobblestone squares, fountains and shade trees had us enthralled. And then there was the piquant cultural anachronism of a British cricket field in the middle of town, which made us laugh.

In *Prospero's Cell*, Lawrence Durrell describes his bohemian life in the 1930s when he and his wife, Nancy, lived on Corfu in a small fisherman's cottage on the northeast coast they named the "White House." Henry Miller and Theodore Stephanides were regular visitors. Of course, we had to pay tribute to the house on "this brilliant little speck of an island in the Ionian," as Durrell called Corfu, surrounded by "waters like the heartbeat of the world itself." I loved that line and often thought it was an apt description of our very own *Ithaca*.

The Balkans, the Bora, and the B— (rhymes with itch)

F ROM CORFU, WE SAILED NORTHWEST UP THE
Adriatic Sea to Croatia, where we thought we were in
the Balkans, but it felt, looked, and tasted more like Italy.
Not surprisingly, because Venice, at the heady peak of its power
from the sixteenth century to 1797, owned the whole Adriatic
coast. Then along came Napoleon, who vanquished the city-
state and appropriated its possessions, precipitating a political
tug of war with the Austro-Hungarian Empire. The cultural
and religious ramifications rippled into the twentieth century,
spawning a treacherous spirit of nationalism that ultimately
replaced Communism as the dominant force in the Balkans and
culminating in the breakup of Yugoslavia.

Nowhere was this more evident than in the town of Mostar,
Bosnia-Herzegovina, across Croatia's eastern border. Here Bosnian
Croat hostility toward the Bosnian Serbs, who wanted to build a
greater Serbia, spread to their Bosnian Muslim neighbors, whom
they suspected of collusion with the Serbs. The bitter fighting saw
both sides bombing each other's houses, churches, and mosques,
destroying families and the fabric of their centuries-old relationships.
The symbol of their once peaceful coexistence had been a stone
bridge that spanned the steep, rocky sides of the Neretva River for
500 years, connecting the diverse cultures and unifying the city with
an elegant arch. For centuries people came from around to world
to see this bright "graceful ribbon of stone." In 1993 the bridge was
bombed, becoming the most visible and symbolically tragic statistic
of the war. By 1995, Mostar was all but destroyed, its population
dispersed and cultural heart dead.

Yet, something in the human spirit refuses to give up. What took nine years to build in the 1500s took ten years to rebuild in the twentieth century. Tediously, and with exacting attention to the details of the original—both in materials and in process—each pale, ever-changing Tenelija stone block was randomly cut and arduously laid in place, replicating the very imperfections of the old bridge that had been the soul of its beauty. *Stari Most* (Old Bridge) lives again, and, like the bridge, the citizens of Mostar are rebuilding their community, patching together their past with allowances for random imperfections.

When we stood on Stari Most in August 2009, much of the old city had been restored: Ottoman houses on both sides of the river had been turned into restaurants and cafés, the narrow cobblestone streets were lined with tourist shops, and couples posed for photographs on the "new" Old Bridge, while bombed-out buildings and charred houses still hovered in the shadows.

Memories of war are still evident in Dubrovnik as well. Croatia's capital city, deemed "the pearl of the Adriatic" by Lord Byron, was mercilessly bombed by the Yugoslav army in 1991 during a yearlong siege. As testimony to the massive destruction, a few pale, rust-and-moss-covered roofs in the rippled sea of new terra cotta tiles stand out like stains on an otherwise clean orange quilt spread out below the encircling city walls. Tourists now stroll by a small museum that dramatically depicts the bombing of the city.

In the world of *Ithaca*, however, anchored up the Ombla River just north of Dubrovnik in a shallow, protected spot surrounded by bulrushes and kept company by ducks and swans, bombs and smoke were hard to imagine. Downriver a cluster of Venetian villas were mirrored in the river like the background in an Italian Renaissance painting. A nearby village, accessible by dinghy, provided access to all our necessities, including a bus to the main gate of the Old Town and the branches of a large abundantly fruiting fig tree hanging conveniently over a low garden wall, which I plundered ruthlessly in spite of Michael's frowning disapproval.

While leaving Dubrovnik and our hidden river idyll was hard, the rest of the Dalmatian coast beckoned us with her necklace of fairytale islands, Roman ruins, medieval cities, unspoiled offshore islands, fishing ports, and sunny beaches—in what the guidebook calls a "matchless combination of hedonism and history." We enjoyed both.

* * * * *

Sailing up the island chain the wind was fickle and the anchorages often crowded. At each stop, however, we were rewarded with glorious sites, great stories, and another name for "big wind": the bora, so-called because it bored down on you out of the blue with 35 to 40 knots. This kept us in the "safe harbor" of Muline on the island of Molat for several days. When the bora dissipated, we moved on to Ilovik, where we picked up a mooring ball under a crumbling tower house next to our buddies Bill and Sam on the *Blue Banana*, whom we hadn't seen for several months. Joined by other cruising friends the next day, we kept the party going until it was time once more to go our separate ways, the BBs south and us north to Rab and Krk at the end of the island chain not far from Trieste as the crow flies. Here, the bora really bore down.

Held off a cement quay by thick mooring lines tied to pilings off the stern, we thought we were secure enough to go to town. But, on our return, it was clear we were not. In spite of the very taut lines, the wind had pushed the boat forward and the bowsprit was now precariously poised two inches over the stone bulkhead, and the tide was going out. Straining every muscle, we were finally able to inch back on the stern lines and pull the boat off the quay with the help of a young Austrian yachtie. Then we lent our quivering arms to his little sloop. Afterward he marveled at the strength of two "old people" and thanked us with a huge Austrian sausage.

In the midst of our struggle, a towering gray motor yacht approached the quay, its Italian crew yelling different instructions to each other and haphazardly heaving lines toward the pier, which was now lined with gawkers who, the night before, had been thinking "Gee, I wish I could live on a boat and sail around the world." Now they were thinking, "Are these people nuts?"

Eventually, the wind settled down and we headed south again to our favorite anchorage upriver in Dubrovnik and on to Montenegro.

* * * * *

Kotor, at the end of a long fjord in Montenegro, was the scene of another drama, more like something out of B-grade movie. Finding a spot to tie up near the Customs dock was our first challenge. Then Michael went ashore to check in while I fended us off the ugly black rubber pier fenders. Laughingly he returned to retrieve his "proficiency license," hoping his US Navy ID would be more convincing than was, apparently, the fact that we had sailed more than halfway around the world and not sunk yet.

After what seemed like hours, he finally emerged from the clutch of little cement houses, limping slightly with a bleeding toe. As it happened, the 6-foot-tall Montenegrin Customs "dominatrix," wearing tight black pants and a blouse three sizes too small, had crushed Michael's foot with a chair after ordering him to "sit" and "remove" something (he was never quite sure what). By the time we finally got tied up to the town quay, assisted by a grumpy, young, bushy-haired *marinaro*, who clearly thought his job was beneath him, we were panting for some stiff "grin and bear-its."

* * * * *

From Montenegro's coastline, we retraced our route to Corfu. Then it was October 6th and we were "flying" under the Rio Bridge that separates the Gulf of Patras from the Bay of Corinth, with 15 knots behind us and the genoa billowing. During a brief stop in Galaxidi, we visited the "Oracle at Delphi," who neglected to predict our near-death experience on the coast east of Galaxidi the next day.

I was below making sandwiches and Michael was behind the wheel doing Sudoku puzzles. The sea was flat, steely gray in the afternoon glare. The engine hummed steadily as the shoreline to port reeled by. I came up with lunch, looked forward, dropped the tray, and screamed. We were just a few yards away from ramming a cliff. Michael immediately got control of the helm and brought us back on course. We couldn't speak. We could barely breathe our hearts were beating so violently. A minute more and we would have been, hopefully, hard aground before we hit the cliff. I yelled, "What were you thinking?" I was so mad and yet I knew it really wasn't his fault.

Recently Dave had been randomly shutting off (no one knew why), leaving *Ithaca* helmless and wandering until one of us would discover that we were off course. When we were sailing with enough wind to keep her pointed up or in the middle of the ocean, it wasn't a big problem, but motoring close to shore or in a confined area could be suicide. The real problem was that the alarm was not loud enough to hear over the engine noise. We should have replaced the alarm in the last port when we had the chance, but we both forgot, but of course, in my mind it was Michael's fault. I was mad that we had not fixed the problem before this and now he was doing Sudokus, and not paying attention. I grumped around for hours but knew it could have just as easily happened to me with my head in a book.

I apologized for yelling, the storm passed, and we carried on to Athens where we tied up in Zea Marina to re-provision. But, before we bought beer or food, we bought a new alarm that was so loud sailors in South America could hear it!

Several days later we were gliding by the cliffs of Cape Sounion south of Athens on the southern tip the Attica peninsula, where the columns of Poseidon's temple blazed fiery in the sunset. Not unaware of its significance in Greek history and myth, we dribbled a few drops of ouzo on the velvety water following the cue of ancient sailors who performed sacrifices at the temple to assuage Poseidon's wrath at sea.

Here, too, Homer tells us, King Menelaus of Sparta buried his helmsman who died at his post while rounding the cape. It was here as well that King Aegeus plunged to his death upon seeing black sails advancing on the horizon instead of white, leading him to believe his son Theseus had been killed by the Minotaur. Thus, these waters came to be named the Aegean.

Zigzagging back across an unusually tranquil Aegean, we could have navigated by the stars, the mast in line with a vertical Orion's belt most nights. Looking up at all the constellations one could understand why the ancients felt the gods and goddesses to be so real in their lives.

By October 25, 2009, we were back in Marmaris preparing for our yearly trip home. I wrote in the log: "Big relief to be out of the Aegean, tied up in Yacht Marine after 3,000 miles this year and 653 hours on the engine—a lot of diesel fuel."

Six months later, in April 2010, we were sailing to Crete.

Crete

APRIL 28, 2010, AGIOS NIKOLAOS MARINA, CRETE.
Only three weeks ago we were sitting on our porch in Annapolis, reluctant to leave our lovely home and family. Finally, we had rewoven ourselves back into the intimacies of normal family life. Grandkids tendered spontaneous hugs rather than shy smiles, boat rides with Danny, lunches with Pete, the old family jokes and camaraderie, the trials of growing children, busy jobs, and young marriages—how their lives have changed. Time is going by so fast. We miss so much.

Saying good-bye to all our old friends at the Marmaris Marina for the last time was a killer, especially to Bill and Sam. I'm not sure when we will see them again.

It's weird to think that we won't be coming back to a place that has been home base for the last three years. I reached up and hugged Bill who said, "See ya, Lady M" with a slight hitch in his voice. Then I hugged Sam. "Good Luck, Kiddo." Another trip home for "scans" has us all worried. God, she is a brave lady. This good-bye stuff is for the birds.

But now, secure and out of the weather, we are exhilarated by the idea of a new place to explore: Crete, land of myth and the famed Minotaur.

* * * * *

"Out on the dark blue sea there lies a rich and lovely land called Crete that is densely populated and boasts 90 cities. One of the 90 cities is called Knossos and there for nine years King Minos ruled and enjoyed the friendship of the mighty . . ." (from Homer's *The Odyssey*).

Myth has it that King Minos, son of Zeus and Europa, attained the throne of Knossos with the help of Poseidon. From there he ruled the whole Aegean basin, colonized many islands, and rid the area of pirates. He married Pasiphae, the daughter of Helios, who bore him numerous children, including the infamous half bull/half human Minotaur, whom Theseus fought in the labyrinth, and ultimately escaped by following Adriane's ball of string.

Archaeology tells us that the Minoans had inhabited Crete since 6500 B.C., when primitive Neolithic people lived in caves and wooden houses, worshipped female fertility goddesses, raised livestock, and made simple pottery. By 2000 B.C. to 1450 B.C., they were living in grand palaces when the rest of Europe was still in primitive huts.

Over the centuries, Crete has been washed with waves of immigrants from North Africa and the Levant, Mesopotamia, and Egypt. Mycenaeans, Romans, Arabs, Venetians, and Turks all left their calling cards on Crete's doorstep. In 1830, it was given to Egypt; in 1913, it was officially united with Greece; and after finally repulsing the Germans in World War II, it suffered the brutal effects of civil war between 1946 and 1949.

Inevitably the modern world caught up with Crete, and over the past thirty years a plethora of hip bars, restaurants, and cement high-rises have sprouted along the northern coast. But Cretan culture remains resilient. Fiercely proud, independent, clannish, and unique, the citizens of Crete cling to their old traditions with dignity and pride. Cretans still play their traditional instruments, dance the slow syrto and pendozali, and compose *mantinadas* (traditional rhyming couplets). Life in the old stone villages of the mountains and high plateaus maintains its slow pace. Men still gather in the *kafeneios*, drink coffee or raki, occasionally firing off a round of gunshot to emphasis a point—though everyone knows that the Cretan women still wield the real firepower. An altercation between womenfolk in the market or town square is a fearful thing to witness.

The Palace of Knossos, the capital of Minoan Crete, is the crown jewel of the island, despite the acknowledged "heavy-handed reconstruction" by British archaeologist Sir Arthur Evans who uncovered the site in the 1900s. Situated on a hill surrounded by pine trees, the original palace was destroyed after a horrific earthquake and rebuilt in 1700 B.C. The "new" multi-storied complex was much more elaborate than the original palace had been. Storerooms, workshops, living quarters, grand halls, and royal apartments (are so maze-like they reminded me of China's Forbidden City) more than justify the myth of Theseus in the labyrinth. Remnants of a sophisticated water system and flush toilets are still visible.

Regrettably, much of the site is now off-limits to tourists. There are minimal explanatory plaques and a disfiguring boardwalk now snakes over the ancient walls. Nevertheless, the vibrancy of the frescos, a technique the Minoans learned from the Egyptians but brought to a much more fully human and seductive level, are unequivocally beautiful. A young man vaults over a bull's horns, forever suspended in that moment; so graceful, one forgives the violent reality of the ritual. Two dolphins cavort across a blue sea in a bedroom. A group of women sit gossiping, their elaborately coiffed black curls draping over their bare breasts. Suddenly two gruff, fat Greek matrons yelled at us, unceremoniously breaking the spell and herding us out the gate like dumb animals. The site was supposed to stay open until 7:00, but it closed at 3:00 due to budget cuts.

Peloponnesian Scenes

AS WE BROKE AWAY FROM THE COAST OF CRETE, fog dogged us into the night. We could hear ships talking on the radio but couldn't see a thing. A blip on the radar would give an approximate location, but a ship's heading is problematic if you can't see its running lights. It was a nervous night. Thankfully the fog cleared the following day and we motored/sailed the rest of the way to Kalamata, in Messina, on the southwest corner of the Peloponnese.

Our first excursion was to Olympia, home to the original Olympics until 394 A.D., when Theodosius II banned them as being too pagan. Until that time, every four years the warring states would halt their hostilities to engage in various sporting competitions, supported by wealthy corporate sponsors, which often resulted in great fame and fortune for the victors. Not unlike our modern world of sports. It is doubtful, however, that our contemporary sporting competitions will leave behind such extraordinary works of art as the fourth-century Hermes by Praxiteles, the beautiful Nike of Paionias, or the pediments and metopes from the temple of Zeus that are reassembled in the attendant Archaeological Museum. Walking under the arched entrance Michael observed, "Just think how many centuries of sports lovers have walked along this path."

Our second excursion took us to the Byzantine city of Mystras, which now ironically looks down from surrounding hills across a valley of olive trees to an ordinary town of cement apartment buildings called Sparta. Mystras was the heart of Byzantine spiritual life for a thousand years after the fall of Constantinople until the Ottoman army invaded in 1460. Likewise, Mystras was once the center of humanistic philosophy and the zenith of late Byzantine art. Now, only shadowy nuns drift through the perfectly proportioned convent of Pantanassa and disappear behind the richly colored fifteenth-century frescoes, many of which languish in low light and remain marred by dark spots of mold and peeling plaster.

A stunning exception is in the Monastery of Perivieptos where Christ the Pantokrator, surrounded by apostles, looks down from the high gold dome with cool, detached intensity. In his book *Mani: Travels in the Southern Peloponnese*, Patrick Fermor describes it this way: "He floats in an atmosphere which is still and spellbound and, if a presiding mood can be identified, it is one of faint, indefinable and glorious melancholia, like the thought of space . . . All trace of apostrophe is lacking; there is no attempt to buttonhole the observer. Western Christs expose their wounds; Eastern Christs sit enthroned in ungesticulating splendor."

No better explanation of the difference between Byzantine and Western Christian art has ever been written.

* * * * *

In the Mani, an area in the central peninsula of the southern Peloponnese, we found yet again a different kind of landscape where barren, rocky mountains plunged down to toy fishing villages, isolated coves and clusters of stone towers stuck up out of the bleak hillside like gnarled fingers. Remote and desolate, it was to the Mani that the wild and rugged descendants of Sparta withdrew rather than succumb to a foreign power. From the seventeenth century on they lived in clans whose feuding was so constant and fierce that the dominant domestic architecture was a defensive tower, many of which remain amid the crumbling clusters of abandoned villages or as lonely sentinels staring out to sea.

Later, in flight from the Turks after the fall of Candia and the final defeat of the Venetians, refugees from Crete settled in the Mani. Bits of Cretan dialect can still be heard in the Maniots' speech and observed in the fiery independence of their personalities. Not surprisingly, the word "Maniot" comes from the Greek word "maniac." Our brief sojourn through the Mani, however, was very benign. No maniacs, just some friendly old people and a shy little dog.

May 16, 2010, Monemvasia, Greece

Just arrived at the Malvasia Hotel after a long eventful drive, feeling lucky to have snagged the last room, but that is the kind of day it has been ever since this morning when we stopped in Kalamata to get some money. As we got back in the car, a young, swarthy Greek fellow appeared and told us in disjointed English that he needed 20 Euros to get home to see his sick mother. "Right, of course you do," we shot a glance at each other and pulled out of the parking lot. A minute later we stopped. "What's wrong with us?" "Supposing it's really true?"

We looked back down the road and saw him, head bent, feet shuffling in the dust. M stopped the car. I jumped out and pressed the 20 Euros into his hand with a "you'd better not be shitting me" look. He was stunned, bowed, smiled a broad, white toothy grin, and was still saying "Efharisto" when I got back in the car. We agreed that whether it was true or not was not our problem. Then wonderful little things started to happen and we laughed about "good Karma."

* * * * *

Around lunchtime we stopped in a little store to buy cheese and salami but there was no bread. We drove and drove over the parched, windy road and through dusty town after dusty town but no bakery, until finally we saw a small handwritten sign that said "mini mart" on what looked like an abandoned house. We stopped, tried the door. It squeaked open to reveal a disappointing number of empty shelves. Two old women and a man were sitting around a table. Reading from our Greek phrase book, Michael managed to communicate that we needed bread. The oldest of the two bent-over old ladies got up on her crutches (the man, of course, didn't move) and hobbled over to a pantry where she pulled out a beautiful loaf of country bread. We smiled and applauded. She grinned. We bought a couple of cold beers and said, "Efharisto." They said, "Efharisto." We waved and smiled. They waved and smiled. Everyone burst out laughing as we banged the door closed and crunched over the gravel driveway.

Down the road we found a little rocky cove and a small shuttered beach-like restaurant with a few old battered tables and chairs on a cracked cement pier next to the water. A perfect place for a picnic:

for Michael, who hates sitting on the ground and will drive until dinnertime to find a picnic table for lunch, and for me there was a winsome puppy who sat demurely with us while we had lunch and modestly accepted a crust of bread in gratitude when we left. Then we got to Monemvasia and found a perfect parking spot right next to the causeway.

We ended the eventful day with dinner on a stone terrace, under a grape arbor surrounded by blooming geraniums, and watched night close over the turbulent sea, praying that our good karma would follow us all the way to Sicily.

Sicily, Scylla, and Charybdis

WHEN WE LEFT THE MARINA AT KALAMATA, Thursday morning about 8:30, it was calm and clear. That afternoon around 3:00, we reached the tip of the peninsula and the picturesque little Bay of Methoni. By then it was overcast and large rollers outside the seawall were stirring up a swell in the anchorage. We rolled around all night but, after checking the weather the next morning, I persuaded Michael that the wind would go down and it would be a fast, mellow passage to Syracuse, Sicily once the initial weather passed through. I was wrong, but he was gentlemanly enough not to remind me.

As we left the harbor, large rollers continued to build under dense gray clouds. First the wind was out of the south, then the north. Then the wind increased to between 18 and 23 knots and shifted to the northwest and west, forcing us to fall off course more and more, until we were heading toward Africa, and further away from Syracuse with each hour. We were not having fun. So much for "good karma." Gradually the sea moderated but the erratic wind kept us motor sailing. A large ship threatened to run us down. We were on edge. It was hard to sleep.

At 5:30 a.m. Dave (our electronic autopilot, you might recall) gave up the ghost. Michael woke me up and I took the helm while he did a preliminary investigation. Finding no immediate fix, he hooked up the wind vane steerer. He was able to hook up the wind vane steerer

May 23, 2010, 65 nm west of Syracuse, Sicily

The wind is predicted to die today. Hopefully that won't happen as "Hans" needs wind to work. It is a beautiful morning, however, and for the moment the boat is moving along at a comfortable pace, although we have

*to keep the engine on to keep up some speed and we really have to "pinch it"
to not lose ground entirely and go backward.*

*Worst of all, our French press coffeemaker has died. So we must ration the
little bit of Nescafé we have until we get to port. We are already on water
rations since the water maker membrane "packed up" weeks ago. My hair
is stiff as a board with salt. All my fingernails are broken and my body is
covered with bruises.*

*Sometimes this cruising lifestyle is more like an Outward Bound survival
course—definitely a test of one's stamina, patience, sense of humor, and ingenuity.*

* * * * *

When we dropped anchor in Syracuse harbor at 2:00 p.m.,
Wednesday, May 25th, we were officially in Italy—sort of. Kudos
and kisses to Hans, who bore the brunt of helmsmanship the prior
twenty-four hours. Only when the wind died five hours out from
landfall did we have to hand steer. As we entered the harbor, Sam
and Bill on board *Blue Banana* and Phil and Janie on board *TSolo*
shouted and blew kisses, and I was in the shower as soon as the
anchor broke the surface of Italian waters. Sometimes a simple hair
wash with meager water, in a tiny, rolling head is the most luxurious
experience in the world.

Phil and Janie, whom we hadn't seen in two years, dinghied over
with Italian wine, bread, local tomatoes and fresh mozzarella floating
in olive oil and basil—the next most luxurious thing in the world.
Later we all went into town to check out the street market, which was
like being dropped into a movie set. Vendors sang and yelled out their
wares to the accompaniment of concertina music. Lines of stalls were
heaped with fruits and veggies, greens, fish, and cheeses of every kind.
We stopped at one vendor, a favorite of our group, who greeted us
like long-lost cousins. Soon big slabs of bread with different samples
of cheese, sun-dried tomatoes, and olives were being passed around
and a large plastic cup of red wine put in my hand. This was my kind
of shopping. Which was reenacted at almost every stall. By 11:00 we
were all ready for a nap. Ahhh . . . Italy.

The next day we had to get serious about fixing our autopilot,
finding a new water maker membrane, and sourcing out a store to

solve Michael's computer glitches. Top on my list, however, was finding a laundry and a new French press. In my wanderings around town, I passed a small appliance store. Surely they would have a French press.

When I enquired in my rusty Italian, the shop owner looked at me, raised his eyebrow in amazement, and pointed out that I was *in Italy*. Why would I ever want a French press? Behind him I saw shelves lined with traditional sturdy, metal Italian espresso pots that I remembered using years ago. We both laughed and suddenly we were best friends and confidants. I said I had to go next door to the barbershop to get some money from my husband. The store owner laughed and said something like, "The woman shops, the man pays." What might have been a sexist remark was said in such a charming, flirtatious Italian way, I couldn't be offended.

May 31, 2010, Syracuse, Sicily

Life continues its delightful pace here. Every day I remember a little more Italian or learn new words and phrases as we struggle through communicating with electronics people, marina people, laundry ladies, and shop vendors. The only problem is that the anchorage is very dodgy when the wind comes out of the south and the marina is completely out of our budget.

* * * * *

Friday we went into town to do some shopping and got a call from the BBs that our boat was dragging! Several other boats in the anchorage had dragged, but we felt sure that we had a good "set" and more than enough chain out. Breathless with panic we ran back to the dinghy landing and powered full throttle into the soaking chop. Sam was at the helm while Bill grabbed our painter (dinghy bowline) and calmly reassured us that they had come aboard, put the engine in gear, and were holding *Ithaca* in place until we were able to return. Once more we thanked God for guardian angels who—in this case—doubled as best friends.

* * * * *

The passage up the coast to Messina and along the north coast of Sicily is historically treacherous. It was said to be here that Odysseus met

Scylla, the six-headed monster, who when ships passed, swallowed a sailor for each head, and Charybdis, the enormous ship-swallowing whirlpool. We should have heeded such warnings. The notorious Strait of Messina would not disappoint.

When we left the marina at Taormina, it looked as though we might have a fairly benign passage, with a few whitecaps and a 10-knot breeze from the south. As we passed Messina, however, things got more interesting, with ferries going back and forth and large ships rounding the narrow neck at the top of the channel. Whirlpools and crazy currents pushed us off course, and an increasing wind of 15 to 20 and then 25 knots compounded the navigational issues: steerage was exceedingly difficult; plus, we could do only 3 knots against the adverse current.

As we approached the head of the strait, marked by a big red tower, we thought we were home free. But, just as we thought we were saying good-bye to Scylla and Charybdis, the wind increased violently as we headed west along the coast toward the Aeolian Islands. Soon we were looking at 35–40 knots out of the south. In an attempt to get closer to shore and in the lee of land—where we would find calmer waters—we headed up and heeled over more. Then the inflatable dinghy flipped over and one line on the dinghy bridle separated. The other end of the bridle was still tied on. We prayed. When we got closer to shore, we raised the main to the first reef, which added speed, but also instability. The boat was harder to control, putting more stress on the dinghy, which snapped the other line, and it departed into a sea of raging whitecaps.

"I told you we should have replaced that line," I yelled over the cacophony of wind and sea.

"Don't worry about that now. The question is do we go back for it or buy a new one in Rome?

"Well, the problem is the outboard is too heavy for the sailing dinghy, so we would have to row everywhere in the meantime and, buying a new dingy in Rome?" I grimaced and rubbed my fingers together in the universal sign of "pricey."

"Okay. But if we don't find it in an hour, it's gone."

After dropping the main sail and securing it in the howling wind, we turned back into the pounding waves and wind, barely making 3 knots, as we stared into the sun's glare and scanned the waves with salt encrusted binoculars. After forty-five minutes, Michael was just about to give up, when I screamed: "I see it. Just off to starboard, bobbing in between the swells and whitecaps."

Finding it was one thing, retrieving it was another. Eventually we were able to maneuver into a downwind position so it would blow down on us, being very careful to avoid getting the lines tangled in our prop. On the first pass, the aluminum boat hook broke under pressure when I used it to hold onto the dinghy, which was bucking and banging against the hull. On the second pass I leaned over the side and grabbed the stern line, wrapped it around a cleat, then grabbed one bridle line, and attached that to the mid ships cleat. Now we had the dinghy secured, but we still had to fashion a new bridle.

We took an old halyard and cut it into two long bits to tie to the towing ring. Then I leaned over the side, held the dinghy up with one hand and somehow tied a bowline through the tow ring on the dinghy with the other hand, while Michael's hands were completely occupied just trying to steer the boat. Once the bridle was safely secured to port and starboard aft cleats, our ancient but ever enduing "rubber ducky" streamed back into the following seas as if its wild walkabout had never happened. Continuing on our way, we were once again amazed that we had survived another Odyssey test.

Gradually the wind went down until we were motoring along the northern coast of Sicily where that night, in a noisy but calm anchorage, we celebrated with a special libation in a ritual of thanks. Many, in fact.

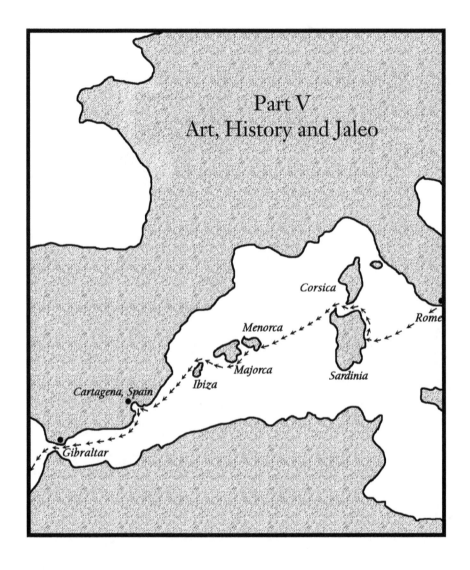

Part V
Art, History and Jaleo

Corsica

Rome

Menorca

Majorca

Sardinia

Ibiza

Cartagena, Spain

Gibraltar

"See Rome and Die"

I HAVE ALWAYS BELIEVED THAT I WAS CATHERINE de Medici in another life. Not an original thought I'm sure, but the fact is, from the first time I ventured onto Italian soil forty years ago, there is no other place where I've felt such a powerful sense of identification—and I'm not even Italian.

After the inevitable questions about pirates and terrible storms, people always ask us what our favorite place was. I have to confess that, while I was entranced by the exoticism of Southeast Asia, the stunning landscapes and outdoor adventures of New Zealand, the pristine palm-fringed islands of the Pacific, and the blazing ancient ruins of Greece and Turkey, I still love Italy the most—its language, its food, its art, its operatic history, its enduring architecture, its stylish and passionate people.

> *"The young men in the Piazza del Popolo*
> *are so fair it is easy to believe that the*
> *breeze that ruffles their hair was made*
> *only to complete them. Their existence*
> *argues for a moment of sweetness before*
> *we turn to dust."*

—From *Italian Days* by Barbara Grizzuti Harrison

That moment of sweetness comes back to me like a welcoming friend when I remember our travels in Italy. But the road to Rome was not easy.

From Vulcano in the Aeolian Islands, we sailed north-northwest to Agropoli, on the Gulf of Salerno. An overnight across the gulf brought us to Capri where, rolling and pitching under Tiberius's cliff-top summer villa, we would have rather been with the tourists on Tiberius's balcony looking down, but we were on the fast track to Rome to meet up with family. The following day, it was back to the mainland—stopping in Gaeta, Formia, and anchoring under Mount Circeo, thought to have once been the island Aiaia where the witch/goddess Circe entranced Odysseus for a year and turned his men into pigs. Now an inconsequential hill, with a full moon rising through an encircling mist, it looked decisively sinister. We were off for Rome early the next morning, destination Fiumicino, just north of Ostia.

Until 42 A.D., the city of Ostia at the mouth of the Tiber River functioned as the port for Rome. Precariously vulnerable to strong winds, tides, and silting, it gradually proved inadequate, motivating Emperor Claudius to construct a new artificial harbor into the Tyrrhenian Sea, about four and a half miles north of Ostia. Two long, curving moles embraced the new harbor like crab claws, and a canal was dug to connect it to the Tiber, facilitating navigation to Rome. In 100 AD, when this harbor proved untenable, the Roman Emperor Trajan excavated a large basin inland and built the Fiumicino canal to connect it to the sea. Over the centuries, much of the coast filled with silt. Now Ostia's and Claudius's monumental harbor are inland archaeological sites. The airport at Fiumicino butts up against the remains of Trajan's basin, and the fishing village of Fiumicino sits astride the still functioning canal.

Up this canal, at the Cantiere Nautico Albula, owned and operated by Max and his partner Enrico, *Ithaca* and her crew would find new friends and a congenial home during a year designated for cultural immersion in all things Italian. But first we had to get there.

Nothing much had changed in the way of navigational challenges since Roman times. Breaking waves across the channel, a strong opposing tide, and random debris in the water still plagued the returning seafarer. In addition, now there was a railroad bridge, a car bridge, and a pedestrian bridge, plus a barrage of navigational hazards, including a large Italian fishing fleet, commercial craft, barges, and one very nervous movie maker.

* * * * *

As we approached the coast, the wind moved to the east, on our nose, and we were motoring into 10 to 15 knots with choppy seas that slowed us down to 3 to 4 knots. At the canal entrance, the wind direction and speed changed again with a vengeance. Now it was blowing 15–20 on the stern. Not good. A wind-against-current situation in the canal would make steerage difficult. Saying a prayer, we surfed into the canal on a breaking wave, only to face what looked like the whole Italian fishing fleet double-parked on both sides of the canal. That, together with a maelstrom of oncoming current, made maneuvering extremely precarious.

It was imperative that we find a place to tie up where we could wait for the eight o'clock bridge openings that evening. It was two in the afternoon. A large sailboat was tied along the quay to starboard, just in front of the pedestrian bridge. We would have to raft up. We approached slowly, yelling that we were coming alongside. There was no response. The people aboard had their backs to us. We yelled louder. No response. We yelled again, more frantically, inching forward. A man on the quay yelled back that they were filming a movie and would be finished in a few minutes. Could we come back later? What? Was he nuts? With the current pushing us downstream, breaking swells to stern, a bridge just off the bow, and no space in which to turn around because a very large fishing boat was off our port beam? Come back later?! Was he crazy?! He clearly WAS a movie maker, not a sailor.

Our only choice was to back down sideways in the current until we could find a place to turn the boat around, go back out of the canal, and surf in again. Upon our return, the movie maker's sailboat was leaving, so we could take their empty spot, but it was not easy. Michael had to maneuver *Ithaca* into the space and hold her there, close enough so I could scramble onto the high cement wall and quickly tie the bow and stern lines to the nearest bollards before the wind pushed us up into the fishing boat in front of us or the current pushed us into the boat behind us—with *Ithaca* bucking like an angry bull all the while. Much to our surprise, it went flawlessly. We went below to congratulate ourselves, unwind, and have a sandwich before it was "show time" again.

Suddenly, a man in brown coveralls yelled at us from the pier. We had to move because a barge was coming. Move where? There was no place to move to! The cruising guide had said it was all right to tie up here and wait for the bridge opening. Michael tried to explain, but the man only understood that we did not intend to move. He went away. More men came. More yelling. Now Michael really "lit his hair on fire," which didn't help communication. "Our engine is too small, the waves too big, and the current is too strong." he explained, gesticulating with his hands like a native. More men came. More yelling. They wanted to take our lines and tie us to the fishing boat on our bow while the barge tied up where we were. Then they would move us back along the side of the barge. It was all a little confusing, half-English, half-Italian, but we had no choice.

The men took our lines. We started the engine and gingerly positioned *Ithaca* alongside the fishing boat without severing our shrouds on its superstructure. The barge positioned itself on the quay. Big black tires lined its gunwales. We pointed to the tires. The men on the barge took them in and we slid back alongside, but the rub rail was also black rubber and bulged out just above our toe rail. So the fenders rode up and down, rolled sideways, squished, squeaked, and got coated with black oily tar as we bounced, bumped, and slid against it. There was nothing to do but watch with dismay as the fenders rubbed black gunk against *Ithaca*'s pristine white hull.

We had about two hours until the bridges opened. It was getting darker and darker, almost impossible to see. All our friendly helpers had long ago vanished into the town. We doubled up the cat's cradle of lines holding us to the barge and waited. As eight o'clock approached, a large powerboat came up the canal and hovered off our port quarter. Then two sailboats motored up the canal into position. Timing was critical. The pedestrian bridge opened. We motioned to the powerboat to go ahead. The sailboats hung back while we took in our lines. The stern line snagged but finally broke free. The current pushed the bow out and we motored under the bridge with no drama.

Now I had to hustle to remove the fenders from the starboard rail, cut off the oily covers, and place them on the port rail, change the mooring lines to port, and move the dinghy to stern in the seven minutes and one more bridge it took us to get to Max's marina. Suddenly a huge catamaran came straight toward us under the car bridge. Michael hugged the stone quay to starboard. It was dark. We couldn't see the marina. Finally, we saw a man standing on a catamaran gesturing with his flashlight to come alongside. Then we heard his voice calmly coaching us into position as our now nude fenders nudged the cat's big white sides. Max and Enrico took our lines and secured the bow two inches behind an inflatable dinghy on the stern of another large cat, while the stern glided in just over a small sailboat snugged under our wind vane steerer. Whew. Engine off. Quiet.

We collapsed in the cockpit, stunned that we were finally there. Tension rolled off us in puddles onto the deck.

"I'm too tired to eat."

"Me too."

"Well, it wasn't THAT bad."

"Right." Michael looked at me as if I were speaking Chinese.

During the next year we made several trips up and down that canal; each was always a challenge—but never "that bad" and always well worth it to be in my favorite place in the world.

*   *   *   *   *

Soon thereafter son Pete and family stopped in Rome for a few days and we did the whirlwind tour, swept along in a river of bodies through the Vatican, the Sistine Chapel, and Saint Peter's Basilica, amazed that St. Peter himself is buried in the bowels of the church directly under the dome where only the pope can say Mass. With the exception of the Coliseum, where they could imagine bloody images of gladiators doing battle with lions, the grandkids, now ages fourteen, eleven, and nine, were not quite as involved as I might have fantasized they'd be.

How could they really comprehend the significance of Michelangelo's *Pietà*, which was for me the high point of that weekend? Christ's body both unbearably heavy and limp, lying like a rag across Mary's lap, her open hands simultaneously accepting and rejecting what she is seeing, her young face suffused with faith. The dichotomy of human pain and spiritual love so perfectly expressed make it a miraculous work of art, especially when you learn that Michelangelo was merely twenty-four years old when he sculpted it. At the time I had no idea how often I would call up that image as a touchstone for personal strength. I stood transfixed until someone pulled my sleeve and said: "Come on, Mertis, let's go get lunch."

A few weeks later Bill and Sam joined us in the marina on their way up the coast. Summertime crowds clogged the steaming sidewalks. Sweating people were packed under the giant dome of the Pantheon. In the Piazza Navona, the river gods of Bernini's Fontana di Quattro Fumi struggled to keep their heads above the swirling sea of tourists, and the Trevi Fountain was so swarmed you could barely see it much less throw in a coin. But Sam was determined, vaguely remembering Frank Sinatra singing "Three Coins in the Fountain," which won the Academy Award for Best Original Song in the movie of the same name in 1955—when she couldn't have been more than a preschooler.

We slurped melting gelatos and waited until a large tour group moved on. I snapped a photo just as Sam threw her coin under Neptune's chariot, guaranteeing a return to Rome. A space cleared and we all threw in our coins, wishing the same thing: that Sam would return to Rome many times. Then we were off for lunch, laughs, and copious amounts of cold white wine.

* * * * *

The rest of the summer Michael and I worked on the boat and got to know our new "home town." Riding our bikes along the canal in the morning and watching the fishing boats come in and off-load their catch while everyone crowded around to buy the freshest and best of what lay spilled out on the pier. Every couple of days Michael rode into town to visit his petite, blonde girlfriend who ran the "Sfuso" shop where she sold local wine out of large aluminum vats and always offered him extra samples before he filled our empty bottles with his choice du jour. How he rode home without crashing his bike is a tribute to fighter pilot determination. And, there was always boat work: installing a new water maker part that Pete had brought from West Marine in Annapolis; trouble-shooting the recalcitrant autopilot, which turned out just to need a new fuse; plus handling numerous other minor and major fix-its while I sanded and varnished, sanded and varnished, sanded and varnished until my fingernails were just a memory.

The reward was ROME. When we weren't working on the boat, Rome was an hour and a half away by public transportation, a fabulous playground we could absorb at will. Magnificent churches, palaces, museums; bookstalls, parks, art galleries, and sidewalk cafés. Often we would make the early Sunday morning trek to Santa Susanna, the American Catholic church in Rome where Mass has been celebrated for 1,700 years. After Mass, we walked along the Tiber under the golden arch of plane trees, which formed a tunnel of fall leaves and through which we could see the Palace of Justice across the river at the end of the Ponte Umberto. Then we would head to the Piazza Navona for lunch, which was always crowded with clowns, magicians, artists, and musicians. It was like one big county fair: people strolling about, eating ice cream cones, taking pictures, walking their dogs; kids playing in the water of Bernini's great Fontana di Quattro Fumi while Saint Agnese in Agone, designed by Bernini's rival Borromini, loomed silently in the background.

The trip back to the boat was another kind of adventure—a forty-minute ride on the metro, then a train to Ostia, and a twenty-minute bus ride back to Fiumicino. Saturday was always particularly crowded with shoppers around the central Termini metro stop. One Saturday it seemed as if all the public transportation was full of young lovers, fondling each other, kissing, or saying passionate farewells. Maybe it was Italian Valentine's Day. A dark-suited old man, who was seated across from such a couple near us on the metro, was clearly mortified by such a public display and kept trying to look everywhere except in their direction. When the seat across from us became vacant, he moved. Laughing, he told us he was eighty and too old for such goings-on. Then he launched into a whole discourse in rapid Italian.

I could understand some of it and responded as well as I could, but at one point I had to confess that I just didn't speak Italian very well. That did not slow him down as he proceeded to tell us about his wife, who was an invalid, his girlfriend who lived in Rome, and some friend who had a big house in Fiumicino. All this was accompanied by much gesturing, rubbing fingers, twirling fingers, kissing fingers, smiling, frowning, and raising bushy eyebrows above his horn-rimmed glasses Eventually, he just kind of sputtered out, a bit dejected as he realized I just wasn't quite following it all. The rest of the way to Ostia he quietly gazed out of the window. What a shame I couldn't have held up my side of the conversation with a bit more conviction and skill. I would have had enough material for a novel.

* * * * *

October 5, 2010, Fiumicino, Italy

Sunday on the Palatine Hill, where Romulus killed his brother Remus and founded Rome in 753 B.C. Standing on the grand portico of the Farnese Gardens overlooking the Forum. Rome, the golden city, stretched out to the surrounding hills on the distant horizon. The whole history of mankind spread out at one's feet from the first humble huts to the grandeur of St. Peter's and the sprawl of the modern city that is contemporary Rome— centuries of human lives creating, destroying, loving, hating, hoping, despairing, birthing, and dying.

Like the stars on a moonless night, breathtakingly overwhelming. I am a speck of dust in the vast continuum of time in which all human toil, passion for fame and power, twists of fate, and acts of nature result in, at best, a few piles of harmonious rocks, at worst, an eroded earth and smog-besmirched sky. But on this sparkling early Fall Sunday afternoon in 2010, it all seems miraculously present, as if everyone from Romulus to Caesar to Berlusconi is here to testify that life goes on, that nothing dies as long as one man is left standing to remember, one log left floating out to the endless sea.

Following St. Francis

O CTOBER 17, 2010, ASSISI, ITALY

Today is my 70ᵗʰ birthday. It's too frightening to think about. Fortunately, we are traveling through Tuscany and Umbria and I can't be bothered to spend any time contemplating the significance or lack of significance of my age. I just feel grateful to be living such a fascinating life. The past week we have been on the trail of the Franciscan monk St. Francis of Assisi and the Renaissance painter Piero della Francesca—two of my great heroes.

* * * * *

The first stop was Arezzo where, after having renounced the debauchery of his youth, thirteenth-century Francis of Assisi became a monk. Thereafter, he roamed the countryside preaching against the excesses of the Church and urging a return to the humble life of true Christian values. It is believed that in Arezzo he calmed village violence by summoning up a giant golden cross, which hung in the sky with arms outstretched over the feuding citizens until hostilities ceased. Ever after, the Franciscans found a permanent home in the area and in the fifteenth century built the Chiesa di San Francesco.

At this point, Piero della Francesca enters the scene when he is called upon to complete the painting cycle of the Legend of the True Cross, a story known and loved by St. Francis. Ten episodes of the History of the Cross are depicted around the nave of the church beginning with the Death of Adam, when his sons planted a seed from the apple tree of the Garden of Eden. It was the wood of this tree that, so the legend goes, eventually became the cross on which

Christ was crucified. Each of the ten panels describes an episode in the story ending with the Annunciation.

Upon its completion, only its didactic value was considered important. In modern times, however, the religious significance is secondary to its sublime aesthetic value. The sense of quiet space and three-dimensionality, the suffused light and volumetric shadows, the serene faces and harmonious sense of color, the pageantry and interrelationship of forms—all contribute to a sense of restrained elegance. A style more humanistic than Byzantine religious art and less flamboyant than the barrages of passionate chiaroscuro so typical of the Baroque. All those angelic faces, rich fabrics, and gauzy landscapes. I wanted to live in that space, in that light. It is the light I love to photograph, the light that camouflages exterior wrinkles and smooths interior ones.

The next day we headed south toward the small medieval hilltop town of Assisi, where you are reminded of the saint's presence everywhere. Born there in 1182, son of a wealthy landowner, Francis died in the countryside nearby in 1226. A small chapel erected near the spot was later smothered by the huge, gaudy Baroque Santa Maria degli Angeli, as if in defiance of his very preaching about a simple life and simple faith.

St. Francis had wished to be buried among the criminals and outcasts on a hill known as *Colle d'Inferno* (Hell Hill), a place of execution until the thirteenth century. Now known as Paradise Hill, it is the spiritual center of the town crowned by the Basilica di San Francesco. Two churches were subsequently built on the spot: the lower church in 1228, and the upper church between 1230 and 1253 In the upper church, Giotto's famous twenty-eight-part fresco circling the walls uses the story of St. Francis' life to translate biblical stories and in so doing changes the course of art history by eschewing the flat, iconic images of the Byzantine and Romanesque period for more natural backgrounds and emphasis on the human quality of Christ and biblical characters. Interestingly, this more humanistic idea in art mirrors St. Francis's own preaching and leads to the full flowering of the Renaissance art of Piero della Francesca.

It just so happened While we were there, it just so happened that a Mass was being conducted in English in the small St Catherine's chapel

in the lower church, intimate in spite of the large crowd milling about. We sat in a front pew and the priest—from Rochester, New York—seemed to be speaking just to me. The reading had been about a woman nagging the judge for justice. The priest used this theme to talk about the importance of "persistence," "hanging in there" in our spiritual lives as well as our personal lives. I thought about how long I have tried to communicate with my sister and been rejected; how long I have been a Catholic and how often I have failed to live up to what I believe. How often the quick, easy quip pops out of my month instead of the kind comment. I can only keep working at it. It was a great birthday sermon.

After lunch, we walked down to the Basilica of St. Claire, all glowing pink and white in the pearly dampness. Even though massive, it struck me as being very feminine with its flying buttresses flung out like all-encompassing arms. St. Claire was the companion of St. Francis and there is almost as much mythology about her as about him. He, the story goes, cut off her long blonde curly hair as she renounced the world for a life of poverty and service to the poor.

From Assisi, we meandered south through the rolling hills of Umbria until we got to the outskirts of Florence. Passing through Pozzolatico and Impruneta, we parked at the Porta Romana and walked along the Via Romana past the antique stores, restoration shops, Boboli Gardens, and Cosimo de Medici's mammoth Palazzo Pitti. I had walked along that street so many times with my sister when, as young Navy wives, we both lived in Florence in the late 70's. We used to joke that when we were old ladies with families long dispersed and grandchildren grown, we would walk down these very streets together, wearing black, arm in arm, gossiping and reminiscing like the quintessential old Italian ladies we saw around us every day.

Now, contemplating Giotto's poignant crucifix in Santa Maria Novella, Bronzino's paintings at the Palazzo Strozzi, and the view from Piazzale Michelangelo- all experiences we had shared so many times together- I felt a deep loneliness. But over the next few days I came to the realization that this was the perfect place to finally say good-bye, to finally let go of the guilt, sadness and disappointment at her lack of communication. I didn't know if I would ever see her or talk to her again, but I did know that compulsive agonizing would not change anything.

Maybe someday, with persistence of prayer, we may once again stroll arm and arm down the Via Romana giggling about the follies of our youth and frown at the tacky tourists sprawled on the steps of the Duomo, but for now, I was grateful for memories.

Vatican Visitation

O F ALL THE SIGHTS IN ROME, THE POPE IS ONE of the most popular. To see him in person is memorable. To have him see you is unforgettable. It was a cold, bright day, so clear you could see all the way down the Via della Conciliazione to the green trees along the Tiber. Rooftops, church spires, and hills on the distant horizon stood out like a tiny toy train village. Arriving early for the 10:30 a.m. weekly audience, we found some seats in the center of the row directly in front of "His" chair, which was positioned on a raised platform in front of the basilica. Looking back we could see hordes of people filling up the square behind us.

About an hour and a half later, everyone suddenly stood up on their chairs, like one of those "waves" at a football game, and started looking off to the north. The big gates of the church behind the podium opened and a phalanx of Swiss Guards filed out. A great roar engulfed us as we saw the white arched top of the "Pope Mobile," like a little toy golf cart, working its way around the outside of the crowd and down an aisle behind us. Thousands and thousands of people stood on their chairs, waved flags and banners, and yelled Papa, Papa, Papa. We could just catch a glimpse of his head through the crowd as the tiny car climbed up the ramp toward the podium between two large roped-off areas of special dignitaries and visitors. Men in black suits were stationed discreetly around the perimeter of the crowd, and the Swiss Guard stood motionless and unsmiling on the steps.

Pope Benedict stepped down from the little mobile and walked out in front of the vast crowd with his arms held up high. An avalanche of sound reverberated across the square. Large TV screens, strategically placed along the sides of the square, provided close-up views as he read in Italian a long description of the life of St. Bridget, whom we were honoring that day. She was a woman who had ten children, was a loving wife and mother, and later went on to become a nun and do good works. More than that I could not get.

When a series of cardinals from different countries introduced their representative groups, the pope addressed each group in their own language and raised his hand to bless them as they stood yelling and waving their flags. At the close of the ceremony the pope led us in the Our Father in Latin. Then he gave a final blessing to the entire audience with emphasis on our children and family members who may be sick or dying. At this point we held up the rosaries we had bought in Assisi to be blessed by the pope for the family.

Gradually the crowd disbursed while the pope stood to receive a line of people who knelt and kissed his ring. Then he got back into the Pope Mobile and slowly proceeded back down the ramp—at which point I, myself, stood on a chair and was able to get a few photos of him blessing the crowd while the music soared and the people cheered. As I looked through the viewfinder, he suddenly looked right back at me, as if to say, "Now, Marguerite, I'm watching you." I snapped the shot.

I have never liked crowds, but I was deeply moved to be part of something so large and powerful; to be there on that sparkling October day in 2010, with people from all over the world who had come in love and respect to this one spot to see Pope Benedict, this one man who represents all goodness, all love, all peace. And he, like a gentle grandfather, thanked us for our good deeds, urged us to care for the poor, and held up the example of St. Bridget to encourage us in our trails. He blessed us and gave us courage that through love for each other we can persevere and make a better world together. Every week he spreads his arms open to the world, takes us in, and gives us hope. Now we have Pope Francis who is opening his arms even wider and, true to his name, taking in every living creature.

* * * * *

Little did we know how soon we would have to put the pope's message to the test. Several weeks later, when we got news from home that our family, as we knew it, had fragmented like pieces of a broken plate, we were overcome with sadness. Pete and Tracy had separated. Cracks that had apparently been developing over the years had been invisible to us. "What? No. That can't be." I exclaimed when Michael hung up the phone. It felt like someone had died. For a long time we couldn't talk about it.

Finally, several days later, after tramping around Fiumicino doing errands, we stopped for lunch at our favorite restaurant near the canal. From our table near the window we watched a light rain start to dampen the sidewalk, then increase to a deluge of water gushing down the gutter.

I fiddled with my silverware and finally whined: "Why don't we just go home now? I'm so depressed."

"Why do you torture yourself this way? There is nothing you can do about any of it."

"I know. Usually it's you that wants to go home. But maybe . . ."

"No problem. We can probably get a space on a flight pretty easily this time of year and be home for Thanksgiving."

"Thank you."

A week later we were deplaning in Baltimore to a huge crowd of Boy Scouts, Girl Scouts, teenagers, parents, and senior citizens all clapping and waving flags to welcome the returning soldiers who had been on the plane with us. It was very touching but a little embarrassing to be walking off the plane to applause of which we were completely undeserving. Then there was our own special welcoming committee as Daniel's smiling face and outstretched arms broke through the barrage of flags.

We all struggled through Thanksgiving and Christmas trying to make life as normal as possible, but there was "no joy in Mudville."

January 2011, Annapolis, Maryland
"March seems to take to Spring the hardest—one day snow, the next day Spring. For that reason, he couldn't stand Spring: it reminded him of too

many promises un-kept, lies told, hearts broken." —*from Song Yet Sung by James McBride*

No one is talking. Everyone is hurting. The joyful, joking gatherings that we loved so much will never be the same. I simply cannot figure out how to deal with it.

* * * * *

This is the last entry in my journal that covered from April 2010 to January 2011. The next one picks up with a description of the towering Dolomites rising behind our balcony window in Aviano, the highest peak still dusted with snow. "We are on our way to Venice," I scribbled and added a smiley face.

Ciao Italia

VENICE. A CRYSTALLINE SPRING DAY. Renaissance loggia lined the Grand Canal like soldiers at parade rest. The narrow streets leading to Piazza San Marco were thronged with people. Lines formed at every entrance. Puzzled, we pushed through to the basilica. Posters announcing the pope's visit hung around the iconic St. Mark's Square and on construction fences in front of the Campanile. The area looked like a demolition zone barricaded with corrugated metal and chain-link fences. Large advertising posters obscured the facades of surrounding Renaissance palaces. No more the vast cafés in the piazza filled with bustling dignified waiters and well-dressed people watching their children chase flocks of pigeons vying for bread crumbs strewn over the gray cobblestones. Even the famous bronze statues of the four horses of the "Triumphal Quadriga" on the portico over the main door of the basilica were fake, the real ones having been relegated to a small galleria behind the balcony.

Originally created in the fourth century on the island of Chios by the Greek sculptor Lysippos, the horses had traveled a circuitous route over the intervening centuries. In the eighth or early ninth century they were moved to the Hippodrome in Constantinople, where they were displayed with their *quadriga*, or racing chariot, until the sack of Constantinople during the Fourth Crusade in 1204, when the Venetians removed the horses and installed them on the terrace of the facade of St. Mark's Basilica. In 1797 Napoleon carried them off to Paris to become part of the design of the Arc de Triomphe, and in 1815, following the collapse of the French Empire, they were returned to Venice. Finally, in 1980, they were moved inside the museum for protection, forced to retreat from the rages of pollution, and replaced by clones.

We had followed pretty much that same route: strolled the shores of Chios, stood under the Walled Obelisk at the Hippodrome, and walked under the Arc de Triomphe, finally tracking down the majestic gilded horses in a church attic—still prancing proudly under the stage lights of a small dark gallery. I must have taken twenty photographs from every conceivable angle. Their powerful, arched heads, eloquent bodies, and gold patina surfaces symbolized the immortal power of beauty that survives in spite of its changing context, a metaphor for Venice, bravely treading water in the rising tide of mass tourism and global warming.

The ride back to the train station on the *vaparetto* (water bus) in the golden operatic light was almost too beautiful to photograph. In spite of the crowds, the tacky shops, the invasive advertising posters, and the many gondoliers who no longer wear their jaunty boaters and cheerful air, nothing can completely obliterate the visual wonder of this most "romantic city in the world." Like an old courtesan, corny and overly made-up, Venice reminds me of Madame Hortense in *Zorba the Greek*, who on her deathbed is still carrying on with heroic charm and courage as if she were twenty. Still able to seduce anyone with one ounce of imagination in spite of her tattered petticoats.

Then it was on to the stately Palladian villas of Vincenza, the luminous sixth-century mosaics of the Basilica di San Vitale in Ravenna, and over the mountains toward Florence—out of the dream onto the autostrada to Fiumicino, a filthy sailboat, and all the problems that accumulate after six months of neglect.

*   *   *   *   *

Our last day in Rome was fraught with frustration, closed museums, crowded buses, and dark churches. The day was not entirely lost, however, as it never is because there were always so many other wonderful and unexpected experiences to be had, in spite of walking for miles in the hot sun and waiting forever for unpredictable buses.

Sitting in a perfect little restaurant on a quiet backstreet in Trastevere, savoring Pollo con Peperoncini alla Roma—tender chicken with big slabs of red peppers in a not too tomatoey sauce—was a fine way to spend the afternoon. Leisurely relaxing under a big umbrella, sipping a lovely chilled white wine, enjoying great food, and watching life slowly parade by. "Who could ask for more?" Michael sighed contentedly.

After lunch and a bit more wine, feeling like a fifties movie star, I stood on the corner and flagged the *navette* (#115 bus) with a kiss to the bus driver. Then we rode up the Janiculum Hill on a curving road lined with balconied villas to the Fontana dell'Acqua Paola and the Piazza Garibaldi, where Rome skirted around us in a 360-degree panorama. We walked slowly around the piazza, reminiscing about all the places we had seen that were now laid out below us. It was a perfect farewell to my favorite place on Earth. We walked down the hill to the bus stop by the river and waited for the bus to Pyramide, which in time came and then filled up with very noisy drunken soccer fans from Palermo. All part of the wonderful kaleidoscopic experience that is Rome.

* * * * *

Now, one of us was chafing at the bit, could practically see the barn and smell the hay. Michael put his head down and was in "move on " mode. His patience with my years of mission creep was wearing thin. He was anxious to finish what we had inadvertently started when we left our pier back in October 1998. It was June 2011 and every year we had another birthday, as my own aching joints and minor bodily malfunctions reminded me on a regular basis. "I want to go home before I have to be mailed home in a box," he said repeatedly.

"You're not old," I would retort.

"This is all great. But we've done it. Don't you get it? I just want to go home."

"It's so depressing at home now."

"But it's home. We have a beautiful house. Great friends. Pete and Tracy will work it all out and it will be fine."

Admittedly, we were brokenhearted about the schism in our family, worried about our grandchildren, and felt in some way responsible. We had been gone all those years, not paying attention to the clues that should have been obvious. Maybe we should have seen it coming. Maybe we could have helped everyone see things from a different perspective, love each other more, set different priorities. In reality, of course, no one can live anyone else's life or even put themselves in someone else's shoes. Still our family was suffering. We needed to be there.

Thus, we decided for forgo the long-held dream of cruising the canals of Europe. Giving the coast of northern Italy and southern France a pass, we headed directly to Spain via Monte Argentario off the coast of Tuscany, Elba, and Corsica. By July 9th we were in Calvi, Corsica. After we tidied the boat, finished provisioning, stashed our clean laundry, stored the French and Italian books, and dug out the Spanish books we hadn't seen since Guatemala, we headed toward the Balearics and Spain. Michael was elated. And so was I, but for a different reason. We had just gotten an email from Pete asking where we were going to be in August because he was planning to bring the boys over for a two-week visit. I literally danced all over the cabin and started making plans of all the fun things we could do, not listening to the warning voice in the back of my mind or Michael's caveats.

After a brief but rolly passage, we made landfall in Mahon, Minorca, and dropped the hook in a protected anchorage below Fort Isabel II. Minorca is a cruiser's paradise, crenelated with deep protected bays and clear turquoise water. The town of Mahon, at the head of a long fiord-like bay, is colorful and historic, with numerous chandleries, markets, and marinas. Many boats stop here, and it was fun to catch up with old friends, especially our friends on *Blue Banana*, with whom we would resume cruising until we sadly parted in Cartagena.

Ten days later we moved on to Mallorca (aka Majorca), another secure anchorage in a good size bay surrounded by the charming Spanish town of Portocolom. It was here that we experienced the first of several very entertaining and always slightly out of control Spanish fiestas.

Hola Jaleo

PORTOCOLOM, MALLORCA, IS A MIXTURE OF bustling summer resort and old colonial town. An adobe church on a dusty, picturesque square near the anchorage became "our" church. The Hotel Formentor, however, was our pilgrimage. Situated on a scenic point overlooking a bay and sandy beach, it was a perfect destination for a Sunday afternoon road trip with Bill and Sam. In the past it had been one of those grand old hotels where the rich and famous of the '30s, '40s, and '50s gathered. Vintage photos of old Hollywood movie stars lined the walls. Back in the late 1970s , when the boys and I were living in a small villa in Florence while Michael was assigned to an aircraft carrier, he and I spent a romantic getaway weekend there and vowed to one day sail back. Unfortunately, since then the Formentor had expanded unattractively and gone a bit down-market. But, in spite of the damp, dripping weather and Sam's obviously declining health, we still laughed and reminisced about the past, buoyed by a good-enough sangria and our mutual enjoyment of being together, knowing that our paths would soon go in different directions.

That particular afternoon we stopped at the house where George Sand and Frederic Chopin had spent a summer. It was a charming little house with a vine-covered garden where I took a photograph of Sam and Bill surrounded by purple morning glories on a terrace overlooking a misty valley. It turned out to be the last photograph of them together that I would ever take.

When I first met Sam, I thought her short hair was a matter of choice, not chemotherapy. As we clocked nautical and land miles around the world together from Southeast Asia to the Mediterranean, I learned more about her story. Sam had been battling cancer since it had been diagnosed in Australia, where both breasts were removed and a flawless reconstruction performed. We met eight months later in Indonesia. That she continued to pursue her dream of sailing around the world is a tribute to her resilient spirit, love of sailing, and courage and determination. Every year she would fly home for scans, come back all clear, and you could practically hear the whole "fleet" heave a sigh. One year it wasn't so positive, but she was determined nonetheless, and returned with a duffle bag full of expensive new medication and instructions for Bill on how to administer it by infusion on the boat, which would temporarily become as sterile as an operating room. This worked so well for so long time that we all believed Sam was invincible.

On one of our many road trips in the Balearics, after a jovial lunch on a shady patio in the middle of an olive grove, we stopped yet again at another old church that I had marked on the map. It was on a gentle hill overlooking a cemetery. I watched Sam walk down toward the gravestones and stare out at the valley below. We all knew what she was thinking, but we couldn't say anything. Slowly she walked back, gave us all a big grin, and made some joke about where we were stopping next on my historical church and art tour. I still replay this scene over and over in my mind wishing that I had at least just walked down the hill and put my arm around her.

* * * * *

August 15, 2011, Portocolom, Mallorca

Reading May Sarton A House by the Sea, a journal of her 60th year in which she writes about confronting the death of her friends and how it makes death a reality in her own life causing her to contemplate: How will I die, when, what will happen to my animals etc. Now begins a process of readying oneself for this inevitability because each day we are more aware of its approach. Daily, little by little, we prepare ourselves for it by letting go of things; not loving with such possessive passion; growing to accept losses with less pain.

I have always thought of my life as a trade-off. I have to give up some things to get other things. Give up seeing my family and grandchildren, house and rose garden, studio and possibility of making art for the challenge and adventure of sailing around the world. But actually, it is more a process of letting go of my past life and concerns and loves. Thinning down for the journey which only looks like a trip around the world when in reality it is a trip out of it.

* * * * *

Back in Mahon we got the bad news that the boys had a change of heart and decided not to join us after all. I should not have been surprised and therefore so disappointed. I know the first rule of survival in life is to never anticipate. But of course I did and I was. I moped around all day worried about Sam and crushed about the boys. Michael, in his intuitive wisdom, suggested we go for a drive, and we found ourselves in the small village of Llucmacanes where the fiesta of "Sant Gaietà" was revving up. There was to be a *jaleo*. What that was, exactly, we were not sure.

A parade was forming just as we arrived, led by two giant papier-mâché characters on stilts named Juan and Rita, accompanied by what looked like a dwarf in a three-cornered hat. The school band followed as black horses and their black clad riders milled about on the street corners. A priest arrived, wearing riding boots and a black cape and hat, and opened the church doors. The townspeople trooped in. We followed. Then the riders filed in and sat in the front pews. The priest meantime changed into his vestments and Mass began.

During the offering, some of the riders—who were carrying beakers of what looked like *pamada* (the local gin and lemon juice drink), with bunches of mint—anointed everyone's head as they passed their hats for the collection. After Mass, they filed out and made an honorary escort for the priest and the "fiesta mayor" to the accompaniment of a vibrant band of mostly horns playing exuberant parade music.

Then the *caixers* (riders) mounted their horses and formed up in a procession behind the *fabioler*, who led the parade past the church sitting astride a donkey, beating a drum and playing a flute. The jaleo had begun. Music swelled as the first pair of horses appeared and performed spiraling turns called *caragols*. The horses pranced and swirled in unison, hooves hitting the dust in time with the music, and rising up on their hind legs in the *fer un bot*. Some horses sustained and extended this pose, actually jumping forward on their hind legs as the crowd roared and cheered. Gradually the competition became more intense and the crowd closed in, grasping at the horses and riders. Apparently, it is good luck to touch the horses' hearts, but it looked like a death wish when the horses swerved into the crowd and reared up unpredictably. The horses were surprisingly graceful and created a sense of choreography as the pairs "danced" together and tried to outshine each other, egged on by the riders and the crowd.

There was also an obvious element of social hierarchy here, the riders presenting an elegant, almost untouchable image above the rowdy crowd. Their dress—the white trousers, white shirts, bow ties, tailcoats, boots with spurs—I read later, is the costume of a brotherhood that goes back hundreds of years. The small whip and the *guindola*, or tricorn hat, identifies the riders as repositories of a tradition that faithfully follows medieval rules and represents the distant historical social classes of the past: the peasantry, the nobility, and the clergy. Their horses seem to be completely aware of their own aristocratic role, heads held high above the grasping throng.

At the end, each pair entered the square in front of the church and proceeded to the bandstand where they were presented with green stalks of bulrushes tied with ribbons and a small silver spoon. The horses twirled and reared up for several more passes as the crowd become even more frenzied. Men carried women on their shoulders alongside the horses as they clawed at the riders. Small screaming children were hoisted up to touch the horses' withers.

When the last pair disappeared down the street, the music subsided. Then all the riders returned to the square and formed another cordon of honor in front of the little taverna across from the church. The priest and the mayor passed between them and proceeded into the bar as the riders clapped and the crowd cheered. Then music started up, the bar was opened, and the dancing began . . . and continued late into the night. We had a few pamadas and walked back to the car completely exhausted and stunned by the drama and chaos that we had witnessed. It didn't escape us that an ambulance was parked under the trees just off the square—a miracle that it was never needed.

Later I looked up the word "jaleo," which has several meanings: "the act of making a noisy disturbance," "any exciting and complex play intended to confuse and (dazzle) the opponent," "a disorder resulting from a failure to behave predictably." It is also associated with flamenco music and dancing from Andalusia where "loud, raucous dancing is accompanied by shouting and clapping to encourage the dancers." It has often occurred to me, since, that the spirit of jaleo must be imprinted in the DNA of the Spanish, judging from the chaotic and dangerous nature of so many of their celebrations, which we were to experience throughout our travels in the country.

*   *   *   *   *

For the rest of August we cruised the varied coastline of Mallorca, explored the museums, churches, the old Arab section of Palma, and battled the tourists in Ibiza. Then suddenly it was September and, after a lovely overnight passage, we were tossing our lines to Sam and Bill on the pier at the marina in Cartagena—steps away from a Roman amphitheater, picturesque architecture, museums, restaurants, elegant shopping. A train station within walking distance put the rest of Spain equally within easy reach. It was perfect.

I was "on the jazz" again with a new country, a new culture, and a fairly familiar language. Michael was happy because we were that much closer to home. At times, however, the disintegrating state of family relationships and the obvious weakening of Sam's health were inescapable and almost too sad to bear. Sitting in the cockpit of *Blue Banana* after a few "grin and bear-its," Bill and Sam confessed that they had decided to sell the boat in Cartagena and fly back to California. This should have been a signal that things were worse than we thought, but it was important to maintain the illusion that, once again, Sam would beat the odds and return to us healthy, enthusiastic, and ready to resume the challenges of the cruising life she loved.

The night before they left, everyone gathered at a local sidewalk restaurant to celebrate Sam's sixtieth birthday—ten of us, seated at a long table under the stars, consumed a steady stream of tapas and told wine-fueled sea stories that only sailors who had shared the same sea-lanes could understand: run-ins with Customs officers, rescues at sea, crooked port captains, charter boat sailors, clueless tourists, tenacious rug salesmen, fierce winds and arbitrary weather, broken gear, dragging anchors, pirates, and shit peddlers. Everyone had a "remember when" story and all of them were funny, even though they might not have been at the time. Silly cards and outrageous gifts added to the general hilarity.

As the bars closed and the street emptied, we all straggled back to our boats and gave Sam a big hug under the full moon. She loved a party and that was a great one. When the taxi came the next morning to take them to the airport, we joked about who had "had the most fun" the night before. We laughed and hugged each other in spite of the tears welling up in our eyes.

"Okay. We'll meet you in Gibraltar in a couple of weeks so we can cross 'the Pond' together."

"Deal?"

"Deal."

Cruisers never say good-bye; we always say, "See ya," because we usually do, sometime, somewhere along the world's wetter paths, and we believed we would.

La Mancha and the
Moorish Soul

S OON THEREAFTER WE WERE OFF ON ANOTHER "therapy trip," rolling our rolly bags across the cobblestones of Madrid's Plaza Major and under an archway to the Hostel Macarena, where we had a delightful room with a balcony overlooking the street. A nice bathroom, fluffy towels, mirrors just where you want them, TV, comfortable bed—everything was perfect except there was no air-conditioning and it was stiflingly hot. The fan worked only on low, so we had to leave the doors open, and the noise from the street all night made it impossible to sleep. The next morning no coffee until 9:00 or 9:30, when a few cafés finally opened. Spaniards stay up all night and sleep in the morning. It was a tough beginning, but, after several whirlwind "art days" in Madrid, we soon got acclimatized. Knowing that my mother and grandmother had spent three years in Spain in the thirties, I imagined them living the same lifestyle. Mother never was an early riser.

* * * * *

Madrid sits squarely in the middle of Spain on the Meseta Plateau, which, shot through with squiggles of mountain ranges, occupies the central half of the Spanish mainland. The cities of Toledo, Avila, and Segovia radiate from its heart, poking up from this vast plateau like marooned islands. La Mancha we know from Cervantes' *Don Quixote de la Mancha*. According to Wikipedia, it is derived from the Arab word *al-mansha*, meaning "the dry land" or "wilderness," and refers to an expansive arid fertile plain in central Spain south of Madrid that reaches to the mountains of Toledo, an area called Castilla-La

Mancha. Interestingly the word *mancha* in Spanish means "stain" or "spot" or "patch," a rather indignant term used by Cervantes to denote the unremarkable origins of his knight-errant, Don Quixote.

Toledo, however, while stained perhaps with the events of history is not a dry, patchy spot. Rising from a bend of the Tagus River, the spires of its alcazar and cathedral pierce a helter-skelter pile of tile roofs like the points of a crown. Walking through the city's narrow cobblestone streets reveals much about the complicated cultural history of Spain.

The Franciscan monastery and church of San Juan de los Reyes was built by King Ferdinand II and his wife Isabella to commemorate the restoration of Spain as signified by the union of their two houses and the birth of their only son, as well as their triumph in battle over the Portuguese. It was intended to be their last resting place until they took Granada in 1492 and decided that was a more significant "venue." It is a late-Gothic beauty blended with lacy Mudejar decoration, ornate but completely unified with nary a swirling cherub or baroque drape. The "yoke and arrow" insignia and double eagle coat of arms of the Catholic monarchs is a major decorative motif, reminding one of the historical significance of this place of worship and that it was Ferdinand and Isabella after all who finally drove the Moors from Spain, even though they appreciated and utilized the Moorish aesthetic.

* * * * *

The towns of Avila and Segovia were also dense with this pastiche of history and cultural mélange, but at the Alhambra, the Moorish soul beats the strongest. As I stood on a cobbled street corner in Granada looking up at the ancient walls and palaces of the Alhambra sprawled across the top of a high cliff, I thought, *Idie and mother must have been here.* It is so sad that we never think to ask the questions of our loved ones that become so important years after they have left us. All I remember is that my mother's mother used to say: "Dixie was such a fat teenager when we were in Spain. I made her walk everywhere." I wondered if she hiked the steep hill to the Alhambra. Michael and I drove up that hill and spent the whole day strolling through the jigsaw puzzle of streets, squares, buildings, pavilions, bathhouses, gardens, pools, and palaces, the most sublime of which was the Palacio de los Leones.

It was here that the sultan and his harem enjoyed celebrations and musical events. A residential palace of perfectly proportioned rooms and courtyards, the sophistication of the decoration represents the flowering of the Nasrid visual arts, where every pavilion and space is a fusion of pattern, superimposed prism shapes, honeycombed with lacy texture, roofs dripping with stalactites, and filigreed horseshoe arches which accentuate the play of light and create an ethereal atmosphere. The central fountain in the main courtyard is surrounded by twelve lions spewing water from their mouths, whence comes the name Palacio de los Leones. It was not hard to imagine veiled Moorish beauties hiding among the slender columns and reclining on silken pillows under the porticos while the water-cooled tiles under foot and the strains of lute music soothed the fevered brow. A contemporary poet, Ibn Furkun, wrote, "The court of the kingdom and its Alhambra have shapes that look like the mansions on the moon."

Beyond the walls of the Alhambra lies the Palacio de Generalife, or Architect's Garden, the Muslim ruler's summer palace that stretches over the hillside across a deep ravine opposite the Alhambra. It was both a country estate belonging to the Nasrid sultans and an agricultural farm. We leisurely wandered the terraced gardens as if we were potentates ourselves, running our hands over the boxwood borders crammed with roses and colorful perennials, pausing by serene reflecting pools, and resting in numerous garden "rooms," delineated by tall cypress trees, each with its own alabaster fountain.

In 1880, Manuel Gomez-Moreno Gonzalez painted *Boabdil's Family Leaving the Alhambra*, which depicts Ferdinand and Isabella's troops making the final assault on Grenada in 1492. Ladies swoon while children are comforted by maids, turbaned couriers embrace, and faithful retainers bow as the mother of Boabdil, the exiled sultan, passes through a tapestry-curtained archway with her head held high. It is a nineteenth-century narrative painting more poignantly significant than aesthetically pleasing. We felt a bit the same way, however, swooning from exhaustion and heartbroken to be exiled from such a magical world when we finally staggered back to our car around 8:00 as the site was closing.

* * * * *

Seville, the capital of Andalusia, on the other hand, is very Spanish. City of castanets, flamenco, flowers, and toreadors. I couldn't help but picture it through my mother's eyes. I still have her black lace mantilla and castanets. Now I imagined her wandering these same streets, being shocked but fascinated by a bullfight in the old wooden Plaza de Toros. I imagined Idie taking time out from her studies at the university to drag a petulant and slightly overweight teenager to the monumental Catedral de Sevilla, the largest Gothic building in the world and third-largest church in Europe, crammed to the spires with wonderful works of art. Animal lover that mother was, did she smile, as I did, at the shepherds, goats, dogs, and chicks in Murillo's *Adoration of the Magi* and at the lion sweetly licking Rufina's feet in Goya's *Santa Justa and Rufina*, honoring the martyred sisters? Did she, too, stand stupefied in front of the monumental retable of gold and think the tomb of Columbus silly in light of the peripatetic history of his bones?

Surely mother and Idie must have rested in the lovely Patio de los Naranjos after their tour of the church. Maybe they even sat on the same bench as we did marveling at the 295-foot-high (90 meters) "Giralda" tower that once was part of a Muslim mosque. Did they climb to the top to enjoy the spectacular view of what then was probably a much smaller city? I suspect not, as mother was always claustrophobic.

After an interesting tapas lunch of cod in black-and-orange sauce and a baked potato in a kind of "pot pie sauce," we marshaled our energy to attack Seville's alcazar, the residence of many generations of kings and caliphs. It was here that the Catholic monarchs set up court as they prepared for the final conquest of Granada. It is, in fact, the oldest royal residence in Europe still in use. King Juan Carlos and Queen Sofia reside here when they visit Seville. It was here also that Ferdinand and Isabella welcomed Columbus on his return from the "discovery" of America. Sala de Audiences houses the earliest known painting of this historical event, depicting Columbus, Fernando El Catolico, Carlos I, Amerigo Vespucci, and Native Americans all sheltering beneath the Virgin in her role as protector of sailors. Did mother giggle at such a funny allegorical pastiche?

The Last of the Med

BACK IN CARTAGENA, ANOTHER CULTURAL anomaly was under way: hordes of costumed townsfolk were roaming the streets and heading for the waterfront. We both did a double take as men in Roman robes, ladies in diaphanous gowns, and burly characters in breastplates carrying shields and weapons paraded by. Even the children were armed and ferocious looking. We grabbed a pizza for dinner and sat watching as still they came. Later on, the masses gathered in front of the town hall—all Romans and Carthaginians in full costume for the opening ceremonies of what we learned was the yearly reenactment of the Roman attack on ancient Cartagena. There were lots of speeches and sword rattling—a little like a pep rally—but we couldn't really follow much of it and walked back to the boat a bit dazed after our travels and long car ride.

Intrigued, I Googled it and discovered that in 300 B.C., Rome, hoping to control its trade routes, attacked Cartagena and thus embarked on the First Punic War. Eventually the war was resolved with a treaty. But in 219, Cartagena attacked Rome. Two years later Hannibal journeyed over the Alps with thirty-seven elephants, 100,000 infantrymen, and 12,000 horsemen to finally claim Rome for the Carthaginians. Then Rome invaded and conquered Cartagena during the Second Punic War. Nowadays, more than 4,000 people take part in a reenactment of parts of this story during one wild week in September. There are battles every night and theatrical performances during the day, ending in a huge final battle and parade through town.

Just steps from *Ithaca*'s foredeck there were flaming arrows, explosions, sword fights, and horses rampaging past dead bodies. It was all surprisingly realistic and a little scary as some people really got into their roles. The spirit of jaleo was in full force. But, as far as I know, there were no real casualties, and Monday morning the town was back to normal, as if a thunderous spirit had inhabited the residents for a week and then passed on to some other place. We were getting ready to move on as well and making preparations for the passage to Gibraltar.

* * * * *

It was a cold, gloomy, tense thirty-six-hour motor sail from Cartagena to Gibraltar and, in my case, painful, as my lower back pain had increased significantly. Luckily, once tied up in the Queens Way Marina we were able to get to a large, modern hospital with English-speaking staff. After an uncomfortable wait of two hours, I could barely walk across the room when they called my name. Even though the Indian doctor who examine me looked like a fourteen-year-old, he had the poise and compassion of a grandfather. After a thorough examination and X-ray, he prescribed some anti-inflammatory medicine and the painkiller Panadol. His diagnosis was that I had "spinal claudication, sacroiliitis, trochanteric bursitis, and arthritis—in the left hip especially." In other words, I am old and my joints are disintegrating. I could actually see most of what he was describing on the X-ray. The sacroiliitis was what was causing most of the pain. The vertebra actually looked collapsed.

Once I got pills that I could actually swallow, the pain lessened and I could at least walk around. I was not, however, supposed to bend over, lift, pull, or twist. Not good news for *Ithaca*'s first mate (or her captain). When we left the hospital, I had a bit of a meltdown and collapsed on a bench in tears. Poor Michael. I felt like I had been hit with a tidal wave of OLD and the future looked very depressing. He was so patient and silently sat next to me holding my hand, letting me work through it until I could laugh again. As in most instances, time heals and soon I was back to normal functioning.

The following Sunday we were grateful to finally hear Mass in English and gustily sing English hymns. I tried to thank God for everything I had and to pray for the strength to accept the realities of my life and things I could not control, realizing how much worse it could be and what others have to suffer, like my dear friend Sam whose daily life was a fight to survive.

That night we called Danny and Lauren on Skype and all my hurts melted seeing their magical smiling faces in real time so far away.

October 10, 2011, Gibraltar

Yesterday we took the cable car up to the top of the "Rock" of Gibraltar. The visibility was the best it has been since we have been here. We could see all the way across the bay to Algeria. The entrance to the Mediterranean Sea lay spread out before us, one of the most significant geographic gateways in the world. A small white sail threaded through the large freighters anchored in the harbor below. "That was us two weeks ago," I said to Michael who was negotiating with a Barbary monkey for his sunglasses. "Except it was a lot rougher with less visibility," he answered, triumphantly repositioning the glasses on his nose. "Who would have thought we'd ever be here?" "Who would have thought we'd ever be a lot of places." Let's turn around and go back." "Are you nuts?" I think the conversation went something like that.

Although the weather has closed in again, our plan is to fill up with water and fuel, check out of the marina, and go to the anchorage for an early departure tomorrow morning. Good-bye Mediterranean. Once again Michael is anxious and happy to be on our way. I am sad. Although my recent bout of back pain is proof that he is right.

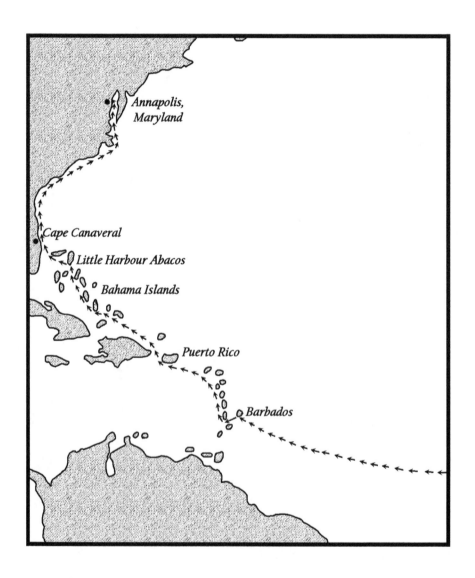

Annapolis,
Maryland

Cape Canaveral

Little Harbour Abacos

Bahama Islands

Puerto Rico

Barbados

292 •

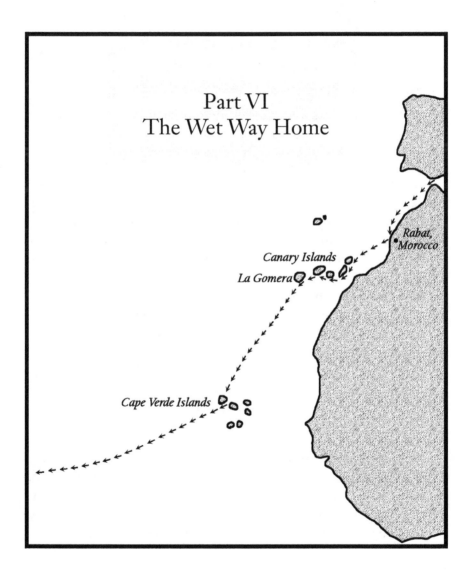

Part VI
The Wet Way Home

Rabat,
Morocco

Canary Islands
La Gomera

Cape Verde Islands

Morocco Madness

O N OCTOBER 11, 2011, I WROTE IN THE log: "Passing Tarifa light, the southernmost tip of Europe where it blows 30 knots 300 days a year, only 20 this morning. Sun coming up. Rolly, rough. Two knots of current against us. Out of the Med into the Atlantic!"

Three days later we were approaching Rabat, Morocco, in thick fog—another sketchy river entrance—when suddenly the fog lifted like a curtain, revealing a horizon punctuated by minarets. The harbor had been closed for four days due to high winds and surf across the entrance. Our timing, for once, was perfect. With a high tide and low wind, entering the channel was not a drama. Still, we were grateful when the marina dinghy guided us over the sandbar and up the narrow estuary past the twelfth-century fort-like Kasbah des Oudaias and historic medina (walled city) with square towers brooding over the harbor entrance. Hundreds of fishing boats, their wooden hulls a patina of peeling paint, jostled for space in the shallows. If we had any doubt, the call to prayer booming from the shoreside mosque confirmed we were back in the world of Islam.

Many adventures ensued: a close brush with the king; a train trip to Casablanca to retrace the haunts of Albert Camus, Edith Piaf, and Antoine de Saint-Exupéry and have the obligatory hamburger at Rick's Café. But my birthday in Marrakesh, and a camel trek to the remote Sahara dunes of Erg Chigaga, were the high points.

* * * * *

From the modern train station in Marrakesh it was an easy taxi ride to the main square, Jemaa el-Fnaa. But we might as well have been dropped off on the moon. A cacophony of bizarre sights and sounds assaulted us as we stepped out on cobblestones: snake charmers played flutes to bored-looking, half-sleeping weaving vipers; water merchants in fringed hats clanged their brass water bowls; cunning soothsayers sat on baby stools telling fortunes; and old men sold dried herbs and secret potions to cure every remedy.

We dove in, wheeled our overnight bags through the square, and squeezed along the crowded alleyways of the medina in search of our *riad*: a traditional Moroccan house built around a garden courtyard, many of which have now been converted into small boutique hotels. Disappointed that our room was no longer available, I complained that it was my birthday and another room in a "nearby" riad miraculously became available. Although finding it was the trick, once there we opened the door to a room worthy of Topkapi. Sunlight poured in through the open balcony window onto two large bouquets of pink roses on a dresser inlaid with mother of pearl. The bed, hung with silk tapestry, was strewn with pink rose petals. In the bathroom, plush white towels hung from ornate hooks and rose petals had been sprinkled artfully around the white marble sink.

After lunch and an exploratory venture through the *souq* (*souk*, or marketplace), we retired to the rooftop garden and ordered two tonics over ice, which we surreptitiously enhanced with our sequestered gin. In the midst of this delicate maneuver, the staff brought out a custard pie decorated with fruit and a candle, and they sang happy birthday while I precariously held the bottle of gin under the table between my knees, feeling a little embarrassed at my transgression in the face of their generosity.

After two secret cocktails, we struck out for the madness that is the Jemaa el-Fnaa at night. The square had been transformed into a carnival. Drum music, flute music, acrobats, and dancers performed in tight groups surrounded by onlookers. At least a hundred food carts had been rolled out and tables set up by waiters who mercilessly pursued customers with rhyming numbers and jingles like "number one hundred seven, closest to heaven," where we finally relented and sat down for rather ho-hum kebabs and chicken couscous. Later we walked through the crowd trying not to linger anywhere too long lest we be asked to pay for the performance, which typically lasted only as long as the next potential customer strode by. We did leave a little money for a lone man playing an oud with a chicken on his head, whom we later realized was a Berber, recognizable by his blue robes and distinctive blue turban. Enthralled with the environment, I wanted to stay, but Michael was "done." This kind of chaos makes him exceedingly uncomfortable. So, we headed back to the sanity and elegance of our hotel room.

The next day was full of summer palaces, museums, old riad architecture, regional craftsmanship, calligraphy, textiles, and leather goods in a souq that rivaled Cairo. Then there was lunch in Mechoui Alley: between eleven and twelve men in white robes set up rows of stalls where they carve up steaming sides of slow roasted lamb served on a big tray lined with paper that doubles as a napkin. A pile of meat/bone/gristle arrives at your table with a bowl of cumin and salt but no knives and forks or napkins. It was the best meal we had in Morocco.

* * * * *

Practically before we could wash the grease off our hands, we were heading for the Sahara Desert with our driver Abdul, destination M'Hamid, an old caravan stop on the edge of the desert border with Algeria which was the base camp for our camel trek to the remote Erg Chigaga, a 25-mile (40-kilometer) stretch of golden dunes, some as high as close to a thousand feet (300 meters). We were both assigned a camel and a blue-turbaned Berber guide who led the camel on foot across the desert. The first day was a two-hour "warm-up." We set off across a barren landscape of buried tamarind trees, windswept and desolate. It was hard to get comfortable and "in the swing." Then the sand transmogrified into a hard, black rocky surface called *rec* (probably for what it does to your body).

A camel trek into the desert to sleep in a Berber tent surrounded by four-story-high dunes may seem romantic, and it was—minus the camel-riding part. A ten-minute ride around the pyramids in Egypt is about all any self-respecting tourist really needs to experience. After the first twenty minutes, the romance wears off along with your first layer of skin. We did learn that camels have different personalities and different gaits. Unfortunately, Michael got the grumpy, jerky one; he was miserable and, for a while, decided walking was preferable.

But seeing him plodding behind us through the heavy sand, seemingly getting farther behind with each step, sent a jolt of panic through my body. "Stop!" I yelled to our guide.

"Here, Michael try mine. It might be easier."

He looked at me doubtfully but swallowed his pride and continued on my more mellow moving steed.

After two hours, we could see small black tents on the horizon. They got bigger as we got closer . . . and smaller as they disappeared over the camel's rump. Rats! We continued another thirty minutes. At dusk, we arrived at a small cluster of black tents. We waddled to our tent, which was furnished Berber style—one large bed smothered in colorful blankets—and bitterly regretted leaving the gin behind. The route to the dining tent was lit with dim solar-powered lights, but the walk to the outhouse tent was trickier. A flickering flashlight over drifting sand dunes made me wish I had been born a man. The next morning, after an additional two-hour trek, we arrived back at base camp and turned in the camels for a 4x4—a much more comfortable ride to the Erg Chigaga. Except . . .

Two 4x4 trucks were following each other across miles of empty desert. There was no obvious road, but the Berber driver seemed to know exactly where we were going. A vague green patch hovering on the horizon like a mirage slowly became more distinct: palm trees and a puddle of blue. An oasis. We stopped. The guides spread blankets and pillows out on the sand near a small, cool pond under arching palm trees, then brought out cold drinks and lunch in covered tagines. After lunch, we stretched out on the pillows, munched on dates, and drifted off into an imaginary "Midnight at the Oasis." But, there was still more desert to cross . . .

The sand dunes got deeper. The 4x4 behind us got stuck. Everyone got out, shoved, pulled, pushed, and dug, to no avail. As we were standing around contemplating what to do, a darkness developed on the horizon like a huge black thunderstorm cloud, except it wasn't. The guides hustled us into the other 4x4 just before a howling sound like a freight train overtook us and visibility dropped to zero. We were engulfed in blowing sand. I had visions of my obituary reading something like, "While sailing around the world Marguerite Welch was buried in a giant sand dune somewhere in the Sahara Desert, and never seen again." Just as I began to hyperventilate with claustrophobic fear, the wind dropped. The sand parted. The guides dusted us off, and we continued to the Erg Chigaga camp. I still don't know what happened to the stranded jeep.

This camp was comparatively grand, with a bathroom en suite, wrought iron bed, and electricity. Viewed from the top of a nearby towering sand dune, though, the whole campsite looked like a handful of puny, toy tents huddled in the trough of a rolling brown sea stretching endlessly to the horizon. One step down the other side of the dune and I would be lost forever, overboard without a life raft.

Fortunately, we did not disappear into the desert and lived on to survive numerous other adventures—fun and not so fun. Back at the marina in Rabat, the weather waiting game began. As in the Fiumicino River, wind and tide governed our departure date. After many mint teas at a small café in the medina watching the waves break over the harbor entrance, we determined that we could probably get out if we were careful and lucky, mainly lucky. We were, and carried on to the Canary Islands in spite of dicey navigational issues, unmarked fishing nets, and a gear failure at midnight (but you've heard enough about those). By November 11th, we had anchored off a secluded beach on the small island of Graciosa off the northern tip of Lanzarote, the second island down in the island chain of the Canaries. The landfall was spectacular.

Tracking Columbus

NOVEMBER 11, 2011, 8 NM OFF GRACIOSA, CANARY ISLANDS

Approaching Graciosa after a very rolly five days, the sunrise is symphonic. Beethovenesque: dark purple clouds against ribbons of torn crimson. Slowly the peaks of the Canary Islands darken against the fading ink of the nighttime sky and melting stars. Then the Sun makes its triumphant entrance with a blaze of trumpets off the port beam, as seabirds carve out swooping arcs above the heaving waves like skaters making figures in the ice. Magnificent, and I am the only witness to this glorious performance. The next time we make a landfall after a long passage we will have crossed the Atlantic Ocean and for all practical purposes completed our circumnavigation, but this landfall I will hold in my heart.

* * * * *

Ultimately, Poseidon had other plans. From Graciosa, we moved on to explore the larger and more touristy island of Lanzarote, where vineyards thrive on volcanic hillsides and each individual vine inhabits a unique microclimate created within its own mini-crater. Cruising past the east coast of Fuerteventura, we continued on to Gran Canaria and the port of Las Palmas, a surprisingly modern city of skyscrapers, traffic, and tourists as well as a historic Old Town of Spanish colonial architecture and interesting museums. It was also home to a large marina, sophisticated markets, and numerous marine services catering to the yearly influx of ARC (Atlantic Rally for Cruisers) participants. It was the perfect venue in which to prepare for the passage across the Atlantic, as so many sailors—most notably Columbus—had done for hundreds of years.

We spent several weeks here getting *Ithaca* ready for her next big adventure, provisioning extensively for the long voyage and having a new mainsail made just to be on the safe side. A new out-haul was installed, the water maker restored, and the freezer topped off with Freon. Soon it was Thanksgiving, which was celebrated by the whole cruising community regardless of nationality. It was a lively event held in a pizza restaurant in the marina, which lent us their facilities and allowed us to bring our own food . . . if we purchased the liquor from them. Needless to say, they did not lose money. After many bottles of various wines and a typically huge lunch, sentimentality reared its beguiling head and soon we were making reservations to fly home for Christmas.

But, of course, it wasn't the way we dreamed it would be. Even though we thought we were emotionally toughened, we weren't. We muddled through the best we could, praying for patience, love, and understanding, but it was hard. Then one night at dinner Danny told us that he and his family were moving to California.

"I won't ever see you," I murmured in disbelief.

"You can come visit us in Carmel, Mom." But, at the time, this reassurance was not comforting. I stared at my plate for a few minutes then went to the bathroom, sat on the toilet, and cried. For years I had mentally compensated for the end of our cruising years with the dream of Sunday night family dinners at Grandma's house. Now one set of grandchildren was barely speaking to us and the other half of the family was moving away. Intellectually I understood the reasons and, from some perspective, even agreed it was a good thing, but emotionally I was speechless with anger and disappointment for days.

In the end, I was grateful that I could go back to the boat and concentrate on sanding, varnishing, sewing canvas, shopping, storing stuff, shopping, storing stuff, shopping, storing stuff, more sanding, varnishing, and more shopping. When there was no room left to store a single can of sardines, the brightwork glowed, and all systems (we thought) were "go," we went. Hopscotching along the rest of the Canaries to get a better angle on the wind, we made what we thought would be our last stop before Barbados—La Gomera.

On January 14, 2012, we tied up in a small marina in the town of San Sebastian for an unexpected final fiesta.

* * * * *

The town of San Sebastian is a small village with a big square next to the waterfront. Its narrow streets radiate from the mouth of a deep ravine, walled in by high, steep dry-brown mountains on either side. The whole island looks like a giant orange juice squeezer, the only flat land being the handful of green valleys hidden deep in the crevices between the mountains.

We were there for eight days, and during that time we drove up every mountain and down every valley, went on walks through the dripping cloud forest, and enjoyed a typical lunch at a remote family inn. After Mass at the same church where Columbus and his men prayed before embarking on their first journey in 1492, and a visit to the house/museum where he spent his last night, we were physically, mentally, and spiritually ready for our last long ocean passage. The whole town must have known because they gave us a fabulous send-off.

The Fiesta of San Sebastian, patron saint of the town, was one of the most joyous, fun, and inventive cultural events we ever experienced in our travels. Concerts, processions, and performances continued for the whole eight days we were there, climaxing in a twenty-four-hour orgy of food and music.

It began at the top of the hill on the edge of town. Men, women, and children of all ages appeared wearing their indigenous village folk costumes. Each group gathered around a float or cart laden with food and wine. Gradually, a parade moved down the main street toward the harbor, handing out yummy morsels and tipples to the spectators gathered along the sidewalk. Each group had its own musicians and dancers. Almost everyone had a musical instrument and was singing La Gomeran folk songs. Many were older people who clearly reveled in this revival of their music, customs, and local cuisine. Ladies wearing coquettish hats and billowing shirts whirled and smiled under the arms of their cavalier partners.

As each group and its cart or float reached the harbor, chairs, tables, grills, mounds of food, and bottles of wine appeared and the real feast began; but the music never stopped. Groups gathered with their guitars, mandolins, castanets, bones, spoons, and a wild assortment of invented instruments, playing music which sometimes sounded a bit like mariachi music, sometimes flamenco, sometimes Cuban, or a mixture of all three. As the evening wore on, some groups took to the stage and played while others danced in the square under the huge spreading fig trees until dawn. Literally. We went back to the boat about 11:00 p.m. and fell asleep to this glorious, exuberant sound. Had we not been committed to an early departure the next morning, we would have hung in there till dawn with the best of them.

Reluctantly, we left La Gomera the next morning, believing that our next port of call would be Carlisle Bay, Barbados, in about three to four weeks. It was not to be. Plagued with broken gear, high winds, rough seas, and a leaking fuel tank, we detoured to the Cape Verde Islands.

African Detour

WE ARRIVED AT MINDELO, SAO VICENTE, CAPE Verde Islands, about 5:30 p.m., and powered around the marina until a *marinaro* directed us to a spot with one very slimy "slime line" (our loving term for many a gross marina mooring line), but at least we were bow into the wind. Even though it was a little jerky on the mooring lines, we were very happy to be flat and level after a week of rolling and rough conditions. Over the past week a series of gear failures—mainly a fuel leak and a broken bilge pump—had made it clear we had to seek refuge.

We had left La Gomera believing that absolutely all systems were up and we had no issues with the boat. Our next port would most assuredly be Carlyle Bay, Barbados. A week later we were stuck in a rather primitive African marina, at the mercy of the very slow and not so capable fridge guys, electrician, and welder—*if* we could find one—when Michael's considerable expertise and experience failed or was challenged beyond his "tool set." Trying to put it all in perspective, I wrote in my journal: *"At any rate, it is great to finally be level, have a shower, and a good strong drink."* Several days later I wrote:

February 4, 2012, Mindelo, Sao Vicente, Cape Verde Islands

It blew like crazy all day yesterday and last night, the gritty desert wind from Africa seeping into every seam and crack, turning the whole boat brown. I can barely see the bow, and the sand is accumulating on deck in dunes. The town itself is pretty dreary, a lot of very poor black people sitting around.

We are Med moored, bow to the pier—noisy, rough, and worrisome, especially at night. Very hard to keep a cheerful outlook as we rock and jerk on the mooring lines, sometimes so suddenly and violently we lose our balance. At least, I suppose, we are not losing our sea legs. I hope we get to use them soon. We are as "fixed" as we are going to be and ready to go if the weather would just improve.

* * * * *

On February 9th, about 2:30 in the afternoon, there was a break. The haze lifted. The wind subsided a bit, and a patch of blue sky appeared. We put two reefs in the main, brought in our lines, motored through the congested harbor, and raised our sails in the turbulent water of the channel between Sao Anton and Mindelo.

Nineteen days later, at 8:30 p.m., Monday, February 27th, we dropped anchor in Carlisle Bay, Barbados.

It was a difficult, challenging passage best summed up by the following journal entry.

Heading for the Barn

F**EBRUARY 24, 2012, AT SEA, 196 NM TO BARBADOS**

Today marks our 15th day at sea since leaving Sao Vicente. For the most part the winds have been 15–20 gusting to 25. Very large swells and breaking seas have kept Ithaca continually off balance, rocking from rail to rail as she slides down one wave and "comes up" into the following one, which pushes her over on her port rail while "Hans" struggles to get her pointed back off the wind and on course.

This dance is accompanied by a chorus of continual squeaks, wails, knocks, shudders, and loud bangs when waves crash against the side of the hull or pour over the stern into the cockpit. Halyards rat-ta-tat-tat against the aluminum mast. The wind vane steerer lines moan. Sitting at the nav station on a dark night you hear the rush, hiss, splash of cresting waves chasing the boat and racing along the hull. Water splashes against the ports and runs along the deck while plates, glasses, bottles, books, canned goods, coffee cups and frying pans slide back and forth in their lockers which have been padded with towels, napkins, rubber placemats, and assorted rolled-up tee shirts to dampen the noise and stay the damage but still the wine glasses tinkle, pots clunk, and the Dremel toolbox beats out a low thunk, thunk, thunk.

The genoa strains and shakes, the sheets quiver then slacken making a loud bang against the deck as the tension of the block releases and tightens, releases and tightens. This is the symphony of sailing accompanied by the almost audible beating of your heart anticipating the "rogue wave" and massive knockdown that menaces out there in the inky black sea.

Night watches are the worst. As morning dawns so does reason, and the monstrous watery mountains chasing the stern seem more manageable in the pinkish-blue light of a new day. Only two more nights and hopefully we will be safely and quietly anchored in Bridgetown Harbor on the western coast of Barbados. But now it's time to hook up the galley strap, straddle my legs out wide and lean against the sink, bracing my body so I can use two hands to fill the coffee pot, turn on the stove, and get breakfast organized.

Another night down . . . I know there is a lesson in this, a metaphor for how little we all are actually "in control" (crash) of our lives. Trust, have patience, hang in there, it could be worse, there is nothing I can do, time heals . . . All these trite sayings come to mind but they do nothing to relieve the tension in my shoulders or the butterflies in my stomach. I am reading a great book, David Mitchell's The Cloud Atlas, but I can't concentrate on it. So I reach for Thomas Merton's Meditations and try to have faith in the boat and God's plan. Whenever there is a lull I try to relax, take deep breaths, be grateful, and pray.

* * * * *

We approached Carlisle Bay in the dark, "bay" really being a misnomer. It was more like a roadstead, open to the sea and not especially protected. It was a battle to the end, with squalls chasing us around the island to the lighthouse, where the seas finally flattened and we followed our waypoints up the coast. We hailed *Machula* on the radio, knowing from mutual friends on the Net that they were anchored nearby. They came out on deck with flashlights and coached us to a safe, deep spot to anchor up near the beach. We circled around, took down the sails, dropped the hook, and it was done. Our last long ocean passage.

Later on, Mark rowed over in his dinghy and handed up a bag of fresh bread, vine-ripened tomatoes, and cucumbers—manna from heaven. Skipping the champagne, we went right to the gin and tonics. Then I finished off the last of my ouzo from Plomari, which seemed a fitting final farewell to the Med and the "big gray heaving sea."

At this point we knew Sam wasn't doing well but had heard from friends that she had rallied, was out of the hospital, and careening around the apartment with her oxygen tank as if she was on a skateboard. We called Bill and learned that she had gone back into the hospital over the weekend with a terrible headache, which turned out to be breast cancer cells in her brain. The weather was still blowing and wild, with no place on the island to safely leave the boat. We would have to wait for better weather to sail to St. Lucia whence we could fly to California. But it continued to blow. Two days later we learned that Sam was in a coma and would not recover.

That afternoon we took a bus to the windswept eastern coast of the island where we sat on a bench and stared at the rambunctious sea—waves crashing against the rocks and palm trees bending in the wind—grateful we weren't out there somewhere in a boat and thinking about how Sam had loved it all. We both felt her presence and knew that she was saying good-bye. By Thursday the weather had improved enough to make the overnight trip to St. Lucia possible, and we flew out to California. We were too late. Sam had died about the time we were sitting on the beach in Barbados.

The "celebration of her life" was held at the unpretentious Monterey Yacht Club on Fisherman's Wharf that she had joined in her teens as the youngest and only woman on the racing team. The rickety floor shook with tearful laughter as the cast of characters in the movie of her life shared their memories, hugged, cried, and welcomed us into her extended family. The weather in Monterey seemed to be mourning her, too, and did not clear in time for us to join Bill on Sam's last boat ride. I sent three gardenias, which I imagined mingling with her ashes just as the white roses had mingled with the remains of my mother fifteen years before. Now when I go back to California to visit my son and his family, I walk along the beach and imagine them hanging out together in the seaweed forest among the playful otters that always made them smile.

* * * * *

From St. Lucia we continued up through the chain of Caribbean islands where we had cruised so many years before, but neither of us were inclined to linger. We had hoped Pete and the boys would join us in the Bahamas, but once again conflicts at home disrupted plans. It felt like we were swimming upstream against an undercurrent of sadness. Life on *Ithaca* continued with the usual weather issues, boat fix-it issues, and money issues interspersed with long days lolling about on beaches, relaxing in beach bars and restaurants, and skimming over miles of tranquil turquoise water. But nothing relieved our unrelenting sorrow.

We crossed the Gulf Stream and headed toward Cape Canaveral with reefed main and genoa doing 6.5 knots, which slowed to 1 knot in adverse current aggravated by bad weather from the north moving down the coast. How poetic. At 2:30 p.m. on June 13th we tied up at Cape Marina, Cape Canaveral. "Back in the USA," but neither of us really felt like celebrating. Then, after a stop in Daufuskie Island to visit Michael's sister and brother-in-law, it was a slow slog up the familiar ICW (Intercoastal Waterway) dodging hurricane warnings, mosquitoes, adverse currents, sandbars, and powerboats. But, as they say, the most dangerous part of any trip is the last mile home.

* * * * *

It had been a very long, stressful, hot, and buggy day. When we reached Dockside Marina in Wrightsville Beach, North Carolina, we just wanted to stop the boat, turn off the engine, and relax. The only spot along the pier was behind *Wrong Brothers*, a very big and loud powerboat with a lot of partying twenty- to thirty-somethings on board. It was Saturday night, and clearly Dockside Marina was really a bar/restaurant masquerading as a marina—no showers, no laundry, no quiet cruiser lounge. Indistinguishable music blared from the bar overlaid by louder music from *Wrong Brothers*. Practically nude girls in very skimpy bikinis hung over the rails and reclined seductively on the bow, to the ogling delight of bare-chested, tanned muscular guys. We felt out of place, tired, old, and overdressed. Luckily, we were so tired the loud music all night did not keep us from sleeping.

The next morning the partyers on *Wrong Brothers* were pretty quiet when we went to church but were at it again by 9:30 when we returned. The tranquil service at the beachside church, with its courtyard garden and deck overlooking the sea, had been rejuvenating, however. The music was soothing and the gracious Southern priest had charm, a down-to-earth attitude, and a sense of humor. More than that, his homily was directed specifically to me, pointing out that I am not in control and can not "fix" everyone else's life, so "Just let it go, Marguerite." I had received a heartbreaking email from home and another one that made me angry. I was disappointed and mad and ready to scratch everyone off my Christmas list. How long will it take me to learn that lesson? For the moment I could laugh about it.

Later that morning we left the party marina and continued up the ICW with a nice breeze behind us. We pulled out the genoa and were cruising along at 7 knots when the western sky darkened alarmingly. Suddenly there was a startlingly loud thunderstorm alert on the radio. We rolled in the genoa. A second later the sky was black. The wind lashed at *Ithaca*, blowing her over on her starboard rail. Visibility went to a boat length. Michael could barely hold the boat centered in the middle of the channel while I peered through the binoculars and coached him from marker to marker. Lightning burst all around us. There were no options. We had to stay in the middle of the channel and keep going. If we were blown out of the channel at high tide and went aground, we would be permanently beached like a sailboat we had seen along the way several days before. In addition, we were in the middle of a military base where big signs along the shore read "Danger. Unexploded Ordinance."

The chart showed a small protected dredged bay up ahead. Two flashing red buoys marked the entrance. Pivoting between the binoculars on deck and the C-map on the nav station computer, I guessed we were just about there. I couldn't think about the 50 knots I saw on the wind speed indicator or what looked like a waterspout coming toward us. I screamed at Michael: "Don't look at anything. Just do what I tell you. Just keep going straight ahead until I tell you to turn."

I continued to alternate between checking our course on the C-map and looking for the markers, calling out the course and water depth. Then I saw the lights and yelled, "Swing the wheel to port." The bow nosed into the wind, the boat righted, and we powered into a calm lake, the wind still blowing and lightning striking all around us. A sudden crack and flash right behind Michael's head shook the boat.

We continued making tight circles in the shallow water until the wind went down and we could find an area deep enough in which to safely anchor. Once the hook was down, we went below to dry off. Shivering with cold and shock, I have never been so scared. Michael looked at me with tears in his eyes and said, "Thank you; you were magnificent," no mean compliment from the Captain who, for the first time, had relinquished command to his first mate. I couldn't help but feel a tinge of pride. I said, "So were you."

Once again, even in our despair and fear, we had survived another Odyssey ordeal together, safely navigating between the six-headed monster Scylla and Charybdis's yawing vortex, with faith, determination, skill, and mutual trust. We laughed and hugged each other. "That wasn't so bad!"

Comparatively speaking the rest of the trip home was a piece of cake.

You Can Go Home Again

C URIOUSLY, MY LAST JOURNAL ENTRY ENDS VERY unceremoniously. A day away from home I wrote: *"I am busy polishing brass, vacuuming, and straightening up. We are so excited to be finally bringing* Ithaca *home."* At 1600 on July 19, 2012, I wrote in the log: "WE ARE HOME!" Large emotions need few words.

We motored up the Severn River past the US Naval Academy with forty-five courtesy flags representing all the countries we had visited run up the forward stay and down the backstay. The New York Yacht Club flag flew at the top of the mast, our home Eastport Yacht Club and Epping Forest Yacht Club flags flew off the starboard yardarm, and Michael's Navy Wings of Gold pennant flew off the port yardarm. A large, pristine American flag on a newly varnished flagstaff dipped gracefully off the stern, replacing her raggedy but well-traveled sister. Hull waxed to a gleaming mirror finish, teak glowing, *Ithaca* proudly wove through the snarl of Sunday summer boat traffic in Annapolis Harbor, dodging dinghies, race markers, powerboat wakes, and narrowly missing Naval Academy knockabouts that threatened to ram us broadside.

Beyond the second Severn River bridge we could just see through the summer haze our white bench on the point where we had welcomed the new millennium. Off the port bow a runabout came speeding toward us. Caroline held a sign that said "Welcome Home ITHACA." Pete, Danny, Laird, and Lauren were all waving and shouting "Welcome home!" They circled several times as we all laughed, cried, waved, and photographed each other.

A mile away we could hear bagpipe music playing and then saw the bagpiper standing on the point under the trees, a family tradition inherited from Lauren's Scottish ancestry. At this emotional moment, mooring the boat in a yachtsman-like manner was a challenge, since both Michael and I were teary-eyed and a photographer from the *Capital Gazette* was documenting every move. As we slowly approached the pier, waiting hands grabbed lines and secured *Ithaca* while I flung over the fenders, and we stepped ashore into a garden of smiling faces and outreached arms. A cork popped and magically there was a champagne flute of sparkling gold in my hand. We were home.

* * * * *

Now, five years later as I complete this book, much has changed and nothing has changed. *Ithaca* still sits proudly at the end of our pier except for summer sojourns to New England. My grandchildren live far away. Dear ones have died. New ones have come into my life. My family has both shrunk and expanded. I am reminded of a quote I found in the *Bible* while we were coming up the ICW, which I copied in my journal.

July 5, 2012, Alligator River, North Carolina
This morning reading the Bible, *I think it was a letter to the Hebrews:*

> *"You, Lord, in the beginning created the earth*
>
> *and with your own hands you made the heavens.*
>
> *They will disappear but you will remain.*
>
> *They will all wear out like clothes.*
>
> *You will fold them up like a coat.*
>
> *And they will be changed like clothes."*

Everything changes in life. Time passes. Clothes wear out. I just have to fold up those old memories and expectations like a much beloved old coat and put them up on the top shelf of the closet. Maybe I'll get a new coat. Something that will be just as warm. I can't see it now but it is all in God's hands.

* * * * *

In fact, that did happen. Through a local tutoring and mentoring program, I discovered the joy of helping kids learn to read. One of those kids lived with us for a year, renewing in us the joys and trials of parenting. Pete remarried and brought a whole new family, including two new charming "step-grandchildren," into our life. Regular visits to family in California and Tucson have given us a good excuse for land travel.

The last page of an earlier journal contains another prescient thought:

June 6, 2012, Little Harbour, Abacos

Reading Susan Sontag's The Volcano Lover I ran across this line describing the main character: "He ferried himself past one vortex of melancholy after another by means of an astonishing spread of enthusiasms." Could this be the intro of a book? What were the enthusiasms, the places most compelling, most resonant? The passion for learning, for experiencing, for photographing, for . . . collecting. I want to write a book about the passion for travel. About how it intersects with one's personal memoir, like reading a good book gets you out of yourself into a different world. Travel—focused, discerning, purposeful travel—drives the ferry around the dangerous shoals of the inner self, keeps one looking outward, not inward where the sea is too deep, too dark, too stormy.

* * * * *

I hope that this is that book.

And finally, this from *A Lady's Life in the Rocky Mountains* by Isabella L Bird: "This is a view to which nothing needs to be added. This is truly the 'Lodge in some vast wilderness' for which one often sighs when in the midst of a bustle at once sordid and trivial."

* * * * *

A fat harvest moon crested over the shadowy treetops and stretched out a shimmering beam across the river, pooling at our feet as we sat hand in hand on the white bench where we had welcomed in the new millennium so many years ago. There was nothing to say really.

I thought, "This is a view to which nothing needs to be added." I need no Rome, no train trip across Mongolia, no ocean challenge. Now, as I age, more limited enthusiasms ferry me "around the vortex of melancholy." I am one with that glistening, ever changing, ever flowing water . . .

> *"And hand in hand, on the edge of the sand,*
>
> *They danced by the light of the moon,*
>
> *The moon,*
>
> *The moon,*
>
> *They danced by the light of the moon."*
>
> Edward Lear, *"The Owl in the Pussy Cat"*

ITHACA

When you start on your journey to Ithaca,
then pray that the road is long,
full of adventure, full of knowledge.
Do not fear the Lestrygonians and the Cyclopes
and the angry Poseidon.
You will never meet such as these on your path,
if your thoughts remain lofty, if a fine
emotion touches your body and your spirit.
You will never meet the Lestrygonians,
the Cyclopes and the fierce Poseidon,
if you do not carry them within your soul,
if your soul does not raise them up before you.
Then pray that the road is long.
That the summer mornings are many,
that you will enter ports seen for the first time
with such pleasure, with such joy!
Stop at Phoenician markets, and purchase fine merchandise,
mother of pearl and corals, amber and ebony,
and pleasurable perfumes of all kinds,
buy as many pleasurable perfumes as you can;
visit hosts of Egyptian cities,
to learn and learn from those who have knowledge.
Always keep Ithaca fixed in your mind.
To arrive there is your ultimate goal.
But do not hurry the voyage at all.
It is better to let it last for long years;
and even to anchor at the isle when you are old,
rich with all that you have gained on the way, not expecting that
Ithaca will offer you riches.
Ithaca has given you the beautiful voyage.
Without her you would never have taken the road.
But she has nothing more to give you.
And if you find her poor, Ithaca has not defrauded you.
With the great wisdom you have gained, with so much experience,
you must surely have understood by then what Ithacas mean.

C. P. Cavafy

Ithaca

THE VOYAGE OF ITHACA -
October 22, 1998 to July 19, 2012

Nautical Miles sailed: 43,822
(in statute miles: 49,978)

Countries visited by sail: 51

Countries visited by land: 9

Longest period at sea: 27 days (Galapagos to Nuka Hiva, French Polynesia)

Sailing Itinerary

Miles Sailed

1998:	ICW, Bahamas	1,118
1999:	Cuba, Mexico (Yucatan Peninsula)	2,044
2000:	Belize, Guatemala, Honduras, Nicaragua, Colombia	2,094
2001:	Panama (including San Blas Islands), Galapagos, French Polynesia, Cook Islands Niue, Tonga, New Zealand	8,675
2002:	New Zealand (boatyard for eight months)	339
2003:	Fiji, New Caledonia, Vanuatu, Australia	4,293
2004:	Indonesia, (including Bali), Singapore, Malaysia	4,788
2005:	Malaysia (tsunami relief), Thailand	688

Acknowledgments

The birth of this book has been accomplished by many mid-wives. Primary among them are Lynn Schwartz and Laura Oliver whose writing classes, thoughtful editing and steadfast encouragement was indispensable, while Linda O'Doughda's attentive line editing saved me from many an embarrassing mistake. Special thanks to all my critique group members and classmates whose insightful suggestions helped me tame an unwieldy text of 700 pages, and to my dear family who endured the birth pangs. However, you wouldn't be reading this without Seaworthy Publications, Inc. Their sensitivity to my writing, willingness to take a chance on my book and consider my input, even when they did not agree, are deeply appreciated. Their choice of Cherie Fox as cover designer was inspired. Thank you, Cherie.

Lastly, but most importantly, I want to thank, my captain, my husband and my dearest love, Michael, without whom all the good things in my life would never have happened.

Photo by Olivia Reed

About the Author

Marguerite Welch is a sailor, writer and photographer whose articles on photography have appeared in numerous art journals. Her short fiction, memoir, and travel writings have been published in Bay Weekly, Wanderlust and Memoir Magazine. She lives in Annapolis Md. with her husband Michael where she sails, gardens, writes, does art projects and gratefully watches the ever-changing colors of the Severn River from her porch swing.